This book is for anyone with the dream of starting their own shoe company.

You will follow the launch of two start-up shoe companies. Each has its own style of shoes and business plan. In each chapter we will describe a requirement or process, then explain how each of our two new shoe brands will tackle this challenge.

You will cover crucial steps such as how to go about creating your shoe brand identity, how to legally set up your shoe company, how to register trademarks and apply for patents, how to get your shoes designed, built, paid for, and of course, how to go about selling your shoes.

You will also learn how to import shoes, how to handle international distribution, and how to pay overseas vendors.

So, what does it really take to start a shoe company?

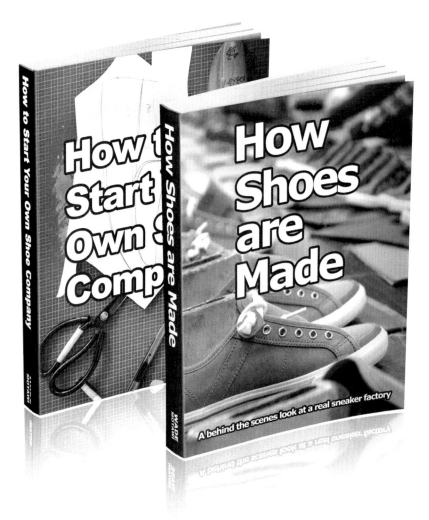

Available now:
"How Shoes Are Made"
"How to Start Your Own Shoe Company"

Coming Fall 2017:
"Designers Guide To Shoe Materials"

WWW.SNEAKERFACTORY.NET

How to Start Your Own Shoe Company

Written and Edited by
Wade and Andrea Motawi

ask_a_shoe_dog@sneakerfactory.net

Dear Readers,

This book was written to educate, inform, and inspire the next generation of shoe designers, shoe developers, shoe makers, and footwear entrepreneurs! Our goal is to help prepare people for fulfilling careers in the world of shoes!

Enjoy!

A special thanks to:

Andrea, Alex & Erik, Karim, Halla, Mom & Dad, Dave, Alfredo, Jason, David, Lizzie, Johnson, Steve, Lenny, Bernie, Simon, Ben, Chad, The Mint Project, the whole crew at Manhattan Giant Pizza.

Thanks to all my working friends in the USA, China, Hong Kong, Korea, Taiwan and Europe.

How to Start Your Own Shoe Company

WADE MOTAWI

DESIGN - DEVELOPMENT - PRODUCTION

MARKETING - SALES - DISTRIBUTION

CHAPTER 1

YOUR SHOES AND YOUR BRAND

Does the world need another shoe company?
There are hundreds, even thousands, of shoe brands in operation. Why make another? Should you really follow your dream to start your own shoe company? The answer is...YES, you should!

If you have a fresh outlook and a way to solve a problem in an original way, read on! The world needs new companies, new ideas, and new personalities to face new challenges in unique and creative ways.

There is always a place for a new shoe company to get started. The billion dollar shoe brands must look for huge opportunities, leaving small brands free to serve niche markets. You can fill a special need or take a fashion risk. Go ahead and make something fresh!

What does a new brand need to survive?
For your new shoe company to survive and thrive in the competitive world of shoes, you will need something special! Originality and uniqueness are a start. You will also need to package your uniqueness in a way that people can understand and appreciate.

What does your new shoe company bring?
Do you have an idea to improve the function of a shoe for a particular activity? Is there a better way to make a running, driving, logging, dancing, bowling or fencing shoe? If you have a fresh twist, go for it! Do you see an untapped market in a foreign country or in your own country? Or maybe you know a footwear buyer or a fashion store owner that has a special need?

Maybe you saw something while traveling that could be a hit at home? If you already own a business, maybe you are looking to expand? An open distribution channel is a good enough reason to make your own shoes. Let's get started!

A great idea

Having a great idea for a new shoe is a small part of what you will need to make a shoe company that will survive.

While you may want to focus on designing every detail of the shoes, you will need to spend more of your time on figuring out the supply chain, sales, marketing, distribution and financial arrangements that will turn your idea into a real functioning business.

This book will walk you through these challenges! *How To Start Your Own Shoe Company* is arranged in chronological order, following the shoemaking process from design, development, production and sales, on through marketing and distribution.

As you read you will learn how to design, source, market and sell your shoes.

Making your plans

Starting a new shoe company will be hard. You can expect to work long hours and late nights. You will meet challenges and you will need to make tough decisions.

We have done our best to explain the business requirements, detail the challenges, and describe your options. We hope you can make this journey with as few surprises as possible. If you have a good plan, you have a chance to succeed! Without a real plan, your shoe company may be doomed to fail.

Creating a business plan

Creating a business plan for your new footwear company may seem like a daunting task, but you can break your plan down into manageable parts. If you have partners, you may want to divide up the plan according to the expertise of each participant.

The master plan needs to cover:
Your brand identity
Product plan
Financial calculations
Sales plan
Distribution plan
Marketing plan

As you make decisions, you will find these plans are interdependent, each supporting the goals of the other. Be flexible as you draft your plans. At this planning stage you should study many different structures for your new shoe company.

Branding plans tell your story

Now it's time to get pen and paper and put down your story. Tell your story back to yourself. If you have a special connection or expertise, this will be the launching pad for your new shoe company. If you have no expertise, but a strong interest, get to work on researching your idea.

What is out there?

Explore your ideas and do some research. With so many shoe brands out there it is important to make sure your idea is new, original and special in some way. Competing against an established competitor without a distinction is the first step on the road to failure.

The internet is an important tool for this research, but don't forget old-fashioned books and magazines. Magazines are a great tool, as they can show you how many different companies are competing in your chosen market. Read *Paris Fashion, Skydiving Today*, or any publication you need to dig deep into your market to understand what is really going on.

Building on your idea

With the idea for your shoe in mind, it's time to sit back a little and think about how best to deliver your shoes. When I say, "deliver," I mean to surround your basic idea with a style and a story that will attract and educate people so they can see how great your new shoe is. This is your brand!

Target markets

Your target market is the particular group of people you are focusing on. Your target market may be lumberjacks, housewives, gamers, fashion models, ballerinas or sailors. Your target market may also be a specific area. For example, shoes for people in Africa, or is there something that makes a shoe special for Australia?

Target customers

Knowing your our target customers will narrow your focus. Your target customers may be kids ages 14 to 18 who play video games, or a special shoe for pregnant women. Take some time to describe your target customer. You must also think about how your customer shops, where they shop, or if they shop. The shoe made for a 14-year-old boy will usually be purchased by his parents. How does this effect the design?

Thinking about your target market and customers will help you design your shoes, your brand, your marketing, and your sales strategies.

Introducing Ricardo

Ricardo is the first of our two shoe company start-up entrepreneurs. In his case he will be turning a pastime activity into new business.

Ricardo is a working professional, a regular guy. By day he is a stock broker for a large trading company in San Diego. Ricardo has a great job that pays well, but after years of working in the financial markets, he is looking for something else.

The good news for Ricardo is that he has money saved up for his shoe project and a wife with a professional career. Because Ricardo has a job and some money set aside, he can launch his shoe company by working nights.

Ricardo's idea

Ricardo has been running triathlons for years, and while training for the swimming, biking, and running events, he has time to think about a concept to make training and running easier. Ricardo is amazed that triathletes will spend $15,000 for a race bike and $5,000 for a "training" bike.

Ricardo sees the possibility of a specially designed line of shoes for these super triathletes. The idea is for three different shoes, related to each other, so the triathlete can move smoothly from training to racing to recovery. Ricardo has shared his idea with his friends who also run triathlons, and they really like his idea.

With his new concept in mind, Ricardo does some research on the internet, checks out a few books, and runs a quick patent search. It seems that Ricardo's new idea for running shoes is in fact... new!

Ricardo knows triathletes have money to spend and he is ready to take the plunge and get started!

Introducing Eve

Eve is an art student and part-time singer in a Boston punk music band. She is finishing college soon and knows that while painting and punk rock are fun, they may not pay the bills. Eve has a unique personal style; wild hair, paint-spattered leather jackets, and big black combat boots. Wherever she goes, Eve likes to stand out and make a statement.

While most people are shocked by her wild fashion sense and hair, some are starting to notice her customized combat boots. Eve always wears black boots but after she ruined a pair while painting, she decided to go for it and turn her paint-spattered boots into another art project.

After one of her shows, someone asked Eve where she got her cool boots. Quick thinking, Eve explained she made them herself and would be happy to make another pair. In just a few minutes, Eve had her first customer. Soon after, Eve made custom-painted designs for her band-mates to help market her shoe design talent.

With her unique style and attitude, Eve decides to expand her custom hand-painted boots from a hobby into a business. Eve will take on the additional challenge of starting a new business without any savings. Let's see how she does.

Brand identity

Before you create your new shoe company you need to think about how you will deliver your message and products. One really important aspect of any company, especially one in the clothing and footwear market, is the brand identity. Start thinking about your new company's brand identity, and what it can do for you.

Your company's brand identity is how you want to be perceived by your customers. It creates an emotional attachment between you and the people who are buying your shoes. Think of branding as the visual voice of your company. It will do a lot of marketing and sales work for you if you get it right, but it can really make life difficult if you get it wrong.

There are brands that are recognized because they have been around for centuries and then there are new brands being created every day. Aim to be the new brand that can turn heads and get noticed in all the right places and you will be able to turn your product into a success in no time at all.

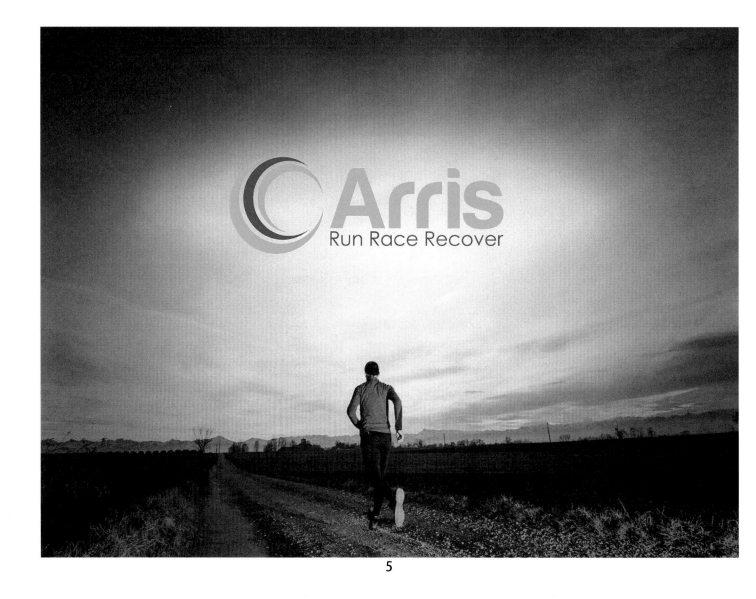

Why should you think about your brand identity before you design your shoes?

The brand identity of your new shoe company will act as your road map. Once you have defined the identity of your brand, every decision you make will be shaped accordingly. Your brand identity is a way to define your business to yourself, your employees, your customers, and to investors. It should deliver a clear statement which describes your brand, and will allow you to focus on what is important to you.

You really have to live and breathe your brand in every aspect of your company.

Your brand identity will allow customers to create an emotional connection to your brand. You must shape your identity to attract your target customers. The values, beliefs, and personality of your brand will attract your customers and reinforce their relationship with your brand.

Your brand does all of these things for you in terms of creating that connection with your customers and driving sales, but it will not be easy. You need to make crucial decisions about your brand identity and work hard to maintain that identity throughout everything you do.

Think of your brand as a person

Thinking of your brand as a person can make it easier for you to establish the goals for your brand. In fact, your brand's personality may be your personality. Many people start a business because it is something they are passionate about, and you may be on a similar path as you develop your own shoe company. The things that you are passionate about in life and in relation to shoes, will come through in your thought process as you develop and create your brand and its' identity.

If you are passionate about design, then use this passion to drive the look of your branding. This will show through in your logo, your shoes, your marketing, your packaging, and the way you want your shoe to be sold.

If your passion is absolute quality, fair trade, environmentalism, motocross lifestyle, tattoos or whatever, this must shine through in your brand identity. Your brand is an extension of you and your passions, and hopefully the passions of your customers!

What is your brand name?

Your company name and brand name may or may not be the same. You may want to create one image with your suppliers and business contacts, and a different brand image with your customer base. Your logos, attitude, images and representatives all reflect the visual look and values the company will bring to the market. This is where you need to think carefully about what you are trying to create. Your brand speaks for you when you are not there. It will sit on your website, on search engines such as Google, on your social media feeds, and people will interact with your brand when you are not there. It is important to let your brand speak positively and strongly for your company.

You must make sure to develop a brand identity that is consistent and appeals to your target market and customers. You need to think about who these people are and what their values are. What will appeal to them and how your brand will communicate this appeal. Often, the easiest way to develop your brand identity is to make a design board with pictures similar to your products. This gives you the chance to brainstorm and think about what it is that you want to create. You should also take a look at some of your competitors and some brands that you admire. Looking at ideas from other successful brands will help you to decide what it is that sets you apart from the rest of the market, and what the key selling points will be for your customers.

A time and place for your brand

You can create a new reality for your brand. You can define a new time and place. Does your product belong with the wooden crates and primitive hardware of an 1850's polar expedition? Maybe your shoes belong posed on the deck of an ultra-modern sailing yacht. You can collect photos from the web, books, or magazines to help set the visual inspiration for your brand.

These are constructive ways to think about what you are creating and where your product will fit in the market. I cannot overstate the importance of spending time on these details to get them absolutely correct. They can determine the success or failure of your shoe company. If your customer can't relate to your shoes or find a compelling reason to buy them, then you will be in trouble. Take the time to get this absolutely right, the decisions you make here will effect everything you do in the future.

Be your own brand

Don't let the identity of other brands dictate or dilute what you are doing. You want to carve out your own niche and be known for your own things. You need to ask yourself, "What are we famous for?" This is not a trick question, but is directly related to your brand. If you cannot answer this simple question, then how will you communicate this brand message to your customers. Your brand and your message need to be unique, and need to come through in everything you do.

The message you deliver, the people you employ, the packaging you use and everything else you do, are part of your brand and the image you deliver to the market each and every day. Think about what a customer will feel when they see your ad, pick up your shoes, or see your Twitter feed. This feeling is a key part of your company. It is difficult to define, but when it feels right your sales will follow.

One company, two brands

One company can have different brands, each with different identities.

The shoe company, Hi-Tec Sports®, operates two totally separate brand identities and this works perfectly for them. They started with the outdoor hiking Hi-Tec® brand that has a loyal following and has their customer coming back time and time again. They then created the Magnum® brand to sell military and service boots.

While the same product team designs and develops the products for both brands, the brand identities could not be more different. Each brand does its own job of targeting completely separate market segments. The company has seen a way to develop two brands and enter two markets, by cleverly thinking about what they produce and how they can appeal to completely different customers.

Brand identity development

There are many great books and websites you can check out to help with your brand identity. Don't worry if you can't figure it out on your own. There are many experts you can hire to help you. There are always people to lean on when it comes to advice and suggestions in situations like this. Do as much research as you can. When you need inspiration, it's best to read, talk, research and rethink what you are doing. It can seem a little daunting at this stage, but your natural passion and energy for what you are doing will come through in your thought process and then into your brand.

Cheryl Dangel Cull has written a few books that I really like for brand identity. They contain many examples and great discussions on brand development theory. This is a great place to start when it comes to what you want to achieve. The more you learn and develop as a business owner, the better your business will be. If you arm yourself with knowledge, facts, and inspiration, then the results that come out of the process will be knowledgeable, factual, and inspired.

Branding design agencies

You may consider using a design agency in this process. They are professionals that deal with these kinds of issues every day. It may be expensive, but they can help you formulate some of your ideas and create a brand that really works for you. From the cost angle it saves money if you can produce all of this yourself, but there may be times when a professional team can help your shoe company, your shoes, and your brand to shine. It is a competitive market, and you want your brand to deliver exactly the right message to set you apart from the competition.

At this stage, you don't need a fully formed identity package, but you should have at least the formation of an idea. Your shoe designers will need some design cues and logo ideas to get started branding your shoes at an early stage, and this stems from the identity that you have created.

A quick word about logos for shoes

Assuming your brand vision includes logos on your shoes, it is a great idea to make sure your logo identity can be neatly applied to your shoes. While many brands insist on bold logo applications, others require understated logos or no logos at all.

Your logo is a huge part of your brand identity. It must be distinctive and say something about the personality of your brand.

You need to be careful about any design with stripes on the side of the shoe. Companies have trademarked 2, 3, 4, 5, and 6 stripes. Watch out!

You also need to make sure your shoe logo can be executed in different colors and different media. If your logo design has many colors, can you make it in black and white? How will the logo look when embossed without color?

Will the logo fit neatly on the side or heel of a shoe? Is your logo easy to scale up and scale down?

A logo design with fine text or very small details may not read well when made by woven label, embroidered, or embossed.

In the book *How Shoes are Made* there is an entire chapter explaining the many ways logos can be applied to shoes. There are many choices, but not all may be suitable for your logo design or the style of your brand identity.

While Ricardo is a regular guy, he is actually sort of boring. He is going to need some help and inspiration to create the brand identity for his new firm.

Ricardo starts by making a list of words and some technical terms he would use to describe his shoe idea. Next he looks through a book about architecture. In a chapter on ancient Greek architecture, he discovers the word "Arris." He likes the sound of it. Ricardo decides to go with it for now.

ARRIS shoes will be clean, lightweight, high-performance shoes. Stripped down to just the essentials, no fancy stuff. In Ricardo's mind, an Arris shoe will be futuristic and sleek.

For just a few dollars, Ricardo has a designer create a series of Arris logos to choose from.

Back in Boston, Eve knows exactly what the brand identity for her shoe will be....it's Eve! Playing off her own name, Eve decides to go with the name "Enigma" and she already knows every boot will have the letter "E" somewhere in the design.

ENIGMA boots are going to be chunky, heavy, and loud. Eve knows every model will have a cool design and unique punk rock style.

KICKING FASHION
IN THE FACE!

Kicking Fashion in the face!

KICKING FASHION
IN THE FACE!

CHAPTER 2

CREATING YOUR SHOE COMPANY

As you create your new shoe company you need to consider what the primary functions of your company will be. In the simplest terms, your new shoe company will:

1. **Design & develop shoes**
2. **Source & import shoes**
3. **Market your brand name**
4. **Sell shoes & collect payments**
5. **Fulfill shoe orders & serve customers**

These main functions must all work smoothly for your new shoe company to thrive! The structure of the company must support each of these functions.

When should you create your company?
You need to legally create your company at the time when you hire people to provide services and start spending money. Up until now your company is just an idea on paper. While it may exist in your mind, or on a note pad, once you need to start spending money, it's real!

Spending money is the trigger. As a start-up, all of your expenses can be written off against any profit you make. You must have a legal company to enjoy this benefit. Everything, meaning EVERYTHING must be documented when it comes to paying your business taxes.

Entire books have been written on the subject of business taxes. You will need to hire a tax accountant. This is a necessity. You could spend many hours doing your taxes and still get it wrong. This is an area where a little professional help will go a long way. For your small business you can hire a tax accountant to help you with both your personal and business taxes. You should expect a tax provider to bill you at least $500 USD per year.

Your tax accountant will explain the process in detail, but you will need to keep an accurate record of all the money you spend. Even your tax accountant's fees can be written off against your company's profits. While you should not expect to see any profit as a start-up, you should not see any corporate taxes either.

Your company needs a name

Your company name does not need to be your shoes' "brand" name. It can be, but it's not required. If you think you may have more brands in the future, then pick something different.

People often confuse the "company" name with the "brand" name. They are not the same. Think of a huge company like Proctor & Gamble™. This company owns hundreds of different brand names, like Tide™, Pampers™, Cascade™, Braun™, Dawn™ and dozens of others. You can call your company almost anything you want, except a name that has already been taken. Often, a company with several brands will change its name to be the name of its most popular product.

What type of company?

For your new shoe company you are going to need to create a legal business and register it with the government. In the USA there are several options open to you. The sole proprietorship and the limited liability company (LLC) are the most common for start-ups. We will describe the advantages and disadvantages to each of these.

Sole Proprietorship

The sole proprietorship is the easiest company to set up. YOU are a sole proprietorship. You don't need to file any tax paperwork. Although you still need to get local permits and licenses to legally do business. The sole proprietorship is simple as it is just YOU. Your personal finances are the company's finances. Should something bad happen to your company, it's actually happening to YOU.

When starting a footwear company, a sole proprietorship may not be your best option. While your shoes will have product liability insurance, you do not want your personal assets available in the case of any lawsuits. A sole proprietorship is okay for your shoe company until you start shipping product to customers.

Limited Liability Company (LLC)

The limited liability company, often called an LLC, is a better choice for your new company. LLC is the least complex business structure. As an owner you will report your share of profit and loss on your individual tax return. You will need to file paperwork with the state's LLC division. Depending on what state you form your LLC in, you may reserve your legal name and file your articles of organization with your Secretary of State's office. Your articles of organization are simply documents that detail how you will run your company. For example, the articles will state who the owners are, what each owner's percentage of ownership and responsibilities within the company are, the voting rights, the profit and loss allocation, and any management rules. Your articles of organization should also state what happens in the case of bankruptcy, selling out, or the death of a participating owner.

Your LLC must have a name that is unique to you and may not contain another company's trademark. The fee to complete and file your state's form for articles of organization can range from $50-$300. Depending on your state's regulations, you may need to file an operating agreement with your articles of organization and obtain any state and local business licenses and permits.

If you live outside the USA you will find there are similar structures for your company. The main point is to make sure your company gives you "limited liability." This will separate your personal finances from the company's finances.

Product liability insurance

When selling shoes, you need an LLC in order to avoid any product liability complications. The LLC will protect your personal assets in the case of a lawsuit or other action that results in a financial loss to your company. You will also need to purchase product liability insurance. This will protect your company in the case of any accidents that may occur while someone is using your shoes. Product liability insurance is mandatory.

The average cost of product liability insurance is $.25 per $100 of retail costs. This amount can be more or less depending on the type of shoe you are making. For example, the product liability insurance for house slippers will be different from that required for tight-rope-walking shoes.

You can search online or ask your local insurance agent to help find a product liability insurance carrier. With many manufacturing companies around, product liability insurance is not hard to find. Your agent will be able to help you with the requirements for your country or state.

Product liability insurance is a must! All your work building your shoe company could be lost if someone suffers an injury while wearing your shoes. See Chapter 12 for more information.

Local government permits

Regardless of the corporate tax structure you pick, you will need to register your new company with your state and local government. In the USA you will need to get a Tax ID number with the IRS, file a Doing Business As (DBA) with your company name, and you may need a local seller's permit.

Doing Business As

All types of businesses can use a DBA. The DBA or "fictitious business name" is a business name that is different from your personal name. Once your DBA registration is complete, your company can use this name to open bank accounts, write checks, enter contracts and collect money. The DBA will require some paperwork with your local government and some small fees. Filing Fees of approximately $100 may include a charge to publish your DBA in a local paper. This is normal procedure. Once again, your DBA name does NOT need to be your shoe brand name. It can be, but it's not required.

Tax Identification Number

To legally file taxes and manage your accounting, your firm will need a tax identification number, usually called the Tax ID or Employer Identification Number (EIN). To get your Tax ID number, you will need to apply to the IRS (USA) or the equivalent in your home country. You can go to the IRS website and fill out the SS-4 form for submission. The EIN is assigned for free and the website will assign you one almost instantly. Keep this number with your important records. It's like the social security number for your business.

Seller's permits

Depending on where you are starting your firm, you may need a seller's permit. You will need to register with your state's Board of Equalization (BOE). This will allow you to collect and pay the sales tax on your taxable sales. When you register, you will receive a seller's permit. The seller's permit proves you are a legitimate reseller and allows you to sell your products to other dealers without charging them sales tax. If you sell to end-user "customers" over the web for example, you must collect sales tax and then forward this tax money quarterly or yearly to your state government. The rules for your home country may be different with VAT tax; etc. While each state has slightly different rules, fees for a seller's permit are low or free.

Bank accounts and credit cards

Now that your firm is created, it's time to open a business bank account at your local bank. You will want to have a checking account and maybe a business credit card to help record all your business transactions.

This may not seem important, but for a small business owner, keeping your personal spending separate from your company spending can save you many hours come tax time.

The major banks have year-end reports for checking accounts and credit cards that will help you organize your expenses. This is a real time-saver. Make sure you take your DBA paperwork to the bank. You will need it to open the account!

 Over at the Arris world headquarters (Ricardo's home office), the "TRIATHLETES SUPPLY CORPORATION LLC" is filing paperwork in the state of California to officially become an LLC.

While Ricardo likes the name Arris for his shoes, he wants to keep his options open if a new name comes up. He has created his LLC now because he will have some major expenses coming for shoe design and development. He may need to bring in some partners or investors, so an LLC is a great choice. Ricardo is also going ahead with all of his local permits.

 Eve is choosing to wait to create an LLC. She will stay as a Sole Proprietorship for now. She is not sure when the Enigma shoe brand will launch but she will go ahead and file her local sellers permits.

Creating and protecting trademarks

To insure your new brand idea is open and available you will need to do a trademark search.

You will need to get your trademark registered to protect your growing brand. In the USA, trademark fees are relatively low: $235 to $325 per trademark and per category. In the UK the fee is £170.

In the USA:
www.uspto.gov

In the UK:
www.gov.uk/register-a-trademark

In Europe:
www.euipo.europa.eu/ohimportal/en/ trade-marks

Listing of worldwide trademark offices:
www.wipo.int/directory/en/urls.jsp

Although not required, prior to filing an application, you are encouraged to search the USPTO's trademark database to see if any trademark has been previously registered or applied for, that is similar to your mark and being used on related products or for related services. Start your trademark search on the US Patent and Trademark office's "TESS" (Trademark Electronic Search System) database.

Think of a few ideas to search. The search may be time-consuming, but it is necessary. You can do it yourself or you can get some help. The website in the USA has great "how to" and FAQ pages to walk you through the process.

It's important to register your trademark so you can take legal action against anyone using your trademark without your permission. In the footwear markets you will need a registered trade-mark to fight against counterfeiters. With your trademark you can also use the ® or (TM) to show that you have claimed, and will defend your brand.

In the future, your trademark may have great value. A properly registered trademark can be sold or licensed.

More information

The United States Patent and Trademark Office has a great deal of information available to you. The application process is explained in detail. They really make it easy. There are many options for filing online and by mail.

Outside the USA

If you live outside the USA, you will need to resister your trademark in your home country. A simple web search is all it takes to find your local trademark office. The rules governing trademark creation are generally similar, but each country has a different process.

When Eve initially searches the TESS database, she finds the name Enigma is used by several other companies. She is very disappointed, but after a closer look she finds that none of the other companies filed for the use as a shoe company.

Eve is going ahead with the trade name "Enigma." Eve needs to save money so she does the paper work herself. Eve pays around $250. She does not apply for additional product categories at this time. Maybe in the future she will apply for Enigma clothing.

Eve will protect the word "Enigma," her two logo patches, and the phrase "Kicking Fashion in the Face."

In the TESS database, Ricardo does not see any other shoe companies who have filed for the trademark Arris. Ricardo decides to go ahead and file for the trademark. He looks online and finds a service to help him file. For a small fee of less than $100 the paperwork is filled out and submitted.

Ricardo goes ahead and registers Arris for both footwear and apparel. Ricardo pays out $100 for the paperwork, $250 for the trademark, plus an additional $50 to add the second product category.

He will protect the name "Arris," the new Arris "ARC" logo, and the phrase "Run Race Recover."

Web domains

While you are working on your trademark, it is also a good idea to visit GoDaddy.com™ or other domain-registering firms to search for a suitable website domain name.

It can be very frustrating to find an open domain name, but keep trying. Don't worry if someone has a website domain that is close to your brand idea. It's the registered trademark that counts.

When picking a web domain, here are a few tips:
Make it easy to type and keep it short.
Don't use numbers or hyphens.
It must be memorable.
It can't be another company's trademark.
Use ".com" if possible.

How much does a domain name cost? Not much! Most web domain names are not expensive, $9.99 to $29.99. Try to stay away from "premium" domains which may cost hundreds or even thousands of dollars. The fact is, the domain name is not as important as it used to be. If you have a good website which is properly built and indexed by Google.com™, your customers will be able to find you.

The value of a domain name is in the quality of your site and the traffic you can generate.

Do you need to buy a hosting plan for your new shoe company's domain? No. You can wait. For now make sure you secure your domain. You will be building your website later.

Do you need more than one domain?
It's not a bad idea to register a few domain names close to your main selection. Some domain registrar companies will try to upsell you more domains and other special features. Most of these are not needed. For now, get your domain registered and move on. However, if you can't find a domain close to your company name, you may need to consider a new company name.

We will talk more about building websites in Chapter 7.

Eve tries to get the domain Enigmashoes.com but it is taken. At Enigmashoes.com Eve finds a broken website that looks like it was abandoned or is under construction. Rather than settle for Enigmashoes.co or Enigmashoes.net, Eve registers Enigmaboots.com. This is a good choice for her. It's simple, it's very close to her brand name, and it is exactly what she makes! She pays $11.99 for a one-year registration.

It is possible for Eve to contact the owner of Enigmashoes.com and make an offer to purchase the domain, but for a small start-up, it may be a waste of time and money.

Arris

When Ricardo searches for Arris.com, he finds it is taken by an internet hardware company. It's okay for the name Arris to be shared by two companies. The trademarks are both valid because they are registered in very different product categories.

Ricardo tries arrisshoes.com and it is available. The double "SS" in the middle of the domain seems a bit strange, so he looks at some other options. Ricardo goes ahead and registers Arrisshoes.com but also selects Arrisrunning.com as his main web domain. He will set-up both web addresses to send customers to the same website.

Ricardo also registers the name of his company, TriathalonSupply.com, just in case. His three domains are $11.99 each for a 1-year registration.

CHAPTER 3

DESIGNING YOUR PRODUCT LINE

Now that you have your company set up and your brand identity roughed out, it's time to design your product line. Yes! You will need a product line. To create one successful shoe design, you may need to make several, maybe even a dozen different shoe designs! You may have sketch pads full of shoe design ideas, but you need to make sure your designs all work together for an overall product plan.

To get your footwear designs started in the right direction, you will need a product line merchandise plan and a footwear design brief that follows a merchandising plan.

What is a product merchandising plan?
A product merchandising plan is a document that explains the structure of your product offering. It can be as simple as a list of your shoe models and prices. It may also have notes on features, colors, and materials for each model. Your plan should also detail when you expect to deliver your merchandise. Your merchandise plan, merchandise map, SKU list, product plan, or whatever you call it, is the basic road map that will set the goals for your footwear design and development.

What is a product design brief?
The design brief is the detailed instruction sheet your product team will follow as they work to create the shoes. The design brief details everything the shoe needs to do functionally, and be stylistically. The product brief explains who the shoe is designed for, how it should look, and any other details you can think of.

Creating merchandising plans

Before you hire a designer, you will need to think about your product merchandising plans. You may have a great idea for one shoe, but that's not enough to get you started.

To make an impact and show some depth, you need to give your customers and more importantly, your dealers, some different choices.

Your first shoe idea may be a great one, but it may also be a flop. If you have a few shoes then you have a much greater chance for success. If you have five models and 3 fail, you still have 2 models you can use as a guide while you work to improve and expand your product offering.

If you are going to create more than one shoe design, you will need to consider how they relate to each other. This is the art of merchandising.

Footwear merchandising basics

Your merchandising plan will come to life depending on the type of shoes you are making and your overall brand strategy. A well-merchandised product line avoids product duplication, covers key price points, delivers options, and gives every item a reason to exist in the product line.

Your merchandising plan will be effected by the type of shoes you plan to make, but also by your brand image. Before you start designing your product line, you should have an idea of what your merchandising plan and brand image will be.

Footwear merchandising strategies

Casual shoes: You can offer the same shoe design at the same price in many different colorways or materials. If you have one very successful model, you can offer it in many colors without cannibalizing or splitting sales from one item to another. Following this product strategy may attract customers interested in your wild colors, even if they are not fans of your particular shoe.

The Converse™ All-Star™ is a perfect example of this merchandising strategy. It consists of one simple shoe made in hundreds, even thousands of different color options.

Flip-flop sandals: The basic rubber sandal can be made in hundreds of colors, many different strap styles, and an infinite number of options for screen printing designs. However, the price for this type of item is nearly always fixed.

Fashion shoes: You can offer women's fashion shoes at similar prices with very different design styles. For example, women's high heel shoes come in a huge variety of colors and styles, so the price may be less important. The merchandise plan is driven more by style options and less by price point.

Hiking shoes: For shoes with similar functions, you can offer models at different price points with different features and materials. Outdoor shoes can be made waterproof or can be made with stronger materials. A hiking product line may have only a few color options; but it will have many different price points based on materials or performance requirements.

Service boots: While military and police service boots may only be offered in black, there are many different features, such as different heights, steel toes, waterproofing, blood proofing, non-magnetic, etc. Each boot will be the same color, but will be a different price depending on the special features.

Fitting strategy: For performance running shoes the styling is very important to attract customers, but fit and sizing may be even more important. If you offer a wide range of sizes in different widths, you may have a segment of the shoe market to yourself with few competitors.

Halo strategy: To follow a halo product strategy you need to make a high-end product that has many features or a new technology. The halo product can be very expensive. You must make it innovative so you can make an impact. It's okay if sales volumes are low, you can adapt the best features to lower-priced shoes with higher sales volume.

The halo product is about boosting your overall brand image. The halo effect will make your other products look better in the eyes of your customers.

Focus strategy: Depending on your product strategy, you can abandon market segments to focus on just one target market. You can commit your company to doing one thing very well. If you are the best at a very specific product category, you can succeed!

Eve's merchandise plan is relatively simple. The Enigma product range will start out with only a few models, each will be offered in just one or two colors. Eve plans to introduce a low-cut "oxford" style shoe on a heavy boot sole, a standard-height leather boot, a standard-height boot with patterned textile inserts, and an ultra-high-top leather boot design. All the models will share one outsole unit, and the boot prices will be set low-to-high based on the boot heights.

Eve's initial product plan for Enigma is only for women's sizes. Later she may add boots for men, but her goal is to make fashion boots for women. She has created a simple list and a visual line sheet.

The Enigma merchandise plan is a mix of strategies. While some models are priced to create feature and style options, other models are fixed at the same price with the graphic style being the main point of difference.

Enigma

Model Name	Colorway	Material Note	WS $	Retail $	Forecast	Sales Forecast
Somerset	Black	Pebble Full Grain	$ 75.00	$ 150.00	300	$ 22,500
Somerset	Brown	Pebble Full Grain	$ 75.00	$ 150.00	200	$ 15,000
Brattle	Mahogoney	Laser Full Grain	$ 75.00	$ 150.00	400	$ 30,000
Brattle	Black	Laser Full Grain	$ 75.00	$ 150.00	300	$ 22,500
Tremont	Black	Smooth Full Grain	$ 57.50	$ 115.00	200	$ 11,500
Tremont	Brown	Smooth Full Grain	$ 57.50	$ 115.00	400	$ 23,000
Beacon	Black	Sub-Action Leather	$ 57.50	$ 115.00	300	$ 17,250
Beacon	White China	Action	$ 57.50	$ 115.00	200	$ 11,500
Revere	Black	Pebble Full Grain	$ 47.50	$ 95.00	400	$ 19,000
Union	Pink Roses	Action	$ 42.50	$ 85.00	300	$ 12,750
Hanover	Spiked Flowers	Action	$ 42.50	$ 85.00	200	$ 8,500
Haymarket	Black Rose	Sub-Action Leather	$ 42.50	$ 85.00	400	$ 17,000
Bowdoin	Black Floral	Sub-Action Leather	$ 42.50	$ 85.00	200	$ 8,500

Fall Collection

Full grain leather 11"
$150.00

"Somerset"

FG - Pebble

"Brattle"

FG - Pebble Laser Lace

Full grain leather 8"
$115.00

"Tremont"

FG - Pebble

"Beacon"

Action leather - Sublimation

Full grain leather Low
$95.00

"Revere"

FG - Pebble

Printed leather 11"
$85.00

"Union"

Action leather - Sublimation

Printed leather 14"
$85.00

"Hanover"

Action leather - Sublimation

Printed leather 11"
$85.00

"Haymarket"

FG Leather
Action leather - Sublimation

Printed leather 11"
$85.00

"Bowdoin"

Action leather - Sublimation

Ricardo's line plan for Arris merchandise is a bit more complex due to his design idea. He will initially offer 4 different models: 1 training shoe, 2 options for racing shoes, and 1 recovery model for post-race recovery runs.

Ricardo knows that of the millions of people who run triathlons every year, 37% are women, so he is planning to open tooling for womens' sizes shortly after.

Ricardo's research into the market for triathlon shoes shows there are many models with crazy bright colors. He needs to decide if Arris shoes will follow this trend, or try to cut in a new direction that may separate his shoes from the others. He's going to task his designer with the extra challenge.

Hmm…this is a big product range for a start-up. We will see if Ricardo can make it happen.

A large product introduction is difficult, but will give Ricardo more chances for success. If Arris starts with only one or two shoes and they both fail in the market, it may take a year for Ricardo to return with new shoes….Can a new brand like Arris survive a year without selling shoes?

Arris Line List

Model Name	Colorway	Material Note	Sizes	WS $	Retail $	Forecast	Sales Forecast
Endro X	Silver	Mesh / PU	7,8,8.5,9,9.5,10,10.511,11.5 12,13	$ 60.00	$ 120.00	300	$ 18,000
Endro X	Green	Mesh / PU	7,8,8.5,9,9.5,10,10.511,11.5 12,13	$ 60.00	$ 120.00	300	$ 18,000
Endro X	Red	Mesh / PU	7,8,8.5,9,9.5,10,10.511,11.5 12,13	$ 60.00	$ 120.00	300	$ 18,000
Phantom	Silver	Mesh / PU	7,8,8.5,9,9.5,10,10.511,11.5 12,13	$ 65.00	$ 130.00	200	$ 13,000
Lightning	Yellow	Mesh / PU	7,8,8.5,9,9.5,10,10.511,11.5 12,13	$ 55.00	$ 110.00	200	$ 11,000
Revo	Yellow	Mesh / PU	7,8,8.5,9,9.5,10,10.511,11.5 12,13	$ 45.00	$ 90.00	300	$ 13,500
							$ 91,500

Creating product design briefs

A product design brief can be a one page document, a 20 page report, or a pasted-up concept board. There is no right or wrong way to write a design brief, as long as you can define and communicate what your shoes need to be. These briefs may be created by the product manager, design manager, owner, or marketing manager. There are two common styles, each with their own purpose:

1. Demographic product brief
2. Visual design brief

The demographic product brief

This brief details the hard facts that will describe the finished shoe. This brief covers the price targets, user's demographics, market competitors, technical details and sales channels. This brief asks and answers three main questions: Who is this for? What should it do? Where will the customer buy it. Once you can answer these questions, it is time to dig deeper. More detail is better!

What is the function of this shoe?
Running, basketball, snowboarding, tennis, bowling, logging, casual or fashion?

Does the shoe have a special feature?
Thick midsole, thin midsole, fat tongue, no tongue, etc.?

Who is this shoe for?
Men, women, a new professional athlete, mall rats?

What is the age of target customer?
Toddler, teenager, college kid, middle-aged, retired?

What retail price is planned for the finished shoe?
Low, mid-range, deluxe or ultra high-end?

When will it arrive in stores?
Spring, summer, winter, fall or holiday selling seasons?

What is the silhouette?
Ultra-low, low-cut, mid-cut, high-top, skinny, puffy?

What is the target environment for these shoes?
Forest, city, desert, track, high school, mountains?

What trends are up and coming next?
Neon, earth tones, transparent, plaid?

What countries will this shoe be sold in?
USA, Canada, China, Europe, Australia?

What materials should be used?
High-tech synthetic, canvas, classic leather?

How many different color-ways are required?

Is a similar competitor's item doing well?

Is there some new technology or patented feature you are working on?

Is there a plan to a manage import taxes?

Visual design brief

The second brief is the "visual brief." It will detail the stylistic direction for the shoe. The visual brief will include photos of other shoes, cars, clothing or anything the product manager and designer can think of to help set the style or explain special design details.

For example, if the shoe is for a professional athlete, you may be inspired by the athlete's personal style or something they like. The visual brief may also be called a "mood board." A mood board can be a computer-made collage or a foamcore board with paper cutouts and fabric swatches tacked on. Photos of the products, users, and use environment should be included.

This information should all be in the designer's mind when pen hits the paper.

The Enigma Design Brief

Eve is a very talented artist and now a shoe designer. Does she need to make a design brief? The answer is, YES. A design brief will help Eve stay on track and allow her to be critical of her own work. She needs to have a practical and commercial eye on her designs. The new shoes she designs for Enigma are not just for her. Eve must think about her customers!

Arris Demographic Product Brief:

What are the functions of these shoes? Running

Do the shoes have special features? The Arris shoes are designed to work together. A complete set of Arris

shoes includes a long distance trainer, a race day shoe, and a post-race recovery shoe.

Each shoe is designed for its special purpose. They share similar upper design and last.

Training shoe: Upper is more supportive, natural fitting, midsole is firm and supportive, rubber sole is thicker and a little heavy.

Race day shoe: Fit is a little tighter, upper is lighter and a little less supportive.

The sole is ultra-thin rubber, midsole is thinner, lighter and a little firmer. Runner will feel like they have wings!

Recovery shoe: Slightly looser fit to account for swollen feet, allowing better blood flow, a semi supportive upper

soft midsole with supportive sidewall. Medium density rubber for durability and a very soft ride.

Who are the shoes for? High level triathletes

Men, women, kids? Men and women, no kids

What is the retail price? $100, $100, $100 purchase together for a discount.

When will they arrive in stores? Spring (January) 2019

What is the silhouette? Low-top jogger with heel notch.

What is the target environment for these shoes? On road running

What trends are up and coming? Study triathlon market. Very bright colors!

What countries will these shoes be sold in? USA, Canada, Europe, Australia

What materials should be used? High-tech synthetic

Is a similar competitor's item doing well? Pearl Izumi EM Tri 2™ selling thru fast!

How many different colorways are required? Maybe 3?

Is there some new technology your engineers are working on? Maybe?

Is there a plan for import taxes/duty? Not sure, shoes will be 100% synthetic

Are there existing outsole molds that can be or must be used? No

Is there a particular new design element or material to try on these new shoes?

Project may require three different shoe lasts to adjust the fitting from training to racing to recovering.

Where will these shoes be sold? Running specialty stores and online retailers.

Arris Ricardo really has no talent as a shoe designer and has no experience in footwear development , so he is going to need some professional help designing his shoe line.

Ricardo's design brief is very detailed with lots of specific information for the designer. The few extra hours of time spent organizing his thoughts will pay off.

A shoe designer's time costs money. A well-written design brief can be quickly absorbed, while an incomplete brief can require a three hour long phone conversation to clarify some details. This can be a waste of time for your designer AND a waste of money for you.

MATERIAL TRENDS - RUNNING   NO SEW TECHNOLOGY | BONDED TPU SURFACES | DYNAMIC STRETCH MATERIALS | STREAMLINED PROCESS

DESIGN TRENDS - RUNNING   STRUCTURAL GEOMETRY | 3D PRINTED BIO STRUCTURES | MULTI-LAYER COMPOSITE POLYESTER RESINS

Getting your shoes designed

If you are not trained as a shoe designer you are going to need some help. You may have a great idea for a new shoe design, but someone needs to make the drawings to communicate your ideas in a favorable and impactful way.

You will need drawings to explain your product vision to your shoe factory, potential customers, investors, and even prospective employees. This is critical. If you can't share your vision, no one will understand what you are trying to do.

Don't be afraid to hire this out. The shoe world has many hired guns that can turn your ideas into actual working shoe designs. Without great designs, your new shoe company is going nowhere. It is very important that your presentation to the factory is complete and professional. If your presentation is incomplete, difficult to understand, or sloppy, the shoe factories will not agree to work with you.

Shoe designers for hire

Don't worry if you need design help. There are many excellent independent designers and design firms that can help you. Web services like Coroflot.com™, LinkedIn.com™, and of course Google.com™, can help you find some design help. You will see there are hundreds of choices; big firms, small firms, and solo designers.

Scope of project

Before you talk to a shoe designer you will need a detailed "Scope of Project." This is simply a list of what you will need designed and the final work product you expect. You may want to see 10 different design "concepts" or design "directions," or you may want to see 4 finished designs, or 2 factory ready technical specifications. Do you need 5 upper designs and 3 outsoles, or 1 outsole and 3 uppers?

Depending on your merchandising plan, you may want one shoe design and 20 colors, or 5 designs and you will design the colors. There are many other things you can add to your scope of project. You may need a new logo design or you may need some retail packaging.

It's a good idea to have your logo design finished before your shoe designer starts working!

 Ricardo's scope of project is just a few lines. The brief should be very detailed, while the scope of project is the simple overview of what the designer will deliver.

Arris: Scope of Project

Four different models: 3 colors each

1 raining style running shoe

2 options for racing shoes:
 supportive or lightning fast

1 recovery model

Two outsoles:
Training and recovery models can share.
Race will need it's own design.
Shoes will all have a family resemblance.

Trainer: most complex (normal lacing)
Race: stripped down (normal lacing)
Recover: maybe puffy tongue
(short lace or slip on)

What to look for in a shoe designer

As a start-up company you are going to need a footwear designer with some experience. While a young gun, fresh out of art school may knock your socks off, you are going to need someone that can design to your product brief, and design a shoe that can actually be made. An experienced designer will be able to design to your price targets and will specify materials with material vendor call-outs in the detailed specifications.

An experienced designer will also have industry contacts. A well-traveled designer will have worked with many factories and will have personal contacts with developers, sourcing agents, and even factory owners.

If you know your shoes will be made in China, you should ask your designer about sourcing in China. If your designs will be made in Italy, it pays to make sure your designer has experience working with European factories. A product specification with Italian materials called out in the hands of Chinese factory may not be productive, like wise a shoe designed with Chinese materials is not appropriate for an Italian factory.

When to hire a crazy young kid

If you can partner a fresh young designer with an experienced developer or senior designer go ahead! You can have the best of both worlds. The young designer can take your designs to new, unique, and wonderful places. While your seasoned professional can make your new shoe designs production ready.

How much does a shoe designer cost?

You should expect to pay between $50 to $150 per hour. It will cost more if you are going for a top star. When you sit down with a designer or design firm, you should have your list of deliverables in mind.

For example, "I would like to see 10 concepts for lightweight hiking boots that cost around $150 retail" Or, you may ask the designer to make your concept for inflatable water-walking shoes come to life.

Some designers may not bill in terms of hours. Instead, they will give you a price for the entire project. The hours required are not important. What is important is that you receive good value for your design dollars.

How the design phases work

The shoe design work should come in 4 phases:

#1   Rough concepts done in sketch form
#2   Refine the best concepts
#3   Select concepts for final designs
#4   Make complete technical specifications

You should always break the design time into phases with regular breaks for updates and reviews. This will allow you to make course corrections and suggestions as you go. This will also allow you to stop or accelerate the process if you see something you like or hate.

You should expect to pay a few thousand dollars. Don't worry, a great design can be worth millions of dollars in the end. You should expect to start with a retainer fee. It is normal for a designer to require a retainer as it's just too easy for a client to take a set of drawings and not pay for them. Don't be offended. A retainer fee is common practice.

Design proposal

Once you have found a designer you like and have presented your design brief and scope of project, you can ask the designer to counter with a design proposal. The proposal will include the design service, estimated hours, and list of deliverables. Don't be afraid to shop around with your design brief. Prices can vary widely depending on how busy the designer is.

How long does it take to design a shoe?

A real footwear pro can sketch up to 10 new shoes in just a few hours, but these will just be ideas. A complete design, ready for the factory, may take 10 to 20 hours from start to finish. A complicated outsole may take a bit more time.

You should plan on approximately 4 weeks of design time from start to finish. The exact length of time will depend on the scope of your project and how many other projects your designer is working on.

 **Arris** Ricardo's challenge is to find and hire a shoe designer that can turn his ideas into a workable product line. Ricardo searches for design firms in San Diego and Los Angeles. He knows it's a good idea to try and find someone local that he can meet with. He also searches the online portfolios found on Coroflot.com™. He finds several designers with production shoes in their design portfolios and contacts them online and over the phone to discuss the Arris project.

After meeting with 3 different designers, Ricardo finds a designer close to his office in Southern California. The designer has experience with running shoes and has worked for a major athletic brand.

With his design briefs and merchandising plan in hand, Ricardo meets with the designer. After discussing the project with Mike, Ricardo decides to go forward. Mike prepares a design proposal detailing the costs, and agrees to meet Ricardo at a local triathlon to study their target customers.

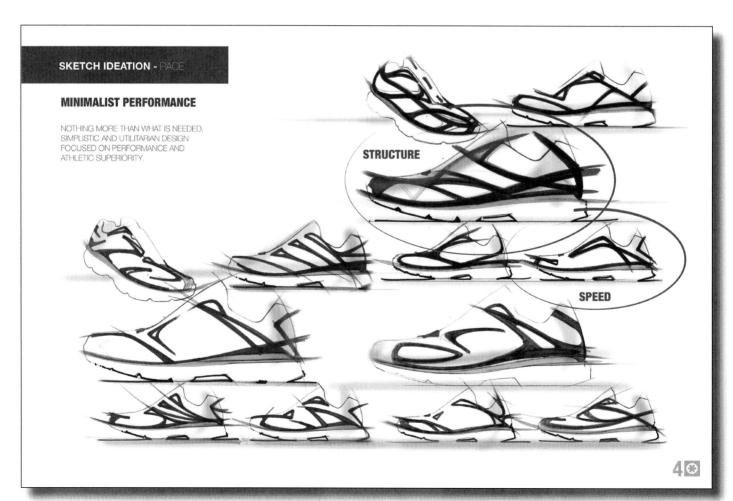

SKETCH IDEATION - RACE

MINIMALIST PERFORMANCE

NOTHING MORE THAN WHAT IS NEEDED, SIMPLISTIC AND UTILITARIAN DESIGN FOCUSED ON PERFORMANCE AND ATHLETIC SUPERIORITY.

STRUCTURE

SPEED

4✷

Mike Smith Industrial Design
7463 Blue Ocean Ave., Suite 7
Encinitas, CA

Design estimate for: Ricardo
Brand: Arris Run Race Recover

Scope of the Project:
Design two high-end running shoe (training) silhouettes
Design will include uppers and outsole from approved concepts
Concepts for the lightweight "race" shoe and comfort-styled "recovery" shoe will be generated.

Phase #1
Sketch first concepts: 8 hours
Mike will deliver to Ricardo photos or scans of hand-drawn concept sketches showing patterns, design detail and possible logo applications.
Ricardo will review designs and offer comments so designs can be finalized.

Finalize design concepts: 6 hours
Mike will deliver to Ricardo .ai and/or PDF format drawings of refined final design concepts for approval.

Phase #2
Approved designs will be made production ready: 3 - 4 hours per model selected.
Mike will deliver to Ricardo complete drawing, tech-pack and complete product specifications ready for first round sample making.

Phase #3
First round product development: 3 to 8 hours (in China)
Assign to factory sample room for sample building
Build "Pull-Over" of patterns
Assemble color-correct samples
Mike will deliver to Ricardo sample shoes for study.
Arris Running will be responsible for factory sample charges, material charges and shipping charges.

(When possible, Mike will provide outline of changes in advance.)

Rates:
Design rate: $150 per hour
Development rate: $150 per hour + travel expenses to be determined
3D CAD design rate: $150 per hour

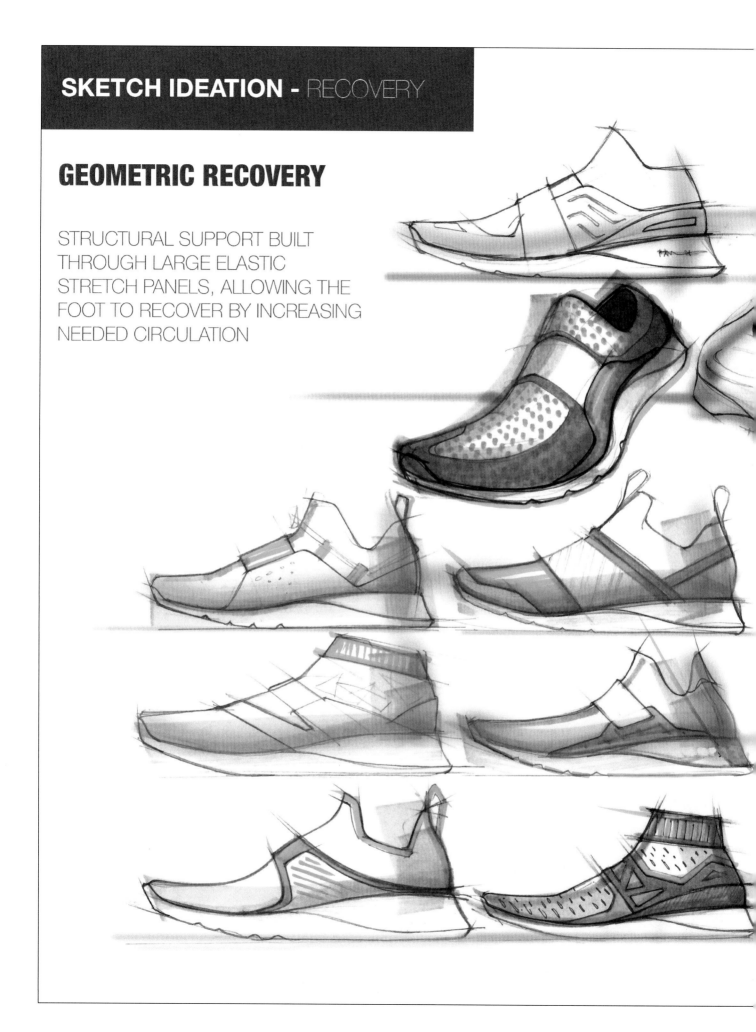

GEOMETRIC RECOVERY

STRUCTURAL SUPPORT BUILT
THROUGH LARGE ELASTIC
STRETCH PANELS, ALLOWING THE
FOOT TO RECOVER BY INCREASING
NEEDED CIRCULATION

STRUCTURED PLATFORM

SPECIFICALLY DESIGN TO ENHANCE AND PROTECT
MUSCLE PERFORMANCE OVER LONG
PERIODS OF TRAINING TIME.

4

ARRIS FOOTWEAR - RECOVERY

RECOVERY SLIP-ON - RETAIL $85.00
MEN'S | WOMEN'S

20 MM WEBBING PILL TAB

TWO COLOR TPU HEAT CUT LOGO

55 MM STRETCH GORE PANEL - FREE FLOATING
ADDITIONAL FOOT SUPPORT

4 WAY STRETCH COMPOSIT MESH MATERIAL
DOUBLE LEYER OUTER & LINING MATERIALS
100% BREATHABLE MESH MATERIAL

OPTIONAL KNITTED VERSION IF POSSIBLE BY FACTORY

EXPANDED EVA INJECTION MIDSOLE
WITH BLOWN RUBBER PODS

BONDED TPU MA
15% - 20% STRET

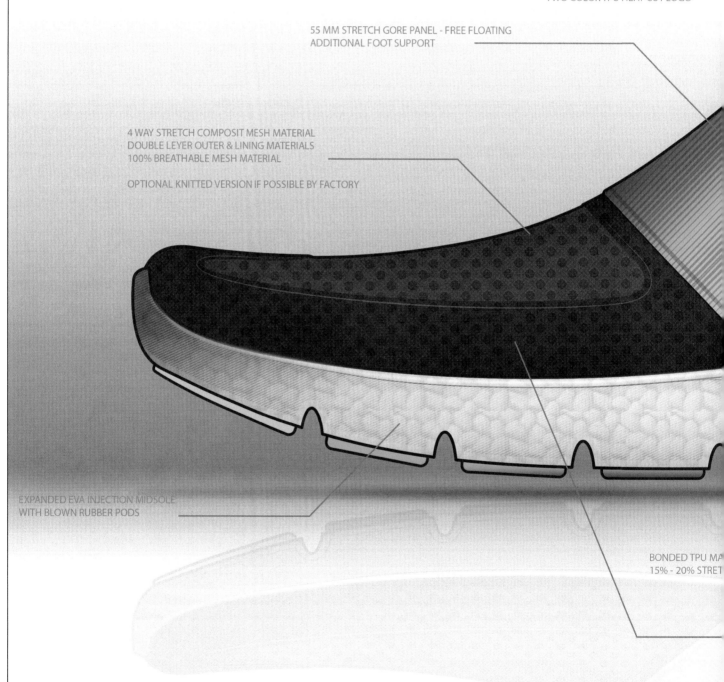

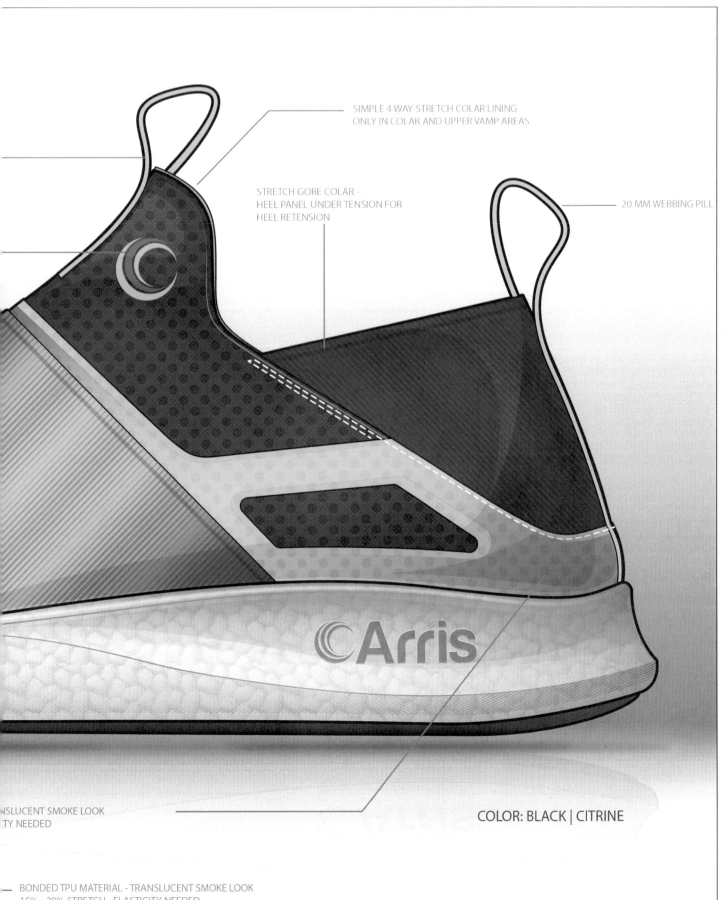

SIMPLE 4 WAY STRETCH COLAR LINING
ONLY IN COLAR AND UPPER VAMP AREAS

STRETCH GORE COLAR -
HEEL PANEL UNDER TENSION FOR
HEEL RETENSION

20 MM WEBBING PILL

©Arris

NSLUCENT SMOKE LOOK
TY NEEDED

COLOR: BLACK | CITRINE

BONDED TPU MATERIAL - TRANSLUCENT SMOKE LOOK
15% - 20% STRETCH - ELASTICITY NEEDED

ARRIS FOOTWEAR - RECOVERY

MEN'S - RECOVERY

COLOR: CARBON | BLACK
UNISEX COLORWAY

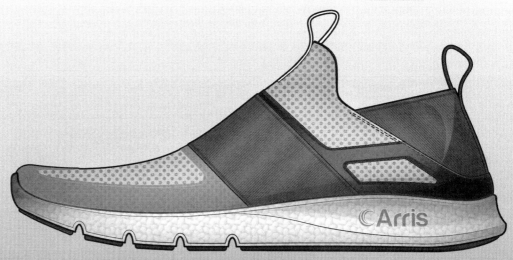

COLOR: LIGHT GREY | ROSSO RED

COLOR: ROSSO RED

WOMEN'S - RECOVERY

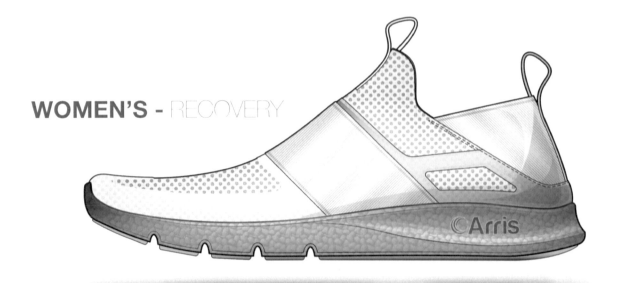

COLOR: WHITE | PALE BLUE

COLOR: BLACK | PEACOCK

COLOR: LT GREY | ROSEBLOOM

Eve is doing her own design work! She's thrilled to have her design brief and merchandise plans in front of her. Enigma boots are very fashionable and she is having fun pasting-up designs. Her plan is to make 50 design concepts and show them to her friends, family, classmates, and the manager at her local alternative clothing store.

38

Development Specification Sheet

	Project Name:	Enigma Beacon
	Factory:	Houjie #1
	Prototype ID:	ENG-Fall 2018-004
	Season:	Fall 2018
	Division:	Fashion
	Color description:	China White
	Country of origin:	China
	Construction:	Cold Cement Cement / Faux Welt
		Board Lasted
	Gender/Size:	W'S7#
	Size run:	7, 7.5,8,8.5,9,10
	Last code:	ENG721
	Outsole code:	IRON-Age-006
	Status:	Photo Sample

	Component Type	Component Specification	Color	Supplier
	UPPER			
1	Toe Top / Mudguard	1.8mm White Smooth grain Action Leather	White	Nan-Ya Tanning
2	Toe Top / Mudguard ART	Sublimation	White/Blue	Cosmo HK
3	Vamp Lining	Cosmo Dream Spacer 100% Polyester	Black	Local
4	Quarter/Eyerow	1.8mm White Smooth grain Action Leather	White	Nan-Ya Tanning
5	Quarter/Eyerow ART	Sublimation	White/Blue	Local
6	Tongue	1.8mm White Smooth grain Action Leather	White	Cosmo HK
7	Tongue Lace keeper	1.8mm White Smooth grain Action Leather	White	Nan-Ya Tanning
8	Tongue Logo	32mm x 32mm Woven Label Stacked "Enigma"	White/Black	Local
9	Tongue Lining	1.0mm Syn - Pig + 4MMKF329+24GT/C	Black	Local
10	Tongue Foam	10mm KFF PU foam	NA	Local
11	Lace Eyelets	8mm Steel	Black	Dae-Sung
12	Medial Vents	8mm Steel	Black	Dae-Sung
13	Shoe Lace	5mm Cotton Waxed Round	Black	Pahio
14	Heel Panel	1.8mm Black Smooth grain Action Leather	Black	Cosmo HK
15	Lining	1.0mm Syn - Pig + 4MMKF329+24GT/C	NA	Cosmo HK
16	Internal Heel Counter	Texon Rite thermoplastic 1.4mm	NA	Texon
17	Internal Toe Puff	Texon Sportflex .35mm thermoplastic film	NA	Texon
18	Eyerow Reinforcement	Super Tuff	NA	Local
19	Upper Thread	bonded nylon 6 250D 3 Ply	Matching	Coats or A&E
	OUTSOLE UNIT			
20	Outsole	#1-44 NBS400 Shore "A" 65 +or-3 SG 1.1 +1.4	Gum	CW Pressing
21	Outsole Color Break	NBS400 Shore "A" 65 +or-3 SG 1.1 +1.4	Black	CW Pressing
22	Outsole Welt	Rubber NBS400 Shore "A" 65 +or-3 SG 1.1 +1.4	Black	CW Pressing
23	Outsole Stitching	bonded nylon 6 850D 3 Ply	Gum	Coats or A&E
24	Insole Strobel	Texon T28	White	Texon
25	Footbed	Cold Pressed EVA Asker "C" 45 Standard Open Mold	Black	Local
26	Foobed Skin	1.0mm Syn - Pig + 4MMKF329+24GT/C	White	Cosmo HK
27	Foobed Logo	Screen Print Logo "Enigma" 65mm Heat Transfer	Black / Red	Local
28	Cement	Water based PU	Clear	Nan-Pou
	PACKING			
30	Inner Box	2016 Box art E-Flue - White Back PVC skin	Black	Lai-Wah
31	Out Carton	Brown	Brown	Local
32	Tongue label	3cm x 3cm White + Black Screen + Weld	Black / White	Local
33	EEC label	2cm x 2cm White + Black Print	Black / White	Local
34	Hangtag	4-Color Print	Color	Lai-Wah
35	Tag pin	White	White	Local
36	Wrap Tissue	10 gram 2 sheets	White	Local
37	Toe Tissue	10 gram 2 sheets	White	Local

Do you need a patent?

If your new shoe idea is something very special and unique, you should work to protect it. Filing for a patent can offer you protection for up to 18 years. There are three types of patents: design, utility, and provisional.

Design patents

The design patent is used to protect a particular look or aesthetic design element. This ONLY protects how the item looks and the patent must be specific. It only protects you from having the look of your shoe copied. You can check out these two Nike design patents on google.com: "Shoe outsole USD329536 S" and "Shoe upper US D333032 S." You will see that the scope of the design patent is very narrow. These patents do not make any function claims. If you follow the link inside the patents, you will find that Nike has thousands and thousands of these "shoe design element" patents.

Design patents are not too difficult to get. You can file and be awarded a design patent for around $5,000. Are design patents worth the cost and effort? For a small firm, maybe not. For a huge firm like Nike with companies trying to copy their designs, yes.

Remember: Your logo design is protected by registering your trademark.

Utility patents

A utility patent is used to protect truly unique ideas for construction or function of a shoe. You can see online that Nike has thousands of utility patents. You can look up this one for "Automatic lacing system US 8769844 B2."

A utility patent can be incredibly valuable. A well-written utility patent can be worth millions of dollars…if you have the money to defend against infringing competitors. A utility patent may cost $15,000 or more depending on the cost for the research and the writing of the claims. If your new firm is based on one amazing new idea, you should do a patent search to make sure you are not violating any existing patents. You can start this on your own but a patent attorney will have to make the final search.

Utility patents are not cheap but if you have a good idea it must be protected.

You can file for a design patent by yourself, but for a utility patent you will need to hire an expert patent attorney to help file your patent application.

Once your patent is issued, you can list the patent number on your product, letting people know your design is protected.

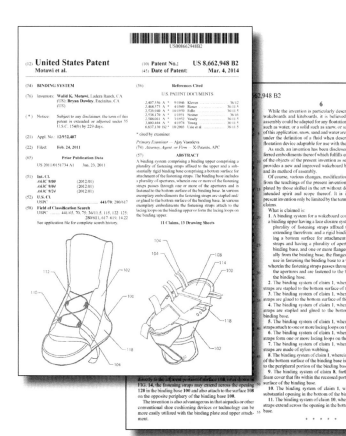

When you review a patent there are a few important things to look for.

#1. The issue date: If the patent is more that 20 years old you can ignore it.

#2. Is the patent a design or utility patent?

#3. Look at the inventor and owners. Use these as search terms to find other patents.

#4. Give the abstract a quick review to get the idea.

#5. The claims are the most important part of the patent. The claims are the legal description of the invention. There are two types of claims: independent and dependent. The independent claims are the critical ones.

Provisional patents

You should also research the provisional patent. The provisional patent is an inexpensive way to "hold your place in line." This allows you to get "patent pending" protection on your design. The provisional patent establishes an early filing date, but does not mature into an issued patent unless you file a regular non-provisional patent application within one year.

The provisional patent does not require professionally written claims. You will see after reading a few patents, that the language used is very dense and specific.

While you are waiting for your provisional patent to be issued, you can use the term "Patent Pending" on your product letting people know your design will be protected.

Preparing your idea for a patent

When describing your invention, you will need to answer a few questions:

What is the name of your invention?

Who designed or imagined the invention?

Was the invention created under a contract?

Do you have the rights to the invention?

What is the purpose or function of your invention?

Do you have the drawings you need to explain the invention?

What are the parts of the invention?

How do the components interact with each other?

How does the invention work?

Have you listed all the ways to construct your invention?

Does the Arris concept need a patent? Yes! Ricardo will need a patent for his 3-shoe system. He worries that someone will copy his idea. There are huge shoe companies that could use the Arris concept. It needs to be protected. Ricardo also wants a patent so he can use the patent number in his marketing materials.

Ricardo starts researching patents online. There are many websites that pull records from the U.S. government patent office database. After a few hours of searching, Ricardo finds a few related items, but nothing that is similar to his idea. He makes notes of any related patents. He knows it's a good idea to give the patent attorney a place to start and he hopes this will save the cost of a few hours of billable research time.

Before Ricardo meets with a patent attorney, he has a few drawings made to describe the details of the Arris concept. His designer is able to make these quickly, as he is familiar with the design. Ricardo also writes down the idea and the major "claims" he wants to include.

The claims are the heart of a patent. They define exactly what the patent does and does not cover. A patent may have just one or two claims, or it may have several pages of claims. The Arris patent is complex and it's going to take some time to get it done. Ricardo quickly files a provisional patent just to be safe.

Eve does not need any patents. Her designs do not introduce any new or unique utility. She can file for design patents but for a small fashion design company it's not worth the effort or expense. If Eve does find a design detail she thinks will be a huge seller, she can file a design patent, or trademark a graphic design or pattern at that time.

CHAPTER 4

PLANNING YOUR SHOE BUSINESS

In this chapter we will review launch-timing for your new shoe line and build footwear costing models. You need to make sure your winter boots arrive in time for the winter selling season and do the math to make sure you can deliver them profitably.

When and how to launch your shoes into the market

All your work getting your shoes designed and built is at risk if your market timing is wrong. The shoe market has buying and selling cycles or seasons.

The common retail selling seasons are fall, holiday, spring, April and summer. Cruise is also a small delivery window for some fashion items but not for shoes. For shoes; fall, spring, and summer are generally the largest delivery windows. Holiday and April deliveries are smaller but still very important.

To ensure your shoes are available in stores for these delivery windows you will need to work the schedule backwards many months. Depending on your sales and distribution plan, you may need your sales reps on the road selling 7-8 months in advance of your planned delivery date.

Delivery seasons

Fall

Can also be called "back to school." This is a large delivery window for many different types of shoes. The fall delivery is critical for football cleats, cross country running, basketball and any other shoe needed by students going back to school or college. Any winter boots and rain gear will also be on the fall schedule.

Fall product must be available to your stores starting in late June so they will be fully stocked for the shopping rush. Your dealers will be switching off the summer product set-up in mid to late July. Fall orders must be placed to the shoe factory February 1st, in order to exit the factory May 1st, and be available for retailers to order in late June.

Holiday

The Christmas shopping season can account for 25% to 45% of yearly sales, and it is important to have fresh product for your dealers. The holiday delivery product is often a tune-up of your top sellers and a great place to roll out special colors or new development items that missed the fall introduction schedule.

Holiday orders must be placed to the shoe factory June 1st, in order to exit the factory September 1st and be available for retail in October. You can expect to pay extra for ocean shipping during the holiday run-up as merchandise floods in from around the world.

Spring

Spring is also a major delivery window. Spring is a key season for summer sport shoes and items needed for winter vacation travel. The new spring merchandise is how your dealers will restock their stores after the holiday shopping rush.

Spring orders must be placed to the shoe factory September 1st in order to exit the factory December 1st, and be available for retail in January.

Summer or April

This delivery is usually the smallest. Retailers will use this April product offering to top up their inventory for the summer selling season. Summer is a chance for shoe companies to offer new colors of top selling models.

Dealers and pre-booking schedule

To meet these seasonal windows on a pre-booking schedule, your development and production teams need to have samples in your sales reps hands 2 to 3 months ahead of your order deadline. If your reps can cover their accounts faster, you can reduce the booking window.

With the typical total production time of 90 to 120 days plus shipping time, you can see why it may take 6 months for a shoe to be in store from when the buyer said, "Yes!"

Direct-to-consumer schedule

Many companies have a direct-to-consumer model that can significantly reduce the time to market, but at the risk of having unwanted merchandise.

If you are selling direct to the consumer, the sales sample production and pre-booking windows are eliminated from the schedule. As soon as you have confirmed your shoe designs for production, you can place the orders to the factory, saving many months.

Again, with a typical production time of 90 to 120 days for orders, plus shipping time, even the direct-to-consumer sales model requires the shoe be confirmed for production 4 months in advance of the planned release date.

In Chapter 5 we will review all the steps of the development process and explain the required time lines in further detail.

Ricardo wants to hit the spring and summer triathlon buying season in the United States. Arris shoes will need to be ready for dealers to take delivery in January. Ricardo follows the sales rep. pre-booking model to make sure he orders the right models.

Because the Arris product range is on the larger side, it is very important to sort out the top sellers from the slow sellers early.

Ricardo must place his sales samples order to the factory March 15th. The order is small so he will ship by air. Large orders usually ship by ocean freight; assuming the development work is on time.

Arris sales force booking window:
May 15th to August 31st
For a large territory, 8 weeks should be enough time to show the shoes and follow up for orders.

Ricardo places his first production order:
August 5th
Shoe production can take 90 to 120 days.

Arris production shoes are on-board ship:
December 1st

Ocean freight lands in Long Beach harbor:
January 1st

Delivery to dealers:
January 15th

Spring Delivery

Month	Week	Activity
MAY	1	DESIGN
	2	DESIGN
	3	DESIGN
	4	DESIGN
JUN	1	DESIGN
	2	DESIGN
	3	Spec Drop
	4	TECH -1
JUL	1	TECH -1
	2	TECH -1
	3	TECH -1
	4	TECH -1
AUG	1	SHIPPING
	2	Design Changes
	3	TECH -2
	4	TECH -2
SEP	1	TECH -2
	2	TECH -2
	3	TECH -2
	4	TECH -2
OCT	1	SHIPPING
	2	Design Changes
	3	TECH -3
	4	TECH -3
NOV	1	TECH -3
	2	TECH -3
	3	SHIPPING
	4	PHOTO SAMPLE
DEC	1	FOCUS GROUP
	2	Photo sample production
	3	Photo sample production
	4	Photo sample production
JAN	1	Photo sample production
	2	Photo sample production
	3	Photo sample production
	4	Photo sample production
FEB	1	SHIPPING
	2	FINAL LINE BUILD!
	3	FINAL LINE BUILD!
	4	Sales Sample
MAR	1	Sales Sample

Fall Delivery

Month	Week
OCT	1
	2
	3
	4
NOV	1
	2
	3
	4
DEC	1
	2
	3
	4
JAN	1
	2
	3
	4
FEB	1
	2
	3
	4
MAR	1
	2
	3
	4
APR	1
	2
	3
	4
MAY	1
	2
	3
	4
JUN	1
	2
	3
	4
JUL	1
	2
	3
	4
AUG	1

Eve is a bit more flexible, but she needs to be ready for the fall selling season. While Eve plans to have a direct-to-consumer online store, she will also offer her boots to fashion stores "at-once." She will deliver to her accounts from her stock immediately upon receiving the orders. While buying shoes without orders can be risky, Eve is confident she can sell all of her boots.

Eve places her first production order:
February 1st

Enigma boots production ship date:
May 1st

Ocean freight lands in Boston harbor:
June 1st

In stock and ready for online sales:
June 15th

Timeline / Production Phases

Month	Week	Phase
APR	1–4	Production
MAY	1–4	SHIPPING / Sales Booking Window
JUN	1–4	Sales Booking Window
JUL	1–4	Sales Booking Window
AUG	1–4	Sales Booking Window
SEP	1–4	Order Deadline / 90 Day Production Time
OCT	1–4	90 Day Production Time
NOV	1–4	90 Day Production Time
DEC	1–4	Exit Factory / Shipping
JAN	1–4	Landing / Check In - Ship to Customers

Month	Week
SEP	2, 3, 4
OCT	1, 2, 3, 4
NOV	1, 2, 3, 4
DEC	1, 2, 3, 4
JAN	1, 2, 3, 4
FEB	1, 2, 3, 4
MAR	1, 2, 3, 4
APR	1, 2, 3, 4
MAY	1, 2, 3, 4
JUN	1, 2, 3, 4

Financial modeling

Before you send any orders to the shoe factory, and before you show samples to potential customers, you need to build your financial models to see if you can make any money! Financial modeling may sound complicated, but once you have a basic understanding, it's easy.

While your new company may not show any profits your first year due to start-up expenses, it's critical that you understand your shoe business sale by sale BEFORE your product launch.

To build your financial models, you will first need to calculate how much it will cost to buy your shoes and import them into your selling market. This is called landing.

Of course, you will not have a free on board (FOB) price for your shoes yet, but you will use the models to work backwards. You will need to give the factory a realistic target price for your shoes.

Once you determine the cost to land your shoes, you will need to select your sales and distribution business model. We are going to focus on the two most common business models: wholesale distribution, and direct-to-consumer marketing.

You will find footwear sales and distribution models detailed in chapter 8 of this book.

Import duty for shoes is reviewed in chapter 5.

Product cost calculations

To build your complete financial model, you are going to need to figure out your real product costs. When you negotiate your shoe purchase price, you need to set the purchase terms with the factory. Usually, your price will be quoted as FOB. The FOB price includes the cost to build, package, and deliver the shoes by container truck to the container harbor. FOB means you will work with the international shipping lines to move your container and not with a local trucking company. Leave the local trucking price negotiations to the factory.

Another common shoe purchase term is "ex-works," which means you or your freight forwarder are responsible for picking up the shoes from the factory. You may buy your shoes ex-works if you are loading a container with other products.

Rarely do you buy your shoes "landed." The landed price includes the importing and shipping to your warehouse. Agents may offer to land the shoe for you, so they can profit from the shipping. Most of the time you will purchase your shoes "FOB."

LANDING CALCULATIONS

Once you have the factory price you need to consider the cost to "land" the shoe. Landing includes all the costs related to bringing your shoes from the factory to your warehouse or your logistics provider. You need to add the cost of ocean freight, inland trucking, harbor fees, insurance fees, import duties, document fees, etc. It's critical to understand these costs, as this will help you work backwards from your shoes' selling price to your factory target price.

Here is a typical landing calculation.

	FOB	Freight Ins. Fees	Container Load pairs	Container Rate	Freight Cost	Duty Rate	Duty	Landed
Arris	$15	0.9%	5000	$4400	$1.02	9%	$1.44	$17.46
	A	**B**	**C**	**D**	**E**	**F**	**G**	**H**

A. The shoe price per pair is $15 FOB boxed and ready to ship from the factory.
B. Insurance and harbor fees are .9% of the value of the shoe, so $15 X .009=$.135 per pair.
C. A standard 40' container holds about 5,000 pairs of shoes, packed 10 or 12 pairs in a case box.
D. The container freight cost from China to the USA with inland trucking is $4,400.
E. The container rate divided by the container load $4400 / 5000 = $1.02.
F. The import duty rate for leather shoes is 9%.
G. Add the FOB and freight together, then multiply by the duty rate = $1.44.
H. Add the duty value, freight, insurance, and FOB. The landed cost is $17.46

In this case, a shoe which initially costs $15 will cost a total of $17.46 to buy, ship and import into the USA. The additional inland freight inside your home country could be $.10 to $.50 per pair, depending on your distribution center's proximity to the landing port. There are also fees for the drivers waiting time which is required when having the container unloaded or dropped off.

If you are using an agent, you may be required to pay duty on the agent's fees. It's best to consult your home country's import regulations. USA regulations require import duty to be paid on any molds or equipment used to make the shoes.

If you purchased any equipment to make your shoes, the value of this tooling needs to be amortized into the price per pair and import duty paid at the same rate as the merchandise. This is called an "assist." If your tooling cost is already being amortized as part of your price from the factory, then no assist is required.

This is the most basic calculation for the landed cost. Once you get started, your freight forwarder can help detail other small fees. Some of the costs of the components are under your control, and some are not.

A. FOB: You can control the FOB cost of your shoe by adjusting its specification.
B. Insurance and harbor fees: You have no control over these fees.
C. Container load: Your shoe packaging design can increase the number of shoes in a container load.
D. Shipping rates: You can shop around and compare rates for discounts. FCL rates are the lowest.
E. Inland freight: Shop around for better inland rates in your home market.
F. Duty rate: Your designs are critical for setting your duty rate. Duty can be 0% to 9% to 37.5%. In many cases, a more expensive shoe can have a lower duty rate, the net effect being a better shoe at a lower price! (See chapter 5 for import duty regulations.)

Overhead calculations

Once your shoes have landed and are inside your warehouse, you are going to have some overhead expenses. It can be difficult to divide your overhead cost into a per pair calculation, but it is a good idea to try. You will know most of the costs if you are using a third party logistics provider (3PL) to fulfill your orders. You will know how much your space rental and order processing costs will be. For a 3PL you can expect to pay between $3 and $4 to fulfill each pair.

If you had to borrow money to buy the shoes, then you should add the interest expense to your overhead. You can expect a 7% interest rate or more to borrow money for your shoe purchase.

Rented office space, employee wages, and office equipment expenses all add up. The more accurate your overhead calculations are, the more accurate your final profit margin calculations will be.

Every company calculates overhead for their products differently. Some companies don't calculate the overhead at all, while some companies figure a percentage rate based on experience. This percentage is usually more than 5% but less than 15%.

Marketing expenses are critical for a young and expanding brand. As a general rule, you should expect marketing expenses of between 10% to 20% of your projected gross sales. This can be a big part of your overhead, so it must be included.

You will need to add your overhead cost to your landed cost before you make your final selling calculations.

If you plan on paying a royalty to an athlete, or are required to pay a license fee to a patent holder, you will need to add this to your landed cost as well.

Don't forget to add your design and development costs to your overhead calculations.

Once you have the overhead and any other charges added, the landed cost may be called a "frozen" or "fixed" product cost.

Selling calculations

How you plan to sell and distribute your shoes is critical to how you make your financial models.

Wholesale distribution margin model

This is a more traditional model followed by most large shoe companies. The shoes are designed and sampled (one size only) and the samples are used by a sales force of in-house salaried reps, or independent commission-based sales reps, to collect pre-orders or pre-bookings. With these pre-orders in hand, the shoe company will place the production orders with the shoe factory. Once the shoes arrive, they are sold to the dealers and the sales reps collect their commission.

Direct-to-consumer margin model

With the modern internet available to help market shoes, the direct-to-consumer model for selling shoes can work. Instead of collecting pre-bookings, the shoes are purchased from the factory in bulk, then sold directly to the end users. This model bypasses traditional retailers and distributors.

Of course, you can also use a combination of the two business models. Some shoe models are sold into the retail chain and some are internet only. Some brands can sell in-store and online without retailers complaining. You have to be careful. Some dealers may drop your brand if they think you are competing with their store by selling on-line.

WHOLESALE DISTRIBUTION MODEL

If you follow the wholesale distribution model, the shoes are warehoused by the shoe company, then sold to shoe stores with the sales reps collecting a commission.

In the wholesale distribution model you will need to set the Manufacturers Suggested Retail Price (MSRP) or Minimum Advertised Price (MAP) for the retailer. Once your planned retail price is defined, you can set your wholesale price. It's important for you to set a realistic price and margin for your dealers. 50% is standard. The goal of most retailers is to "keystone" the product. Keystone is 100% markup from wholesale to retail with a 50% profit. Keystone is not always possible, but very few retailers will plan on less than a 40% profit when they sell your shoes.

When a retailer cuts the selling price down by 50%, the retailer is selling the product at 0% profit or even at a loss.

Here is a basic selling calculation that does not account for any discounts or sales commissions.

Landed Cost	Frozen	Wholesale	Retail	Profit	Margin	Forecast	Sales	Profit
$17.46	$18.68	$40	$80	$21.32	53.3%	5000	$200,000	$106,600
A	B	C	D	E	F	G	H	I

A	The shoe's FOB or landed cost, $17.46
B	Landed cost times 7% overhead charge, $17.46 x 1.07 = $18.68 frozen or fixed cost
C	Wholesale selling price to dealers is $40
D	Retail (MSRP or MAP) is $80. The 100% mark up is called keystone
E	Wholesale price minus frozen cost, $40 - $18.68 = $21.32 in profit
F	Profit divided by the wholesale cost, $21.32 / 40 = 53.3% margin
G	How many pairs do you plan to sell? 5000
H	Pairs to sell times wholesale cost, 5000 x $40 = $200,000 in sales
I	Profit times pairs sold, $21.32 x 5000 = $106,600 total profit

The margins analyzed below are calculated from an "average" wholesale price to dealers. This accounts for 10% in commissions and discounts. This is a more realistic calculation. You can see what happens to the profit margin.

FOB	Frozen	Wholesale	Avg. Wholesale	Retail	Profit	Margin	Forecast	Sales	Profit
$17.46	$18.68	$40.00	$36.00	$80.00	$17.32	48.11%	5000	$150,000	$86,600
A	B	C	D	E	F	G	H	I	J

A	The shoe's FOB or landed cost, $17.46
B	Landed cost times 7% overhead charge, $17.46 x 1.07 = $18.68 frozen or fixed cost
C	Wholesale selling price to dealers is $40
D	Wholesale price minus 10% (5% commission and 5% discount) = $36 average wholesale price
E	Retail (MSRP or MAP) is $80
F	Average wholesale price minus frozen cost, $36 - $18.68 = $17.32 in profit
G	Profit divided by the wholesale cost, $17.32 / 36 = 48.11% margin
H	How many pairs do you plan to sell? 5000
I	Pairs to sell times average wholesale cost, 5000 x $36 = $180,000 in sales
J	Profit times pairs sold, $17.32 x 5000 = $86,600 total profit

DIRECT-TO-CONSUMER MODEL

In the direct-to-consumer model you will be in control of the retail price. You may make a simple calculation and say, "Wow! I'm going to be rich!"

Landed	Frozen	Retail	Profit	Margin	Forecast	Sales	Profit
$17.46	$18.68	$80.00	$61.32	76.65%	5000	$400,000	$306,600
A	**B**	**C**	**D**	**E**	**F**	**G**	**H**

A	The shoe's FOB or landed cost, $17.46
B	Landed cost times 7% overhead charge, $17.46 x 1.07 = $18.68 frozen or fixed cost
C	Retail (MSRP or MAP) is $80
D	Retail price minus frozen cost, $80 - $18.68 = $61.32 in profit
E	Profit divided by the retail cost, $61.32 / 80 =76.65% margin
F	How many pairs do you plan to sell? 5000
G	Pairs to sell times retail cost, 5000 x $80 = $400,000 in sales
H	Profit times pairs sold, $61.32 x 5000 = $306,600 total profit

Watch out! This simple calculation is missing a few important details. In the direct-to-consumer sales model you still need a "store." While your web store may be inexpensive, it will not be free. To compete in the online shoe market, you will need some paid online advertising such as search engine ads. You may also need a warehouse or a 3PL to fulfill your orders to your customers.

Another issue to consider is that you will own the shoes until you sell them. This means you will need to find capital to invest in your inventory. In the pre-book distribution model many of the shoes you buy from the factory are sold before you buy them.

FOB	Frozen	Retail	Credit 7%	Freight	Web Conv	3PL	Profit	Margin	Forecast	Sales	Profit
$17.46	$18.68	$80	$1.31	$1.00	$5	$18.13	$35.88	44.85%	5000	$400,000	$179,400
A	**B**	**C**	**D**	**E**	**F**	**G**	**H**	**I**	**J**	**K**	**L**

A	The shoe's FOB or landed cost, $17.46
B	Landed cost times 7% overhead charge, $17.46 x 1.07 = $18.68 frozen or fixed cost
C	Retail (MSRP or MAP) is $80
D	Frozen cost times 7% interest rate on money from bank, $18.63 x .07 = $1.31 interest per pair
E	Freight inbound to 3PL, $1.00 per pair
F	Web advertising cost per conversion, $5.00 per pair
G	3PL provider expenses (AMAZON FBA™) including listing fee, $18.13 per pair
H	Retail price minus frozen cost, interest, freight, web, 3PL, = $35.88 profit
I	Profit divided by the retail cost, $35.88 / 80 = 44.85% margin
J	How many pairs do you plan to sell? 5000
K	Pairs to sell times retail cost, 5000 x $80 = $400,000 in sales
L	Profit times pairs sold, $35.88 x 5000 = $179,400 total profit

Do you plan on offering any discounts? What about free shipping? A 20% discount off your retail price or an offer of free shipping could reduce your profit by $15. Your margin is quickly down to a dangerous 24%.

What is an acceptable profit margin?

Footwear profit margin goals for every shoe company are different. Margin goals will vary depending on the distribution arrangements, the market position for the brand, and the price point.

There is no right or wrong answer. The highest margin possible is not always the best answer. There are many good reasons to have a high margin target and just as many to set a lower margin goal.

What is the standard margin? 50% and above is great! 40% to 50% is still good. Below 40% may not be so good, but then again, this depends on what market you are in.

Do you have big plans for marketing and advertising campaigns? If so, you may need to set your margin well above 50% to pay for it.

The couture high fashion and ultra luxury brands can command high margins. They need to! Big international ad campaigns and celebrity endorsements are very expensive!

Nike™ can command high margins for Jordan™ shoes, but less for their kids shoes.

Is your super-brand hot in the retail market? Are you growing very fast? Are you having a hard time meeting demand? If your company is growing too fast or is getting out of control, higher margin targets can bring in higher profits while slowing growth to a level you can manage.

Do you have new technology that nobody can copy or an exclusive on a new material? If so, you can keep your margins high.

High-end products with high-end features can command higher margins from high-end customers.

The margin rate will also depend on the retailer for your shoes. Are you targeting discount stores or specialty retailers? Specialty shoes can command higher margins over commodity shoes at discount stores.

If your shoes are hot sellers and in demand, you can command higher margins and you don't need to offer retailers any discounts. The top luxury brands are never on sale, and can also offer the retailer high margins.

If you are in a competitive market, you may need to offer discounts.

When is a lower margin okay?

There are times when a lower margin is okay, even advised. Of course, sometimes the shoe company has no choice and must cut margins.

A good time to accept a lower margin is when you are trying to grow your market share aggressively. Footwear buyers and customers know a good value when they see it. The dealer may pass on the great price to their customers or hold onto the extra margin for themselves. This is okay. A happy retailer always buys more!

Are you looking to create customers for life? It's not a bad idea to have aggressive prices on kid's shoes. If you can make a brand connection to a child at a young age, you may have just made a customer for life.

It is standard practice to take a lower margin up front for Special Make Up (SMU) or Made To Order (MTO) products. SMU or MTO shoes are sold before you even place the order with the factory. If you are selling in bulk container loads, and factory direct to your customer, it is okay to take a lower margin. You may need to, if you want to land a big sale.

You can expect lower margins at lower price points. This is a fact of the shoe trade. Discount shoppers demand more value than high-end consumers.

Keep in mind that rainy weather will slow down sandal sales, while sunny days will make winter boots hard to sell at full price.

Shoe companies are often forced to accept lower margins. Sometimes the model is old or obsolete, or a competitor is offering a superior product at the same price. Distressed merchandise must also be discounted. This includes broken size runs, discontinued styles, or shoes delivered late in the selling season that must be sold quickly.

Many companies have adopted aggressive discount strategies. They have learned it is better to offer discounts during the selling season to move product quickly. A summer sandal may sell well in late July with a 25% discount, but will be impossible to sell in September, even with a 60% reduction.

Eve is planning to have her own online store as the main outlet for Enigma boots, and will offer fashion retailers wholesale discounts when they buy Enigma boots in bulk. She will need two different margin calculations to plan both distribution plans.

Eve has not listed any of her research, development, marketing, or sales expenses on her margin calculations. Her R&D spending is low, and she plans to start small with her marketing plans. She will ramp up once she has some profits coming in.

Wholesale Distribution

Model	Color	Material	FOB	Frt Ins Fees	FCL	FCL Rate	Ship Cost	Duty Rate %	Duty	
Somerset	Black	Pebble Full Grain	$35.00	$0.35	4000	$4,400.00	$1.45	8.5%	$2.98	
Somerset	Brown	Pebble Full Grain	$35.00	$0.35	4000	$4,400.00	$1.45	8.5%	$2.98	
Brattle	Mahogany	Laser Full Grain	$35.00	$0.35	4000	$4,400.00	$1.45	8.5%	$2.98	
Brattle	Black	Laser Full Grain	$35.00	$0.35	4000	$4,400.00	$1.45	8.5%	$2.98	
Tremont	Black	Smooth Full Grain	$30.00	$0.35	4000	$4,400.00	$1.45	8.5%	$2.55	
Tremont	Brown	Smooth Full Grain	$30.00	$0.35	4000	$4,400.00	$1.45	8.5%	$2.55	
Beacon	Black	Sub-Action Leather	$30.00	$0.35	4000	$4,400.00	$1.45	8.5%	$2.55	
Beacon	White China	Action	$30.00	$0.35	4000	$4,400.00	$1.45	8.5%	$2.55	
Revere	Black	Pebble Full Grain	$22.00	$0.35	4000	$4,400.00	$1.45	8.5%	$1.87	
Union	Pink Roses	Action	$18.00	$0.35	4000	$4,400.00	$1.45	8.5%	$1.53	
Hanover	Spiked Flowers	Action	$18.00	$0.35	4000	$4,400.00	$1.45	8.5%	$1.53	
Haymarket	Black Rose	Sub-Action Leather	$18.00	$0.35	4000	$4,400.00	$1.45	8.5%	$1.53	
Bowdoin	Black Floral	Sub-Action Leather	$18.00	$0.35	4000	$4,400.00	$1.45	8.5%	$1.53	

Internet Distribution

Model	Color	Material	FOB	Frt Ins Fees	FCL	FCL Rate	Ship Cost	Duty Rate %	Duty	
Somerset	Black	Pebble Full Grain	$35.00	$0.35	4000	$4,400.00	$1.45	8.5%	$2.98	
Somerset	Brown	Pebble Full Grain	$35.00	$0.35	4000	$4,400.00	$1.45	8.5%	$2.98	
Brattle	Mahogany	Laser Full Grain	$35.00	$0.35	4000	$4,400.00	$1.45	8.5%	$2.98	
Brattle	Black	Laser Full Grain	$35.00	$0.35	4000	$4,400.00	$1.45	8.5%	$2.98	
Tremont	Black	Smooth Full Grain	$30.00	$0.35	4000	$4,400.00	$1.45	8.5%	$2.55	
Tremont	Brown	Smooth Full Grain	$30.00	$0.35	4000	$4,400.00	$1.45	8.5%	$2.55	
Beacon	Black	Sub-Action Leather	$30.00	$0.35	4000	$4,400.00	$1.45	8.5%	$2.55	
Beacon	White China	Action	$30.00	$0.35	4000	$4,400.00	$1.45	8.5%	$2.55	
Revere	Black	Pebble Full Grain	$22.00	$0.35	4000	$4,400.00	$1.45	8.5%	$1.87	
Union	Pink Roses	Action	$18.00	$0.35	4000	$4,400.00	$1.45	8.5%	$1.53	
Hanover	Spiked Flowers	Action	$18.00	$0.35	4000	$4,400.00	$1.45	8.5%	$1.53	
Haymarket	Black Rose	Sub-Action Leather	$18.00	$0.35	4000	$4,400.00	$1.45	8.5%	$1.53	
Bowdoin	Black Floral	Sub-Action Leather	$18.00	$0.35	4000	$4,400.00	$1.45	8.5%	$1.53	

Landed	Retail	Wholesale	W/S -7% Com	Profit	Margin	Forecast	Sales	Profit
$39.78	$150.00	$75.00	$69.75	$29.98	42.97%	250	$37,500.00	$7,493.75
$39.78	$150.00	$75.00	$69.75	$29.98	42.97%	250	$37,500.00	$7,493.75
$39.78	$150.00	$75.00	$69.75	$29.98	42.97%	250	$37,500.00	$7,493.75
$39.78	$150.00	$75.00	$69.75	$29.98	42.97%	250	$37,500.00	$7,493.75
$34.35	$115.00	$57.50	$53.48	$19.13	35.76%	250	$28,750.00	$4,781.25
$34.35	$115.00	$57.50	$53.48	$19.13	35.76%	250	$28,750.00	$4,781.25
$34.35	$115.00	$57.50	$53.48	$19.13	35.76%	250	$28,750.00	$4,781.25
$34.35	$115.00	$57.50	$53.48	$19.13	35.76%	250	$28,750.00	$4,781.25
$25.67	$95.00	$47.50	$44.18	$18.51	41.89%	250	$23,750.00	$4,626.25
$21.33	$85.00	$42.50	$39.53	$18.20	46.03%	250	$21,250.00	$4,548.75
$21.33	$85.00	$42.50	$39.53	$18.20	46.03%	250	$21,250.00	$4,548.75
$21.33	$85.00	$42.50	$39.53	$18.20	46.03%	250	$21,250.00	$4,548.75
$21.33	$85.00	$42.50	$39.53	$18.20	46.03%	250	$21,250.00	$4,548.75
						3250	$373,750.00	$71,921.25

Landed	Retail	Profit	Margin	Forecast	Sales	Profit
$39.78	$150.00	$110.23	73.48%	250	$37,500.00	$27,556.25
$39.78	$150.00	$110.23	73.48%	250	$37,500.00	$27,556.25
$39.78	$150.00	$110.23	73.48%	250	$37,500.00	$27,556.25
$39.78	$150.00	$110.23	73.48%	250	$37,500.00	$27,556.25
$34.35	$115.00	$80.65	70.13%	250	$28,750.00	$20,162.50
$34.35	$115.00	$80.65	70.13%	250	$28,750.00	$20,162.50
$34.35	$115.00	$80.65	70.13%	250	$28,750.00	$20,162.50
$34.35	$115.00	$80.65	70.13%	250	$28,750.00	$20,162.50
$25.67	$95.00	$69.33	72.98%	250	$23,750.00	$17,332.50
$21.33	$85.00	$63.67	74.91%	250	$21,250.00	$15,917.50
$21.33	$85.00	$63.67	74.91%	250	$21,250.00	$15,917.50
$21.33	$85.00	$63.67	74.91%	250	$21,250.00	$15,917.50
$21.33	$85.00	$63.67	74.91%	250	$21,250.00	$15,917.50
				3250	$373,750.00	$271,877.50

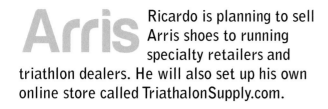

Ricardo is planning to sell Arris shoes to running specialty retailers and triathlon dealers. He will also set up his own online store called TriathalonSupply.com.

Ricardo will keep his online store separate from ArrisRunning.com. He plans this mixed distribution model so he can make extra markup by selling the shoes himself, but avoid upsetting his triathlon and running specialty retailers by competing against them.

Ricardo needs to make two different margin calculations. With a 3PL handling the logistics, and independent reps charging a 7% sales commission, Ricardo can see a profit margin of between 36% and 53% for his shoes.

This is not a great margin, but it does include the Arris operational overhead, marketing expenses, and sales rep. commissions.

For a start-up brand, Ricardo should also plan on 10% of FOB for research and development, 7% of the wholesale cost for sales commissions, and 10% of gross sales for marketing expenses.

Wholesale Distribution with 3PL

Model	Color	Material	FOB	Shipping Calulations					Duty%	Duty	Overhead			
				Ins Fees	FCL	FCL Rate	Cost				R&D	Marketing	3PL	
Endro X Training	Silver	Mesh / PU	$17.00	$0.35	5000	$ 4,400.00	$1.23	20%	$3.40	$1.70	$2.81	$4.00	
Endro X Training	Green	Mesh / PU	$17.00	$0.35	5000	$ 4,400.00	$1.23	20%	$3.40	$1.70	$2.81	$4.00	
Endro X Training	Grey	Mesh / PU	$17.00	$0.35	5000	$ 4,400.00	$1.23	20%	$3.40	$1.70	$2.81	$4.00	
Phantom Race	Silver	Mesh / PU	$15.00	$0.35	5000	$ 4,400.00	$1.23	20%	$3.00	$1.50	$2.81	$4.00	
Lightning Race	Yellow	Mesh / PU	$15.00	$0.35	5000	$ 4,400.00	$1.23	20%	$3.00	$1.50	$2.81	$4.00	
Revo R+R	Yellow	Mesh / PU	$14.00	$0.35	5000	$ 4,400.00	$1.23	20%	$2.80	$1.40	$2.81	$4.00	

Direct Internet Distribution with 3PL

Model	Color	Material	FOB	Shipping Calulations					Duty%	Duty	Overhead			
				Ins Fees	FCL	FCL Rate	Cost				R&D	Marketing	3PL/Web	
Endro X Training	Silver	Mesh / PU	$17.00	$0.35	5000	$ 4,400.00	$1.23	20%	$3.40	$1.70	$5.63	$4.50	
Endro X Training	Green	Mesh / PU	$17.00	$0.35	5000	$ 4,400.00	$1.23	20%	$3.40	$1.70	$5.63	$4.50	
Endro X Training	Grey	Mesh / PU	$17.00	$0.35	5000	$ 4,400.00	$1.23	20%	$3.40	$1.70	$5.63	$4.50	
Phantom Race	Silver	Mesh / PU	$15.00	$0.35	5000	$ 4,400.00	$1.23	20%	$3.00	$1.50	$5.63	$4.50	
Lightning Race	Yellow	Mesh / PU	$15.00	$0.35	5000	$ 4,400.00	$1.23	20%	$3.00	$1.50	$5.63	$4.50	
Revo R+R	Yellow	Mesh / PU	$14.00	$0.35	5000	$ 4,400.00	$1.23	20%	$2.80	$1.40	$5.63	$4.50	

For Ricardo's direct internet sales plan he needs to make a few adjustments. The R&D expense remains the same, but Ricardo figures the marketing and operations expense of the website will be 20% of gross profits. With the 3PL handling the logistics, he will need to cover the cost of processing credit card transactions, so he adds $0.50.

The margins look great! Ricardo will be able to offer free shipping and discounts. He will also need to set aside a budget for returns and shipping.

He needs to plan for a 20% customer return rate for his online sales.

Landed	Retail	Wholesale	W/S -7% Com	Profit	Margin	Forecast	Sales	Profit
$30.49	$120.00	$60.00	$55.80	$25.31	45.35%	300	$36,000.00	$7,592.25
$30.49	$120.00	$60.00	$55.80	$25.31	45.35%	300	$36,000.00	$7,592.25
$30.49	$120.00	$60.00	$55.80	$25.31	45.35%	300	$36,000.00	$7,592.25
$27.89	$130.00	$65.00	$60.45	$32.56	53.86%	200	$26,000.00	$6,511.50
$27.89	$110.00	$55.00	$51.15	$23.26	45.47%	200	$22,000.00	$4,651.50
$26.59	$90.00	$45.00	$41.85	$15.26	36.46%	300	$27,000.00	$4,577.25
						1600	$183,000.00	$38,517.00

Landed	Web Retail	Profit	Margin	Forecast	Sales	Profit
$33.81	$120.00	$86.20	71.83%	300	$36,000.00	$25,858.50
$33.81	$120.00	$86.20	71.83%	300	$36,000.00	$25,858.50
$33.81	$120.00	$86.20	71.83%	300	$36,000.00	$25,858.50
$31.21	$130.00	$98.80	76.00%	200	$26,000.00	$19,759.00
$31.21	$110.00	$78.80	71.63%	200	$22,000.00	$15,759.00
$29.91	$90.00	$60.10	66.77%	300	$27,000.00	$18,028.50
					1600	$183,000.00	$131,122.00

CHAPTER 5
MANUFACTURING AND IMPORTING YOUR SHOES

With your designs in hand, it is now time to find a factory...right? Wrong. With your new shoe designs in hand, take some time to show them around. Let your friends and family have a look, show them to your neighbors. This can give you some new insight and confidence to move forward. Most of all, when you show your designs, you will be practicing your sales pitch. This is a great time to have some industry people take a look. Try a local shoe store manager. If you have any contacts in the shoe business, go ahead and talk to them, and collect some feedback.

Once you have your sales pitch polished, you are going to need working capital to get started. Shoe factories, agents, tooling shops, airlines, material suppliers, and shipping companies will all require payment, in some cases in advance of services. Make sure you have capital available. We will review capital requirements a bit later, but you need to be prepared to raise it. You will need to pull together a detailed business plan to show that you are ready to build and operate a business.

Are you ready to look for a shoe factory?
The shoe factory sales people will be working hard to "qualify" you. They want to make sure you are serious and that there is potential in your project and potential in YOU! Make sure your sales pitch and business plans are complete before you start meeting with the factories.

Factory meeting checklist
Going into a meeting with confidence in yourself and a polished business plan will help you to present the professional image you want to project for your company. Make sure to have the following information:

1. **Project Brief:** A list of exactly what you want to accomplish. How many styles and colors etc.
2. **Designs:** Complete detailed drawings with all colors, materials and constructions.
3. **Outsole designs:** Must be complete in 2D drawing form.
4. **Pricing:** Target FOB, wholesale and retail prices must be calculated.
5. **Schedule:** Dates for your retail release schedule.
6. **Capital:** Estimated capital requirements and a plan for raising it.

Finding a factory to make your shoes?

The real truth is that finding a factory for a new shoe project may be very difficult. If you are new to the shoe trade and don't have any personal connections, it will be hard to find a factory that will accept your project. But don't worry, there are a few strategies you can follow to get your project placed in the right factory.

Designer contacts

If you selected an experienced shoe designer or footwear developer to work with, then he or she should have many contacts. In just a few years working in the shoe trade, a footwear designer may have worked for several different brands and a dozen different shoe factories.

Shoe designers and developers with some overseas experience will know footwear agents, trading companies, or people that know people. The shoe business is built on relationships and personal contacts. Shoe factories and material suppliers are always working together, and one contact can lead you to other contacts.

Internet searches

Google is not a bad place to start your search for a shoe factory. However, your average shoe factory in China or Italy may not have an easy-to-find website. If you are looking for a factory in China, you should head directly to Alibaba.com™. Alibaba has listings for thousands of factories. You can search by product, county and province.

You will find dozens of listings, but beware, many are not actually factories. They are trading companies or agents. These firms are not necessarily bad, but you should dig deep into the listing to make sure you know what you are dealing with.

Business network and social media sites

Web sites such as LinkedIn.com™, Coroflot. com™, Malakye.com™, or even Facebook.com™ can provide you with leads for footwear factories or footwear sourcing agents.

The shoe-making world is a huge network of friends, co-workers, associates and acquaintances. One contact in the trade can lead you to another. Keep looking!

Footwear agents and trading companies

Another way to find a factory is to NOT look for a factory, but instead look for a footwear agent or trading company that will present your project and help you find the right shoe factory.

Search engine research is not a bad place to start looking for an agent. Again, Alibaba.com™ is a great place to start your search. You will find there are many firms that list themselves as "trading" or "sourcing." These firms will have many contacts. They may also offer quality control help or provide a review for a factory you may have found online. Most importantly, you need to make sure they have footwear experience. It pays to get references when shopping for an agent.

Working with an agent

There are some basic terms you need to expect when working with agents.

Confidentiality agreements will be signed. Your agent will protect your project from the eyes of competitors. A busy agent may be working with several shoe brands, and may even be working with your competitors.

Sample delivery charges will be your responsibility. FedEx and UPS bills are not cheap for shoes shipping from Asia to the USA or Europe. Plan accordingly.

Costs for shoe outsoles or upper molds are expensive and must be paid for in advance.

The cost of your shoe samples must be paid before shipping from the factory.

Monthly product management or product development fees may be required, depending on the agent. Development costs may vary wildly, you should shop around.

The production minimum order quantity will vary from 500 to 6000 per style, and 500 to 1000 pairs per colorway.

You can expect production lead times of 90 to 120 days. Then add time for shipping.

For any new customer, the production shoes must be paid for in full before shipping.

The "right" shoe factory for your project

Just as you need to find the right designer for your project you will also need to find the right factory. Most shoe factories have a particular expertise. The skills and equipment required to make sport shoes is very different from the skills and equipment required to produce women's high heels or leather work boots.

A factory's assembly line and equipment may be set up for cold cement or vulcanizing process but seldom both. A hiking boot factory will have equipment suited for cutting heavy leather and waterproof sealing, while a factory for snowboard boots will have oversized assembly line equipment suitable for tall boots.

There are factories that specialize in women's fashion shoes, sandals and men's dress shoes. Each factory will have relationships with material suppliers and mold factories appropriate to their specific expertise.

Where will you find the factory for your shoes? The style of shoe you plan to make will help determine where in the world your shoes will be made. Athletic shoes are almost always made in Asia. The shoe factories in China, Vietnam, Indonesia, Korea, Taiwan and Thailand have easy access to the labor and high tech materials required for modern athletic shoes. This type of shoe is generally not made in Europe.

High fashion leather shoes can be made in Asia but high end, high style, high quality shoes are made in Europe.

Shoe factories in South America are very capable of making leather casual and fashion shoes. South American leather hides are exported to Asia and Europe for manufacturing shoes.

Shoe factories come in all sizes, from just one or two lines squeezed into a single story building, to huge 20 or 30 line factories that look more like a small town or college campus. In China there are shoe factories with over 20,000 workers in one facility.

What factory size is best for your shoes?

Small factories may be hungry for orders but may lack the internal product development expertise to make complicated shoes. These factories may not have all the expensive machines that a monster factory will have, but the small factory will have an owner that you can meet. If you can build a personal relationship with the owner, you can get your project placed.

You might think that large shoe factories would ignore small brands but this is not always the case. While you may never meet the owners, and you may not get the most experienced technicians working on your project, large factories do support some small brands. The small brands may be served by junior staff members and may have to accept "fill in" or off season production times, but you may find yourself sharing production space with Nike™ or another super brand.

Shopping for quality

The quality of product coming out of a shoe factory does not usually vary. If you are in a big factory with Nike™ shoes, great! You will be able to enjoy the same high quality standards. Are you in a factory with "No Name" cut price brands? Watch out!

When selecting a factory, one of your first questions to ask should be, "who else do you make shoes for?" If you don't have a chance to visit the factory in person or cannot send a representative to walk the line, then your next bet is to look at what they make for other companies.

If they cannot send you a photo or won't tell you any other brand names, you may need to look for a different factory.

Do factories help start-up brands?

Shoe factories need volume to make money. Small orders just can't cover the time and expense of development. The development process for a 500 pair order is the same as a 25,000 pair order.

However, every new customer has a chance to be the next Nike™ or the next flop. The factory sales manager has to decide if your new company is a winner or a loser. Is your company new? Is your company an existing company that is already selling shoes or an existing clothing brand looking to expand into the shoe trade?

Shoe factories prefer to do business with established companies but new companies can get service if they approach a factory correctly.

Factories are always looking for orders. With a successful Kickstarter™ campaign you may have orders in-hand when you approach a new factory, 1000 or 2000 pairs is not a big order but it will put you ahead of most other footwear start-ups. We will cover Kickstarter™ campaigns later in the book.

Ricardo's designer has many years of experience in the trade and is able to help with shoe factory introductions. Because Arris is a high performance athletic brand, the shoes will need to be made somewhere in Asia.

Ricardo is able to meet with 2 agents and a shoe factory representative in Los Angeles. He also attends a shoe material show in Portland, Oregon with his designer, and gets lucky with an introduction to a Chinese shoe factory that can make the technical Arris running shoes.

Ricardo is well-prepared for this introduction with complete designs, a detailed business plan, and a reasonable timeline for his product launch. He also prepared a rough budget with capital requirements planned out. He didn't end up showing this to the factory, but it is good to have on hand.

When Ricardo and his designer meet with the factory manager they make a good impression, and the factory agrees to take on his project.

Ricardo's designer has worked with this factory before, so the Arris team is able to proceed with development without having to visit the factory.

While Ricardo would like to visit the factory, he is just too busy getting the Arris company set-up. He has decided to contract with a freelance shoe developer who will help get the Arris project moving in China.

The new home for Arris shoes in China will be a medium-size, 10-line factory named Very Well Shoes Inc. located in the south of China near the city of Humen. Very Well Shoes Inc. is in the center of the shoe industry, surrounded by material suppliers and footwear component sub-contractors.

Eve has a hard time finding an agent or a factory to take her seriously. Her crazy hair, wild Enigma designs, and lack of financial backing are all risks which agents and factories are not willing to take. She will have to find another way.

Eve tries a crowd-funding campaign, but even with a cool video clip featuring her boots and her punk rock band, her project does not fund.

Eve is not one to give up on her dream. If she can't find a shoe factory, maybe she can find an existing shoe company that can help.

She goes back to the internet and runs a search for any companies that make military boots. She starts to contact their marketing departments in hopes of doing a design collaboration.

After another hard month of many rejections, Eve makes contact with a young marketing manager at Iron Age Boots who likes the idea. The marketing department at Iron Age Boots sees the potential of expanding their brand with a unique twist on the punk rock military look.

Maybe Iron Age Boots can be the next Doc. Martens with a harder edge?

Iron Age Boots sends Eve some samples for her to work with. In just a few weeks she is ready to make a presentation to the owners.

Eve is no dummy and she brings more than just her design work to this meeting. She is able to present the entire Enigma business plan. It's a good thing she does! After meeting her and seeing her work, the owners of Iron Age Boots agree to support the collaboration project, introduce Eve to their factory, and help launch Enigma.

The shoe development process

The shoe development process is simply the transformation of the designer's drawings into the complete shoe. This includes the commercialization which is the creation of all the production sizes once the prototype design has been confirmed.

Do you need a shoe developer?

What is a shoe developer? A shoe developer is a shoe-making technician that can push your shoe design through the development process with the factory.

While the designer is responsible for the outside look of the shoe, the developer is responsible for all the technical shoe-making details. A developer will be communicating the designer's vision to the factory, while at the same time making sure the shoe is well-constructed, fits well, meets the target price and is produced on time.

Shoe brands will have developers work with designers, and then communicate with the shoe factories' internal development staff.

Your shoe designer may be able to offer you this development service. The shoe factory or the agent you use may also have developers available to see your project through.

Large shoe-making firms will have designers and developers set-up in teams. Usually the designer will have moved onto the next season's design project, while the developer will push the current project forward. Often the developer works magic, transforming a crazy designer's impossible drawing into a real shoe.

In general, the developers job is to allow the creative shoe designer to keep making the cool new designs and away from all the time-consuming technical work and trips to the factory.

Arris The Arris product line is complicated and very technical. A high-performance running shoe is not easy to make and winning over the very demanding triathlete community will be a difficult challenge for Arris.

To make sure the Arris development runs smoothly, Ricardo will hire a US based developer to work directly with the factory. Ricardo wants to be involved, but he is not a shoe-making expert. To be successful, he is going to need professionals with experience specific to running to make the Arris shoes perform.

Ricardo's developer will work closely with the Arris designer to create the technical specifications, and with Ricardo to make sure the shoes follow the product brief, are the right price, and meet the targeted import duty classifications.

The Arris development will be time-consuming and will require many rounds of samples and several trips to China. Ricardo needs to make sure he has the capital arranged for a long development process.

Eve will make samples in China for her collaboration project. Iron Age Boots does not own the factory but they have had a stable working relationship with several factories for many years.

Eve will work with the in-house staff of Iron Age Boots in America to get her designs ready for the Chinese factory. Once the designs are ready, Eve is invited to China to work on the development inside the shoe factory and to start work on her Enigma branded products for women.

Getting your samples made

An established shoe brand will have no trouble getting pattern development and samples made for free. Factories look at existing shoe companies as a low risk with possible high rewards. They know it's already a real business with real customers.

Outsole development tooling will almost always be billed. A sample tool could cost $1500 for a rubber sole to $3500 for a rubber and EVA midsole unit. If new lasts are required the shoe brand will be billed. The tooling and lasts costs must be billed because they are prepared outside the shoe factory.

A newcomer to a factory may need to buy samples. Each factory will have a different policy. You could expect to pay 200% of the real FOB price plus all shipping charges. So, if a basic shoe costs $15, the sample would cost $30, and shipping from China could cost another $30 or more.

It may be better for a newcomer to find an agent with factory contacts. The agent will manage the factory relationship and help the newcomer avoid getting into trouble with the factory.

A big factory may make small orders for an important customer. I've worked for companies that produce 5 million pairs a year and if we asked the factory to make a small order, they would do it as a service. Generally they seek to avoid small orders.

There are some factories that can accept small orders. They have smaller operations and will charge more for this service. Materials will have to be bought from the local market, and tooling will have to be chosen from what they already have "open" and available. You won't always have a great selection.

The shoe development timeline

How long does it take to develop shoes? Once the shoe factory starts, you should see a new pattern pullover in just a week or two. A complete shoe, color correct, with outsole tooling will take 6 to 8 weeks. Each following revision round can be 2 or 3 weeks depending if the tooling needs adjustments or new materials need to be ordered.

If you have an entire product line or range to develop, you can expect the process to take 6 months to have a complete set of photo-ready samples.

Tech sample round

The tech sample round is the first stage following the design cycle. This round will give the designer the first chance to see their shoe designs come to life. It generally takes 6 to 8 weeks to create a new shoe from the design drawings. This sounds like a long time, but keep in mind the typical R & D group may develop 30 new models at a time. The first phase is to produce one sample of each new shoe. A simple sneaker may have a prototype outsole mold or a borrowed sole unit from an existing shoe. This will still give the developer a good idea of what the shoes will look like.

Over the course of the 6 to 8 weeks, the designers and developers will have a chance to see pattern trials, outsole blue prints, and material swatches. Both designers and developers may travel to the factory to review progress, and speed up development. After many weeks, the samples may be hand-carried or mailed to the designers by air freight.

This can be a fun time for the team. Like gifts, the samples will arrive and be unpacked with great excitement! While some projects look great, others are failures. Typically, the design team will have a week to review the new samples, recommend changes, and prepare for the photo sample meeting.

With the new sneaker samples in hand, the product team will meet with the sales and marketing teams, to decide which new designs will go forward in development. The result of this phase will be a complete line of shoes ready to be photographed for the sales catalogs.

From the first phase, only 30% of the new items will go forward. Many items are changed, scrapped, or combined with others, until only the best ideas go forward.

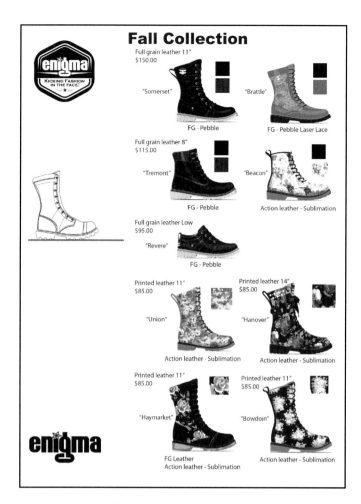

Fall Collection

Full grain leather 11"
$150.00
"Somerset"
FG - Pebble

"Brattle"
FG - Pebble Laser Lace

Full grain leather 8"
$115.00
"Tremont"
FG - Pebble

"Beacon"
Action leather - Sublimation

Full grain leather Low
$95.00
"Revere"
FG - Pebble

Printed leather 11"
$85.00
"Union"
Action leather - Sublimation

Printed leather 14"
$85.00
"Hanover"
Action leather - Sublimation

Printed leather 11"
$85.00
"Haymarket"
FG Leather
Action leather - Sublimation

Printed leather 11"
$85.00
"Bowdoin"
Action leather - Sublimation

Photo sample round

The photo sample round is another 6 to 8 weeks of work. The goal of this phase is to improve the new designs and make all the color/material choices. The designer and the product manager work together to "merchandise" the product line. Merchandising occurs when the new designs are arranged with the existing products to ensure a balanced mix of colors, materials, design themes and price points.

For the photo sample round, the team may create 6 new colors to review, and the best 3 or 4 will be selected.

As with the tech phase, the photo sample patterns will be adjusted and the outsole tooling will be opened, recut, or repaired. The developers will often travel to the factory to check all the details. Usually, the developers will send the new collections to the factory, then arrive 4 to 5 weeks later to review progress. This gives the shoe factory enough time to make pattern collections, and acquire the correct color materials required to make the samples. The developers will review both the raw materials and the test patterns, before giving the factory the green light to make the samples.

Photo samples are made only for review by the R & D team. The materials and logos may be painted or simulated without having to order hundreds of yards of custom-dyed material. The developers may work at the factory to oversee the final assembly.

This is a good time to get costing for your shoes. With the designs, materials and constructions nearly finalized, the factory can create an accurate costing sheet. Before a shoe can be added to your product line, you will need to have the costing details and duty calculations made.

Photo samples can be used to help you raise money for your start-up. With color-correct photo samples, you can finally show the real shoes to potential investors, or you can preview the samples with potential buyers. You can also use these shoes to launch a crowd-funding campaign.

The final line build

With the photo samples now back in the design center, it is time to merchandise the final product line. Like a giant puzzle, the new shoes and old shoes are arranged on the wall. When the line build is being worked on, there can be a hundred different shoes selected, and 200 more on the floor rejected or postponed.

Once the line is arranged, the sales and marketing teams will have their say. Long hours, heated discussions, dented egos and wounded pride may result...but, in the end, the line is settled.

The surviving shoes are quickly reviewed for any design changes, then organized for the photographer to get started. Once the line is set, it is time to order the salesman's samples.

Depending on the size of the company's distribution network, anywhere from 10 pairs to a few hundred pairs of each new shoe will be ordered. Men's size 9 and women's size 7 are the common sample sizes.

Sales sample production

Depending on the amount of samples to be produced, this phase will take 9 to 10 weeks. Following the final line build, the developers will send off the last few changes for the shoe. Hopefully the changes are small, so the factory can get started ordering materials. Unlike the photo samples that could be a mix of painted material and substitutions, the sales samples have to be the real deal. All color and materials must be correct.

Within a week of receiving the order, the factory will have ordered the materials. This is a key issue to follow up on, as the lead time for some materials can be 4 to 5 weeks. While the factory is waiting for the new materials to arrive, the final pattern adjustments are reviewed and confirmed.

The factory will also be making 1 set of metal cutting dies to make the sample size shoes. The mold factory will be finishing any modifications to the outsoles. This is also the first time the shoe will be made outside of the factory sample room. Some stitching problems are only discovered once the production stitching staff try to mass-produce the samples.

As with the photo sample round, the developers often visit the factory just in time to confirm the materials for the sales sample shoes before they are stitched. The developer can also request the sample room to make one last sample to review the details before the sales samples are produced. This is a critical time to review the progress of the samples. Mistakes or delays can hurt a new shoe's chance of success.

Only the best, most experienced stitchers, are selected to work in the sample room. They must work quickly, as the customers are always in a rush. Are the samples handmade? Yes, and so is the production!

The final development phase

Commercialization is the last phase in product development before shoes go into production. Up until now, your new shoe design has only been made in one size. Once the order has been placed it is time to make or "grade" the other shoe sizes. Grading a shoe requires time, effort and money. The factory will not make the size grade until the order has been placed.

Grading is almost always done in a rush. While it may take 6 to 9 months to develop the final design, the final size grade will be complete in 30 to 45 days. Grading requires all the patterns and outsoles to be made and test fit. Every design detail needs to be checked for every size. The factory will also make sure there are no assembly problems.

This is also the time when the factory will require payment for the new outsole tooling, cutting dies and shoe lasts for each size.

Keep samples and confirmation samples

You will need to confirm the fitting samples for each shoe size, and check the design's visual proportions. Some shoe designs may look great when made in size 7, but make look distorted when graded up to size 12. Every size must be checked.

When the design is finally ready, you will have a matching set of confirmation samples. 1/2 of the pair is your "keep sample" to keep in your office, and the matching 1/2 pair will stay in the factory.

This shoe is the factory's guide to your expectations of what the production shoe will look like. The confirmation samples should be tagged, signed and stored in a safe place. The factory may produce additional pairs for you to sign, these will be used by the material-purchasing team, stitching department, assembly line and QC inspection staff.

The Arris products will require extensive fit testing, wear testing, durability testing, and some lab testing. A technical running shoe is not easy to produce, but the factory Ricardo chose for the Arris products has experience making this type of performance athletic footwear.

Ricardo's product development is going to take many months. He has created 3 different shoe designs and needs to make sure each of the three models functions as he plans. Ricardo has a long list of features to refine, and will need new outsole equipment to make the Arris shoes.

New shoe lasts will require multiple rounds of fit testing to get them just right. Small changes are a simple matter of adding or removing material to the last to refine the fitting. Major changes, such as bottom contours or width adjustments, may require outsole tooling changes. Each development round will cost more money and require more time.

Depending on the required changes, a sample round may take a week or a month. Several sample rounds can easily add up to 6 or 9 months.

To help move the development process along quickly, Ricardo has approved a travel budget for his developer. Trips to Asia can be expensive but are well worth it.

2017 estimated round trip airfare from California to China $1200 (economy)
$100 airport shuttle or parking
$100 per night China hotel
$50 per day meals
$100 per day car service (if required)
$100 per day translation service (if required)

A two week development trip may cost $3500 to $4500. This may seem expensive, but incorrect tooling or delayed samples can cost Ricardo significantly more.

Eve will have an easier time developing her product line. The Enigma program landed at a factory that specializes in making heavy-duty boots. Eve is able to use lasts the factory has in-house. This saves Eve a great deal of time and money. While the lasts are not perfect, she can get her brand started. Eve knows she will need to make a sleeker last with a tall heel later, but for now she can get started. Eve has also decided that she can use an "open" mold for her outsoles.

The boot factory has an outsole tool with a removable logo plate allowing Eve to insert her logo into the tooling without the expense of buying an entire set of outsole molds.

Eve does run into some development issues. The boot factory has never been asked to make colorful boots with printed patterns and embroidery before, so it will be a bit of a struggle to get the looks she wants.

Eve does some research on Alibaba.com to find a company that can help the boot factory with the design details. Eve needs to make Enigma boots special.

Even a very professional shoe factory may need help with material research. If you are looking for something uncommon, be prepared to find it yourself.

Shipping your production shoes

Once your production run is finished the shoes are packed and placed into an ocean freight container. You have seen these giant boxes. They are exactly the size of a 40-foot trailer on a semi truck. The standard size is 40 feet by 8 feet by 8 feet and holds about 5000 pairs. There is the half-size, 20-footer, and the extra large 40-foot-high cube (about 1 foot taller than the standard 40). It is best to ship a full container load (FCL) versus a less than container load (LCL) or loose freight. Try to avoid LCL, as it's more expensive, takes longer, and merchandise is not protected as well as when sealed in a metal shipping container.

What is freight forwarding?

Once your shoes are in the container, they will be trucked to the freight harbor. This is handled by the freight forwarder or the factory's freight forwarder. The freight forwarder is the company that arranges shipping, and handles the export and import documentation. They are responsible for passing the shipping documents to customs officials of the exporting and importing countries. The forwarder contacts the shipping lines and schedules your container to meet the vessel traveling to your import harbor.

Why you need a freight forwarder

Forwarding involves directing the shipment of palletized freight between the initial shipper and final consignee. In most cases, the final consignee will be the buyer. A freight forwarding company will arrange everything you need for the secure storage and efficient delivery of your stock. This includes all aspects, from the warehousing of a company's products, to the shipping of said goods to their various locations.

There are many options when it comes to selecting the company you will partner with. You want to make this process as smooth as possible, so you need to look at what a freight forwarder can offer you in terms of their service. For example, freight forwarders like ProPack take care of important shipping-related paperwork, expedite border crossings, track shipments, and keep their clients informed about the status of their products throughout the process. This means that you have a great overview of what is going on with your products, and you can keep any other interested parties informed, such as the end customer.

How to find a forwarder

There are companies the world over that call themselves freight forwarders. A quick internet search can give you a huge list of potential suitors when it comes to looking after your shoes and getting them to their final destination. You will want to know a little more before choosing the company that appears at the top of this list. The shoe factory may be able to help you. They have experience in making goods for export markets, and will have working relationships with different freight forwarders. You want to seek out as many referrals and recommendations as possible. If the freight forwarder is known by the shoe factory, it will ease the transition of goods from the factory to the forwarder.

How to pick a freight forwarder

Best price and less hassle are great reasons to choose one freight forwarder over another. They will save you time and money and get your business moving forward fast. In addition to this, you want to know that the company you are working with has great customer service. There will be times when you want to know what is going on, or you need to ask advice or assistance.

The freight forwarder you are dealing with has to deliver great customer service and help you when you need it most. Ask them for references that you can contact to check out how they have performed in the past.

Eve's development partner and factory already have a working relationship with a forwarder. She will go with their suggestion. Eve's boots will be shipping in both full container loads (FCL) and less than container loads (LCL). LCL shipping is more expensive and will take longer to arrive in Boston, so Eve will do her best to avoid it if possible.

Her boots are shipping directly to her rented space. Eve will need to make sure she has people on hand to help unload. The trucking company will deliver the container and include two hours of driver waiting time while Eve and her helpers unload the cargo container. After 2 hours of waiting time Eve will need to pay $60 per hour for the driver to wait at her location.

The trucking company can leave the containers, but Eve will have to pay extra for the return trip and pickup.

 Ricardo will be shipping directly to his contracted 3PL. Ricardo has selected a freight forwarder with an office in Los Angeles, close to his home and the Long Beach container port. His 3PL already does business with this freight forwarder, so receiving the containers of shoes should be smooth. Ricardo does need to take extra care to make sure his shoes are correctly labeled for receiving at the 3PL. While Ricardo does have to pay a receiving charge, he knows his logistics are being well looked after.

UPC bar codes

Before your shoes ship from the factory, the boxes will need UPC bar codes. The UPC is the Universal Product Code. Retail stores will require that you have UPC numbers for your products. Each model, color, and size will need its own UPC code.

If you plan to sell your products on Amazon or other retailers, you must set up product bar codes. If you plan on setting up a 3PL to handle your logistics, you will also need UPC codes.

The bar code is used by retailers to control their receiving, stocking and checkout processes. Your shoe master carton will need the UPC number. The inner box will also need the UPC. Sandals on hooks will need the bar code on the shipping bags and on a hangtag.

Universal product codes are assigned by a US based non-profit company GS1 US. GS1 US charges membership fees that begin at $250, plus an annual renewal fee that is around $50. A membership form can be filled out online on GS1's website, **www.gs1us.org.**

Once your company is a member, you will be assigned a 6 or 9-digit prefix. Your UPC numbers will all have the same prefix. The next 5 digits are yours to assign to each of your products. You can start with 00001 or you can create your own coding system.

Once the numbers are assigned, you can order the bar code stickers from specialty printers or just send the number to your shoe factory. Almost all shoe factories have a bar code printing system, and they will make your product labels on demand.

What shoe sizes do you need to order?

As part of your product merchandising plan, you need to think about what shoe sizes you will offer to your customers. For some shoe brands, offering a wide range of sizes and widths is part of their footwear marketing model. For example, New Balance™ is famous for offering huge size ranges with many widths. For the biggest shoe brands selling millions of pairs of shoes, the costs associated with making the extra sizes is so small it's not a concern. For smaller companies and start-ups, every extra shoe size is a significant amount of money.

To support large productions runs and ensure fast delivery, you need to have multiple outsole tooling copies. To support a production run of a million pairs, there may be 10 sets of cutting dies and 5 or more copies of the outsole tooling. A little used size 6.5 may have only one tool, while a popular size 11 may need 10 sets of rubber pressing tools and 15 sets of tooling to make EVA midsoles.

Shoe brands will use a standard size "curve" to order the right amount of each size. These charts are only a general guide. Every shoe brand will develop their own custom curve based on their sales history. The size curve for endurance running shoes will run a little smaller than a size curve for military boots. Different countries and cultures will have different size runs. For example, the size curves for Asian markets will be smaller than those required for the American or European markets.

MEN'S SHOE SIZE CURVE

US Sizes	Japan Size	Korea Size	Euro Sizes	UK Sizes	OZ Sizes	Inches	CM	Curve
7	23	250	40	6.5	6.5	9.625"	24.4	1%
7.5	23.5	255	40-41	7	7	9.75"	24.8	1%
8	24	260	41	7.5	7.5	9.9375"	25.4	2%
8.5	24.5	265	41-42	8	8	10.125"	25.7	4%
9	25	270	42	8.5	8.5	10.25"	26	15%
9.5	25.5	275	42-43	9	9	10.4375"	26.7	15%
10	26	280	43	9.5	9.5	10.5625"	27	11%
10.5	26.5	285	43-44	10	10	10.75"	27.3	10%
11	27	290	44	10.5	10.5	10.9375"	27.9	14%
11.5	27.5	290	44-45	11	11	11.125"	28.3	11%
12	28	295	45	11.5	11.5	11.25"	28.6	13%
13	29	300	46	12.5	12.5	11.5625"	29.4	2%
14	30	310	47	13.5	13.5	11.875"	30.2	1%

WOMEN'S SHOE SIZE CURVE

US Sizes	Japan Size	Korea Size	Euro Sizes	UK Sizes	OZ Sizes	Inches	CM	Curve
5	21	220	35-36	3	3	8.5"	21.6	2%
5.5	21.5	225	36	3.5	3.5	8.75"	22.2	2%
6	22	230	36-37	4	4	8.875"	22.5	6%
6.5	22.5	235	37	4.5	4.5	9.0625"	23	6%
7	23	240	37-38	5	5	9.25"	23.5	10%
7.5	23.5	245	38	5.5	5.5	9.375"	23.8	12%
8	24	250	38-39	6	6	9.5"	24.1	13%
8.5	24.5	255	39	6.5	6.5	9.6875"	24.6	11%
9	25	260	39-40	7	7	9.875"	25.1	13%
9.5	25.5	265	40	7.5	7.5	10"	25.4	10%
10	26	270	40-41	8	8	10.1875"	25.9	10%
10.5	27	275	41	8.5	8.5	10.3125"	26.2	2%
11	28	280	41-42	9	9	10.5"	26.7	3%

Balancing a size run

Occasionally, a shoe company will need to re-balance their stock of a shoe model. While the "gut" sizes (10,10.5,11) may sell out, the extreme ends of the size curve may remain unsold. This broken size run cannot be sold at full price. Fill-in orders from the shoe factory will be needed to correct the inventory.

The Arris product line requires many new pieces of outsole tooling to produce each size. In order to reduce the tooling start-up costs, Ricardo will start with a smaller size run. If the shoes really take off and customers demand more sizes, he can add more tooling later.

US Sizes	Japan Size	Korea Size	Euro Sizes	UK Sizes	OZ Sizes	Inches	CM	Curve	Pairs
7	23	250	40	6.5	6.5	9.625"	24.4	0%	0
7.5	23.5	255	40-41	7	7	9.75"	24.8	0%	0
8	24	260	41	7.5	7.5	9.9375"	25.4	2%	20
8.5	24.5	265	41-42	8	8	10.125"	25.7	4%	40
9	25	270	42	8.5	8.5	10.25"	26	15%	150
9.5	25.5	275	42-43	9	9	10.4375"	26.7	15%	150
10	26	280	43	9.5	9.5	10.5625"	27	13%	130
10.5	26.5	285	43-44	10	10	10.75"	27.3	10%	100
11	27	290	44	10.5	10.5	10.9375"	27.9	15%	150
11.5	27.5	290	44-45	11	11	11.125"	28.3	11%	110
12	28	295	45	11.5	11.5	11.25"	28.6	13%	130
13	29	300	46	12.5	12.5	11.5625"	29.4	2%	20
14	30	310	47	13.5	13.5	11.875"	30.2	0%	0

Order   1000

The Enigma development expenses and start-up charges are fairly small due to the use of existing equipment. Eve could afford to offer more sizes but she would rather not carry the stock of the small and large sizes. Like Ricardo, she is going to play it safe and start with a narrow size run.

US Sizes	Japan Size	Korea Size	Euro Sizes	UK Sizes	OZ Sizes	Inches	CM	Curve	Pairs
5	21	220	35-36	3	3	8.5"	21.6	0%	0
5.5	21.5	225	36	3.5	3.5	8.75"	22.2	0%	0
6	22	230	36-37	4	4	8.875"	22.5	6%	30
6.5	22.5	235	37	4.5	4.5	9.0625"	23	6%	30
7	23	240	37-38	5	5	9.25"	23.5	12%	60
7.5	23.5	245	38	5.5	5.5	9.375"	23.8	12%	60
8	24	250	38-39	6	6	9.5"	24.1	14%	70
8.5	24.5	255	39	6.5	6.5	9.6875"	24.6	12%	60
9	25	260	39-40	7	7	9.875"	25.1	13%	65
9.5	25.5	265	40	7.5	7.5	10"	25.4	10%	50
10	26	270	40-41	8	8	10.1875"	25.9	10%	50
10.5	27	275	41	8.5	8.5	10.3125"	26.2	2%	10
11	28	280	41-42	9	9	10.5"	26.7	3%	15

Order   500

Import duty and shoe tariffs

Import duty is a fee charged to the importer of any product coming from a foreign country. The fee is paid to the government of the importing country. This fee is dependent on the country of origin, material classification of the shoe, and import regulations of each country. Here we will review the duty regulations for importing shoes into the USA from China. The rules to classify shoes are common for most countries while each importing country may have different duties.

For a shoe to be imported, it must first be "classified." This tells the government what you want to import and what the import duty fee is. A large shoe company will have an in-house import specialist that will review the shoes and assign the classifications. It's very important for you to know the duty classification, as the duty must be added to the shoe price.

Heading/ Subheading	Stat. Suf- fix	Article Description	Unit of Quantity	Rates of Duty		2
				1		
				General	Special	
6404 (con.)		Footwear with outer soles of rubber, plastics, leather or composition leather and uppers of textile materials: (con.)				
		Footwear with outer soles of rubber or plastics: (con.)				
6404.11 (con.)		Sports footwear; tennis shoes, basketball shoes, gym shoes, training shoes and the like: (con.)				
		Other: (con.)				
6404.11.90		Valued over $12/pair...........................	....	20% 1/	Free (AU, BH, CA, CL, D, IL, JO, MA, MX, P, PA, R, SG) 4% (OM, PE) 10% (CO) 20% (KR)(s)	35%
		For men:				
	10	Ski boots, cross country ski footwear and snowboard boots.....................	prs.			
	20	Other.................................	prs.			
		For women:				
	40	Ski boots, cross country ski footwear and snowboard boots.....................	prs.			
	50	Other.................................	prs.			
		Other:				
	70	Ski boots, cross country ski footwear and snowboard boots.....................	prs.			
	80	Other.................................	prs.			
6404.19		Other:				
6404.19.15		Footwear having uppers of which over 50 percent of the external surface area (including any leather accessories or reinforcements such as those mentioned in note 4(a) to this chapter) is leather..............|..	....	10.5% 2/	Free (AU, BH, CA, CL, CO, D, E, IL, JO, KR, MA, MX, OM, P, PA, PE, R, SG)	35%
	20	For men.................................	prs.			
	60	For women..............................	prs.			
	81	Other.................................	prs.			
6404.19.20		Footwear designed to be worn over, or in lieu of, other footwear as a protection against water, oil, grease or chemicals or cold or inclement weather.......................	....	37.5% 3/	Free (AU, BH, CA, CL, D, IL, JO, MA, MX, P, R, SG) 1.9% (PA) 7.5% (OM, PE) 18.7% (CO) 37.5% (KR)(s)	66%
	30	For men.................................	prs.			
	60	For women..............................	prs.			
	90	Other.................................	prs.			

Tariff number

Classification information

Duty rate

Duty free countries

Shoe classification

Your shoes must be classified according to the Harmonized Tariff Schedule (HTS) This is a huge book, over 8 inches thick! It is helpful to use the computer PFD file or the online search tool from the USA HTS website to classify your shoes.

http://hts.usitc.gov

There are many chapters for shoes. Classification can be complicated and a little daunting. For the common shoe types, there are only a few HTS codes you need to know. Some of the rules may seem a little strange but that's how it goes.

Once your shoe is classified, you can assign its HTS code to the shipping documents. Your freight fowarder will add the charges to your customs clearance invoice.

The HTS is a 10 digit code that looks like this: 6402.19.05.30.

This cheap leather shoe also has an 8.5% duty.

The same design made from R/P or synthetic PU materials would be 20% + $.90, if its price is less than USD $12.50. If the price is more than $12.50, the duty is just 20%.

If you are a shoe designer, developer, or product manager, you need to know this stuff! Maybe adding $.05 to a shoe price can save you +.90 in import duty.

6402.19.05.30 is for men's golf shoes imported at 6% duty.

Shoe classifications are based on material, function, gender, size, construction and value.

When reviewing a shoe, you need to consider its majority material (over 51%). Is it natural leather or made from rubber plastic (R/P)? Leather shoes have an 8.5% to 10% duty (based on the FOB price).

This mesh shoe has a 20% duty.

This expensive leather shoe has an 8.5% duty.

This rubber Zoris style sandal falls into the 0% duty category.

This textile running shoe has a 20% duty.

This action leather shoe has an 8.5% duty.

This shoe is a mix of materials, but is over 51% leather. The duty rate is 8.5%.

As a shoe designer or product manager you should sit down with your import classification specialist and get to know how this works in detail. When planning your product line, designing duty-efficient shoes can save your company big bucks. You can pay less duty to the US government and provide more value to your customers!

You can find shoe import classification specialists working freelance. Expect to pay about $50.00 for each shoe model you are having classified.

This suede leather shoe has an 8.5% duty.

This canvas shoe has a 20% duty +$.90.

The bad news for Ricardo is that almost all of the Arris running shoes will be in the 20% import duty classification. The Arris product line is made up almost entirely of textile upper with synthetic PU leather trims and logos. The shoes are over $12.50 so they fall into the 20% duty class. This will add an extra $3.00 on top of a $15.00 FOB shoe.

Import tariff rules apply to everyone. No company, big or small, can avoid paying import duties. Ricardo's competitors will pay the same fees.

Some countries receive special treatment when importing goods into the USA or Europe. The shoes may have a lower duty rate, maybe even 0% duty. However, moving production to these less developed countries often results in expenses well beyond the duty saved.

Ricardo can take some steps to reduce his duty costs. For the Arris recovery shoes, Ricardo's designer and developer can look at some other material options. Instead of mesh for the uppers, they will try perforated suede leather or some type of perforated synthetic suede.

Both material options are more expensive than mesh, but the duty rate for leather is 9% and the duty rate for a 100% synthetic shoe (not mesh) is 6%. Duty rules can be a bit complicated. It is important to review the duty expense and material costs against the performance of each material.

Eve has a much simpler time with the duty regulations for the Enigma product line. The boots Eve is working on are almost entirely made of leather. For women's leather shoes the duty rate is 8.5% of the FOB price.

A shoe which is 55% leather and 45% fabric or synthetic leather will be classified as leather for US duty regulations. EU rules are slightly different for leather. In the USA, customs officials only count the exposed surfaces. In Europe, customs officials also count material covered by other materials.

Eve has some boot designs with fabric inserts. These designs will still be classified as leather duty in the USA, as long as over 50% of the surface is leather.

Many companies use the duty rules to save some money. The fabric insert material will cost less than leather, but the shoe will be still be classified into the lower 8.5% leather duty rate. You may find some low-end white action leather sport shoes or black leather boots with the medial quarter panels made from a matching, but inexpensive, synthetic leather. You will find this technique used on many inexpensive shoes.

CHAPTER 6
START-UP COSTS AND RAISING CAPITAL

How much starting capital do you need to launch your new shoe brand?

This may be the most important question as you prepare to launch your new shoe company. Starting capital can be hard to come by, and start-up costs for a shoe company can vary wildly, depending on your plans.

Footwear development and production costs
In this chapter, we will detail how much it will cost to develop your shoe line. These costs include expenses for development, tooling, travel, samples, production and shipping.

The capital calendar
Knowing when you will need money is just as important as knowing how much you will need. We will study the capital calendar for a footwear start-up. As you plan your new shoe business, you need to know exactly when to find investors, when the factory will require payments, and when you can expect to see money coming back into your company.

Raising seed money
Where can you get the seed money to launch your new company? We will look at how you can raise money to get started. Should you borrow from your friends, family, or a bank? Maybe you should launch a crowd-funding campaign.

Finally, once you have the money for your shoe company, how do you go about sending it to your shoe factory or agent? We will learn about letters of credit and overseas wire transfers.

Getting started: $0-$100
Putting pen to paper, online research, observing your target customers and studying your target market can all be done for almost nothing. Some gas money and a few lunch meetings with contacts can go a long way in helping you crystallize your plans!

Legally creating your company: $500
The paperwork can be a little frustrating, but the fees are generally low.

Trademarks: $250-$500
Trademark fees are standard. There is no avoiding them. Trademark costs can rise rapidly as your shoe company expands into foreign markets.

Web domains: $9-$100,000
While web domains start at $9 per year, a prime domain name could cost $100,000.

Designing your shoes: $0 to $20,000
This amount depends on your designer or design firm and scope of project. Upper designs are simple. Outsole tooling may be complicated. Do you have a few shoes, or an entire product line?

Product development: $2,000-$60,000
A development contract with an agent could cost $2,000 per month. A contract developer or full-time hire could cost $3,000 per month. Factory travel; $2500, factory pattern development charges; $1000 to $5000, and sample tooling; $0 to $50,000.

Tooling and lasts: $0 to $150,000+
Depending on your product, this cost can be $0 to $150,000 or more. If you are using existing lasts and molds then the cost for new production equipment could be $0. If you need new lasts, outsoles, and injection molds your production tooling could cost many hundreds of thousands of dollars.

Cost to buy your shoes:
For a new brand getting started, you should expect to pay a minimum of 50% of the total purchase price of the shoes when you place your production order. The total cost will be the price of the shoes, import duty, taxes and shipping charges.

Marketing costs:
Photography, catalog, web site production and trade show exhibit fees can add up fast! Marketing expenses for a growing company can be 10% to 20% of your gross revenue.

The capital calendar
The capital calendar is key to planning your financial operations. It lets you know when your shoe business is going to need more capital input.

You don't need all the money upfront, but you do need a plan. A capital calendar will let you plan with your investors and banks, or time your crowd-funding campaign. A detailed capital calendar will help make sure there are no surprises for you and your partners as you go through the design, development, production, marketing, and sales processes.

The capital calendar will also tell you when you can expect profits to come back into your new shoe company!

THE CAPITAL CALENDER

May:
The design phase will require payments to your designer. Starting with a retainer to begin the project. You'll also need to pay company start-up fees, including money for local permits, trademarks and web domains.

June:
The design phase is complete. Your designer will need final payments to complete the specification packs.

July:
Shoe factory and/or agent shoe development charges.
Contract shoe developer fees and travel expenses.

August:
Sample tooling for outsoles and samples shipping charges.

September:
Shoe developer travel expenses.
Samples tooling for outsoles and samples shipping charges.

October-November:
Shoe developer travel expenses.
Samples tooling for outsoles and samples shipping charges.

January-February:
Photo sample invoice and shipping samples.
Patent filing charges.

March
Product photography and catalog production.

MAY	1	DESIGN
	2	
	3	
	4	
JUN	1	Spec Drop
	2	
	3	TECH -1
	4	
JUL	1	
	2	
	3	
	4	
AUG	1	SHIPPING
	2	Design Changes
	3	
	4	TECH -2
SEP	1	
	2	
	3	
	4	SHIPPING
OCT	1	Design Changes
	2	
	3	TECH -3
	4	
NOV	1	
	2	SHIPPING
	3	PHOTO SAMPLE
	4	FOCUS GROUP
DEC	1	
	2	Photo sample
	3	production
	4	
JAN	1	
	2	SHIPPING
	3	FINAL LINE
	4	BUILD!
FEB	1	Sales Sample
	2	Production
MAR	1	
	2	

March-May:
Sales sample invoice and shipping samples.
Shoe developer travel expenses.
UPC barcode set-up fees.

June-August:
While the salesmen are booking sales, the factory is working to make the mass production sizes.

Sales rep and distributor sample payments received!

Trade show exhibiting fees
Sales related travel
Product demo expenses

September:
Production order placed. 25% to 50% of the total invoice cost must be paid in advance to cover the production tooling.

November:
Production order complete. The balance of the production shoe cost must be paid before shoes are shipped.
Website development.

December:
International & direct shipment payments received!

January:
With the shoes shipped, the freight forwarder will require payment for import duties and shipping charges.

Customer payments received!

APR	2	Production
	3	
	4	
MAY	1	SHIPPING
	2	
	3	
	4	
JUN	1	Sales Booking Window
	2	
	3	
	4	
JUL	1	
	2	
	3	
	4	
AUG	1	
	2	
	3	
	4	Order Deadline
SEP	1	90 Day Production Time
	2	
	3	
	4	
OCT	1	
	2	
	3	
	4	
NOV	1	Exit Factory
	2	
	3	Shipping
	4	
DEC	1	
	2	
	3	Landing
	4	Check In - Ship to Customers
JAN	1	
	2	
	3	
	4	

Footwear development costs

The development costs for footwear are driven mainly by the time it takes, tooling required, and travel expenses.

A very complicated shoe design will require many pattern trials, and maybe several rounds of tooling modifications. Each sample round may need to be air-shipped back to the designers for study.

Unique tooling designs are difficult to get right the first time. Mold designs often change as problems are revealed and solved. Every scrapped tool costs money.

A new shoe last shape will require fitting trials and sample revisions. Each round consumes time and money as air-shipping the samples adds up.

Travel can be very expensive! If you are going to Asia or to Europe, you can expect a week-long trip to cost a minimum of $3000 to $4500, or double that if you plan to fly business class.

Arris Arris development expenses are going to be big. Ricardo needs new lasts and tooling for his 3 new models.

His tooling development expense will not be much beyond the cost of his production molds because he is not introducing any new technology. However, the three Arris lasts needed to make the three types of shoes, will each require several sample rounds. Each test upper will require air shipment back to Ricardo's office for testing.

Ricardo is also sending his developer to China twice. Each trip will cost $3500 plus the developer's wages. The complex Arris development will cost Ricardo over $20,000 for setup, samples and shipping (tooling not included).

Enigma development expenses are minimal. Eve is using existing lasts and outsoles. She will travel to the factory once for $3500 and she will have to pay some printing and textile setup fees, sample fees, and shipping charges. Her total development expenses will be less than $6000.

Production startup costs?

There are two main factors that will determine your footwear mass production start-up costs: Tooling and mold costs, and labor and production costs. Let's look at these cost components in turn.

Shoe equipment costs

If you need outsole tooling and lasts, then your start-up expenses may be very high. If you are using what we call "open molds," then your start-up costs can be significantly reduced.

Open outsole molds are available to the factory for customers to use, but may have some significant limitations. Depending on the style of shoe, open molds may be used to make high-quality footwear. Leather wingtips or classic work boots with die designs can be made with "open" rubber-bottom molds.

Factories may offer modern, big brand look-alike molds, but you will need to be very careful. These molds may look nice, but you will need to check the fitting. Tooling made for Chinese local market goods may not fit a last compatible with your market. While the outsole molds are free to use, a compatible last will still need to be developed and purchased.

The cost of new tooling depends entirely on the design. A simple one-piece rubber cup sole mold may cost just $1,000 to $1,500 per size.

A two-part rubber and EVA outsole unit will require the same $1,500 mold for the rubber parts, then a second $2,500 mold for the EVA parts. A modern high-tech basketball shoe with molded parts may be $10,000 per each size of outsole, midsole, welding, injection and emboss tooling.

A complete size run of tooling will require 8 to 12 sets for production. The tooling cost for a unique design can be very expensive, up to $100,000 or more.

During development a sample mold will be needed to confirm the design before the set of production molds is opened. The prototype sample molds may be used for production, but not if they need significant modifications. These molds must all be paid for, even if they are used to press just a few sample parts. A mold may be used just once and then scrapped if there is a design problem.

If you are making small runs, the factory may require you to purchase the material cutting dies. These are not so expensive. They cost between $500 and $1,000.00 for a complete set.

If your project requires a new last, the factory will require payment for the set of production lasts. You will need a single set, including one of each size for development and then a production set once you place an order.

A standard production assembly line running larger orders of 1500 pairs per day will require 500 to 750 pairs of lasts for smooth operation. Small runs will still require 200 to 300 pairs of lasts. When the assembly line is running, the factory cannot afford to have workers waiting for a last to come back to the start of the line.

Tooling costs

In China there are hundreds of tooling factories making shoe equipment. The market is competitive and quality can vary widely. Prices are stable. The labor rate for workers is fixed, so price is determined by complexity and raw material quality. If a mold price is very low, watch out for poor quality metal. Below are the basic costs you should expect. If costs seem higher or lower, shop around for another price.

A shoe factory may lower the tooling cost to win the orders. A low margin customer is better than no customer, and they will find a way to make a profit on the orders later.

Rubber cupsole mold: $1200 to $1500

EVA compression tooling: $2500 to $3500

Injection EVA tooling: $3500 to $4000

Flat sheet mold rubber or EVA: $1000

Footbed molds with logo: $3000 per set

Upper emboss mold: $300 to $1000

Last development fee: $0 to $1500

Plastic last: $5 to $7 per pair

Cast metal last: $2 to $3 per pair

Cutting dies: $1000 per set

Metal hardware (stamped): $300 to $700

Metal hardware (cast): $800 to $1200

Logos (fine mold/micro injection): $100 to $200

Injection plastic shank mold: $1000 to $2500

RF emboss welding tooling: $100 to $500

CNC 4K knitting set-up: $300 per size

Sublimation print set-up: $300 per design

Woven label set-up: $0

Embroidery programming: $0

Eve will need some cutting dies, logo welding tools and a stamping mold for custom logo hardware. While the factory would normally charge new customers for cutting dies in advance, because she is working with an established brand that enjoys a good relationship with the factory, they will waive the cutting die charge.

~~Upper cutting dies 5 sets = $3500~~
Enigma logo welding tool = $500
Hardware stamping mold = $500
Total = $1000

Arris The Arris product line requires a large amount of new equipment. Ricardo will make one size of each last until he has production orders.

Upper cutting sample dies = $500
Arris logo welding tool = $500
Arris footbed pressing mold = $500
Hardware stamping mold = $500
Training shoe rubber sole = $1200
Training shoe EVA midsole = $2500
Training shoe last development = $1500
Racing shoe rubber sole = $1200
Racing shoe EVA midsole = $2500
Racing shoe last development = $1500
Recovery shoe rubber sole = $1200
Recovery shoe last development = $1500

Development tooling total = $15,100

Hardware stamping mold = $1500
Upper cutting sample dies = $3500
Arris logo welding tool, 3 sizes = $1500
Training shoe rubber sole, 8 sizes = $9600
Training shoe EVA midsole, 8 sizes = $20,000
Training shoe production lasts = $3000
Racing shoe rubber sole, 8 sizes = $9600
Racing shoe EVA midsole, 8 sizes = $20,000
Racing shoe production lasts = $3000
Recovery shoe rubber sole, 8 sizes = $9600
Recovery shoe production lasts = $3000
Arris footbed mold = $3000

Production tooling total = $87,300

Product costs

The start-up product costs are driven by the factory's minimum order quantity (MOQ). Order minimums for shoes are based on the minimums for the different shoe materials.

For a material like suede leather, the MOQ may be 1000 sq. feet. This is enough leather to make about 500 pairs.

For mesh or PU material, the MOQ may be 100 to 500 meters.

For individual samples or small sample runs, shoe materials can be purchased in the local markets, but choices may be limited. Larger material vendors will have sample labs for small batches of materials. To produce a sales sample run, the factory may purchase the MOQ of a material with the expectation that the customer will use this material for the first production run.

The product cost calculation should include photo samples, sales samples and the production order. Depending on the factory policy and the customer's order history, the price for the photo samples and sales samples may be the same as the FOB price or may be the FOB price times two.

Purchase price of 2000 pairs of shoes?

Roughly, the factory price for your shoes will be 25% of the retail selling price. So, if your shoes will cost $100 in the store, plan on $25 for the shoe with shipping and import duty included. So....$25 x 2000 pairs = $50,000!!!!

The factory will require 25% to 50% payment upon order placement to cover the material purchasing. The balance will be required before the shoes can ship.

You can see it adds up fast! Yes, you can start your own shoe brand, but don't expect to do it by yourself. You are going to need lots of help!

Eve's sample order is for 5 pairs of each model. The total cost is $2,053. Eve needs to pay the factory $1,770 with $283 going to cover freight and duty charges.

The production order for one container of boots will cost over $100,000! $88,500 will be going to the shoe factory, with $15,000 going to the freight forwarder to cover shipping and duty.

While this is a large amount of money, the profit (less marketing expenses, discounts and operational expenses) could be nearly $84,000.

For Eve to break even she will need to sell about half of the 3250 pairs.

Enigma Sample Order

	Shoe Name	Colorway	Material Note	FOB + PACK $	Freight $	Duty %	Duty $	Tax $	CustIns In Frt$	Landed $	Order	Total Cost	Factory Invoice	Freight forwarder
1	Somerset	Black	Pebble Full Grain	$35.00	1.45	9.5%	3.33	0.012	0.32	$40.11	5	$200.53	$175.00	$25.53
2	Somerset	Brown	Pebble Full Grain	$35.00	1.45	9.5%	3.33	0.012	0.32	$40.11	5	$200.53	$175.00	$25.53
3	Brattle	Mahogoney	Laser Full Grain	$35.00	1.45	9.5%	3.33	0.012	0.32	$40.11	5	$200.53	$175.00	$25.53
4	Brattle	Black	Laser Full Grain	$35.00	1.45	9.5%	3.33	0.012	0.32	$40.11	5	$200.53	$175.00	$25.53
5	Tremont	Black	Smooth Full Grain	$30.00	1.45	9.5%	2.85	0.011	0.32	$34.63	5	$173.14	$150.00	$23.14
6	Tremont	Brown	Smooth Full Grain	$30.00	1.45	9.5%	2.85	0.011	0.32	$34.63	5	$173.14	$150.00	$23.14
7	Beacon	Black	Sub-Action Leather	$30.00	1.45	9.5%	2.85	0.011	0.32	$34.63	5	$173.14	$150.00	$23.14
8	Beacon	White China	Action	$30.00	1.45	9.5%	2.85	0.011	0.32	$34.63	5	$173.14	$150.00	$23.14
9	Revere	Black	Pebble Full Grain	$22.00	1.45	9.5%	2.09	0.008	0.32	$25.87	5	$129.33	$110.00	$19.33
10	Union	Pink Roses	Action	$18.00	1.45	9.5%	1.71	0.006	0.32	$21.48	5	$107.42	$90.00	$17.42
11	Hanover	Spiked Flowers	Action	$18.00	1.45	9.5%	1.71	0.006	0.32	$21.48	5	$107.42	$90.00	$17.42
12	Haymarket	Black Rose	Sub-Action Leather	$18.00	1.45	9.5%	1.71	0.006	0.32	$21.48	5	$107.42	$90.00	$17.42
13	Dowdoin	Black Floral	Sub-Action Leather	$18.00	1.45	9.5%	1.71	0.006	0.32	$21.48	5	$107.42	$90.00	$17.42
											65	$ 2,053.68	$ 1,770.00	$ 283.68

Enigma Production Order

	Shoe Name	Colorway	Material Note	FOB + PACK $	Freight $	Duty %	Duty $	Tax $	CustIns In Frt$	Landed $	Order	Total Cost	Factory Invoice	Freight forwarder
1	Somerset	Black	Pebble Full Grain	$35.00	1.45	9.5%	3.33	0.012	0.32	$40.11	250	$10,026.29	$8,750.00	$1,276.29
2	Somerset	Brown	Pebble Full Grain	$35.00	1.45	9.5%	3.33	0.012	0.32	$40.11	250	$10,026.29	$8,750.00	$1,276.29
3	Brattle	Mahogoney	Laser Full Grain	$35.00	1.45	9.5%	3.33	0.012	0.32	$40.11	250	$10,026.29	$8,750.00	$1,276.29
4	Brattle	Black	Laser Full Grain	$35.00	1.45	9.5%	3.33	0.012	0.32	$40.11	250	$10,026.29	$8,750.00	$1,276.29
5	Tremont	Black	Smooth Full Grain	$30.00	1.45	9.5%	2.85	0.011	0.32	$34.63	250	$8,657.10	$7,500.00	$1,157.10
6	Tremont	Brown	Smooth Full Grain	$30.00	1.45	9.5%	2.85	0.011	0.32	$34.63	250	$8,657.10	$7,500.00	$1,157.10
7	Beacon	Black	Sub-Action Leather	$30.00	1.45	9.5%	2.85	0.011	0.32	$34.63	250	$8,657.10	$7,500.00	$1,157.10
8	Beacon	White China	Action	$30.00	1.45	9.5%	2.85	0.011	0.32	$34.63	250	$8,657.10	$7,500.00	$1,157.10
9	Revere	Black	Pebble Full Grain	$22.00	1.45	9.5%	2.09	0.008	0.32	$25.87	250	$6,466.40	$5,500.00	$966.40
10	Union	Pink Roses	Action	$18.00	1.45	9.5%	1.71	0.006	0.32	$21.48	250	$5,371.05	$4,500.00	$871.05
11	Hanover	Spiked Flowers	Action	$18.00	1.45	9.5%	1.71	0.006	0.32	$21.48	250	$5,371.05	$4,500.00	$871.05
12	Haymarket	Black Rose	Sub-Action Leather	$18.00	1.45	9.5%	1.71	0.006	0.32	$21.48	250	$5,371.05	$4,500.00	$871.05
13	Dowdoin	Black Floral	Sub-Action Leather	$18.00	1.45	9.5%	1.71	0.006	0.32	$21.48	250	$5,371.05	$4,500.00	$871.05
											3250	$ 102,684.15	$ 88,500.00	$ 14,184.15

Arris Sample Order

	Shoe Name	Colorway	Material Note	FOB + PACK $	Freight $	Duty %	Duty $	Tax $	CustIns In Frt$	Landed $	Order	Total Cost	Factory Invoice	Freight forwarder
1	Endro X	Silver	Mesh / PU	$34.00	4.05	20.0%	6.80	0.012	0.32	$45.18	15	$677.70	$510.00	$167.70
2	Endro X	Green	Mesh / PU	$34.00	4.05	20.0%	6.80	0.012	0.32	$45.18	15	$677.70	$510.00	$167.70
3	Endro X	Grey	Mesh / PU	$34.00	4.05	20.0%	6.80	0.012	0.32	$45.18	15	$677.70	$510.00	$167.70
4	Phantom	Silver	Mesh / PU	$30.00	4.05	20.0%	6.00	0.011	0.32	$40.38	15	$605.68	$450.00	$155.68
5	Lightening	Yellow	Mesh / PU	$30.00	4.05	20.0%	6.00	0.011	0.32	$40.38	15	$605.68	$450.00	$155.68
6	Revo	Yellow	Mesh / PU	$28.00	4.05	20.0%	5.60	0.010	0.32	$37.98	15	$569.67	$420.00	$149.67
											90	$ 3,814.11	$ 2,850.00	$ 964.11

Arris Production Order

	Shoe Name	Colorway	Material Note	FOB + PACK $	Freight $	Duty %	Duty $	Tax $	CustIns In Frt$	Landed $	Order	Total Cost	Factory Invoice	Freight forwarder
1	Endro X	Silver	Mesh / PU	$17.00	1.05	20.0%	3.40	0.006	0.32	$21.77	300	$6,532.15	$5,100.00	$1,432.15
2	Endro X	Green	Mesh / PU	$17.00	1.05	20.0%	3.40	0.006	0.32	$21.77	300	$6,532.15	$5,100.00	$1,432.15
3	Endro X	Grey	Mesh / PU	$17.00	1.05	20.0%	3.40	0.006	0.32	$21.77	300	$6,532.15	$5,100.00	$1,432.15
4	Phantom	Silver	Mesh / PU	$15.00	1.05	20.0%	3.00	0.005	0.32	$19.37	200	$3,874.63	$3,000.00	$874.63
5	Lightening	Yellow	Mesh / PU	$15.00	1.05	20.0%	3.00	0.005	0.32	$19.37	200	$3,874.63	$3,000.00	$874.63
6	Revo	Yellow	Mesh / PU	$14.00	1.05	20.0%	2.80	0.005	0.32	$18.17	300	$5,451.84	$4,200.00	$1,251.84
											1600	$ 32,797.56	$25,500.00	$7,297.56

Ricardo has hired 8 salesmen to visit dealers across the USA. He will need sales samples brought in ahead of the main production run. He has gone ahead and ordered 15 pairs of each model so he has enough for his reps, for his in-house salespeople, and a few pairs set aside for important buyers to wear test.

Ricardo wants his sales samples to arrive fast, so he has decided to air ship them. This increases the freight cost to $4.05 per pair, but cuts 4 weeks off the delivery time.

The factory making Arris shoes also has a policy to double charge for samples made in the sample room versus on the assembly line. While $3,814 seems expensive for samples, Ricardo will get some of this money back when the sales reps pay for the samples.

Ricardo could have limited the sample run by not ordering every color of the Endro X, but he wants to make a big impression with the dealers. 6 models is a very small shoe line so he wants to show them all.

The first Arris production order is very small. Ricardo is lucky to have a small MOQ. He agrees to use any leftover materials on future orders, so the factory accepts the low order quantity for the first order.

Ricardo's tooling and first production order have totaled more than $100,000. The Arris product plan calls for sales of $90,000 with a profit of $56,000. The Arris brand will not turn a profit during its first season unless he can increase his sales forecast!

Ricardo runs the numbers again. He needs to sell 4000 pairs to cover the development, tooling and cost of goods. An operating loss is not the end of his company, as long as he can find capital to operate.

Start-up capital calendars

Ricardo and Eve have very different capital requirements. They both need a significant amount of money to bring their shoes to market, but they don't need the money at the same time.

Eve's development expenses are minimal as Enigma boots are not complicated and the development requires little travel, but Eve's boots are expensive to produce. She will need to raise $97,000 to buy and ship the boots. Her total, before marketing expenses, is around $109,500.

As mentioned before, the Arris product design and development is complicated and will require lots of tooling, travel, and technical expertise. Ricardo needs to hire experienced designers and developers to make sure the Arris project is moving in the right direction.

Ricardo's expenses are front loaded in his process. The design, development, and resources required to make one set of samples has consumed over $30,000 in capital. To complete the development and produce the product line sales samples, Ricardo will need another $5,000.

With the Arris sales force working to collect orders, Ricardo will face some critical decisions.

If his salesmen fail to book orders, Ricardo must make a choice to either write off the $35,000 as a total loss and go back to work as a stockbroker, or Ricardo can change his designs, make new samples and go forward investing another $86,300 to make the production tooling.

In total, Ricardo will need over $165,000 to bring Arris to market. This includes $15,000 he allocated for marketing his new brand.

Arris

May:
The design phase $4500 Company startup fees, trademarks and domains. $500

June:
The design phase complete your designer will need payments to complete the spec packs. $4500

July:
Shoe factory and or agent shoe development charges. Contract shoe developer fees and travel expenses. $3500

August:
Samples tooling for outsoles and samples shipping charges. $17,000

September:
Shoe developer travel expenses. Samples tooling for outsoles and samples shipping charges. $3,500

December:
Shoe developer travel expenses. Samples tooling for outsoles and samples shipping charges. $3,500

January-Febuary:
Photo sample invoice and shipping samples. Product photography, web and catalog production. $1,200

---

enigma
KICKING FASHION IN THE FACE!

November:
The design phase: $0.00 Eve does this herself. Company startup fees, trademarks and domains. $400

December:
Shoe factory or agent shoe development charges. Contract shoe developer fees and travel expenses. $2,500

February:
Samples tooling for outsoles and samples shipping charges. $1,500

March:
Shoe developer travel expenses and samples shipping charges. $2,500

July:
Photo sample invoice and shipping samples. Product photography, web and catalog production.
Samples $600
Catalog photos $1000

Spring Delivery

Month	Wk	Activity
MAY	1 2 3 4	DESIGN
JUN	1 2 3 4	Spec Drop / TECH -1
JUL	1 2 3 4	TECH -1
AUG	1 2 3 4	SHIPPING / Design Changes
SEP	1 2 3 4	TECH -2
OCT	1 2 3 4	SHIPPING / Design Changes
NOV	1 2 3 4	TECH -3
DEC	1 2 3 4	SHIPPING / PHOTO SAMPLE / FOCUS GROUP
JAN	1 2 3 4	Photo sample production
FEB	1 2 3 4	SHIPPING / FINAL LINE BUILD!
MAR	1 2 3 4	Sales Sample Production

Fall Delivery

Month	Wk	Activity
OCT	1 2 3 4	DESIGN
NOV	1 2 3 4	Spec Drop / TECH -1
DEC	1 2 3 4	TECH -1
JAN	1 2 3 4	SHIPPING / Design Changes
FEB	1 2 3 4	TECH -2
MAR	1 2 3 4	SHIPPING / Design Changes
APR	1 2 3 4	TECH -3
MAY	1 2 3 4	SHIPPING / PHOTO SAMPLE / FOCUS GROUP
JUN	1 2 3 4	Photo sample production
JUL	1 2 3 4	SHIPPING / FINAL LINE BUILD!
AUG	1 2 3 4	Sales Sample Production
SEP	1	

March-April-May:
Sales sample invoice and shipping samples. Shoe developer travel expenses. UPC set up fees. $3,800

June-July-August:
While the salesmen are booking sales the factory is working to make the mass production sizes. The production tooling must be paid for. $86,300

September:
Production order placed 50% in advance. $15,000

November:
Production order complete. The balance of the production shoe cost must be paid before shoes are shipped. $15,000

January:
With the shoes shipped the freight forwarder will require payment for import duties and shipping charges. In bound 3PL charges. $7,000

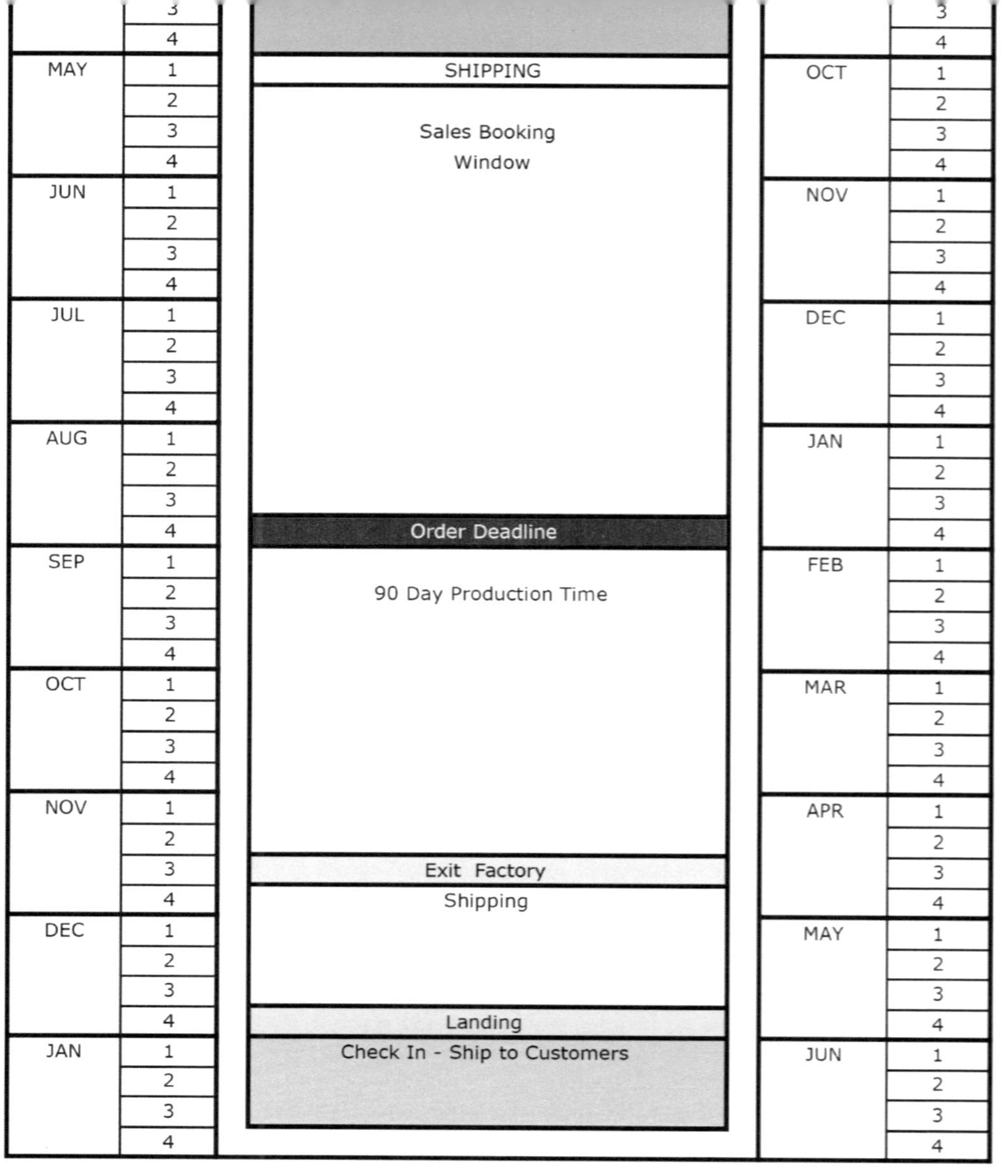

October:
Sales sample invoice and shipping samples. Shoe developer travel expenses. UPC set up fees. $4000

November-January:
While the salesmen are booking sales the factory is working to make the mass production sizes. The production tooling must be paid for. $1,000

February:
Production order placed. 25% to 50% in advance. $44,000

April:
Production order complete. The balance of the production shoe cost must be paid before shoes are shipped. $44,000

June:
With the shoes shipped the freight forwarder will require payment. Import duties and shipping. $15,000

Rental charges for the Safe House. $10,000

Inland freight to the Enigma Safe House. $800

Timeline (left column of months)

Month	1	2	3	4
MAY				
JUN				
JUL				
AUG				
SEP				
OCT				
NOV				
DEC				
JAN				

Timeline (right column of months)

Month	1	2	3	4
OCT				
NOV				
DEC				
JAN				
FEB				
MAR				
APR				
MAY				
JUN				

Timeline phase labels:
- SHIPPING
- Sales Booking Window
- Order Deadline
- 90 Day Production Time
- Exit Factory / Shipping
- Landing
- Check In - Ship to Customers

Raising money for your shoe company

When it comes to starting your new shoe company, raising seed money is one of the first things you need to consider. As you go about the early stages of designing and developing your shoes, you need to be thinking, "How am I going to pay for this?"

You need to make sure that you have properly planned in advance. Running out of money in the middle of your project will be a huge disappointment.

Know your costs

Every investor you talk with will ask you, "How much money are you looking for? What exactly is it for? When do you need it?" And most importantly, "When can I expect to get paid back?" Having a detailed capital calendar will allow you to report this information properly to your investors. It will also help you both to see if your project is running according to plan or not.

In chapter 2 we reviewed the basic business set-up costs. In chapter 3 we learned how much a new design may cost. In chapter 4 we made a financial plan, and in chapter 5 we reviewed the cost of development and production. When you will need to spend money is detailed in the capital calender found in chapter 6.

By now you should have a much clearer idea of what this new business is going to cost. If you don't have a number in your mind, you should take some time and make your calculations.

Planning and preparation are a must. Without a detailed list of costs you won't know how much money to ask for. Without properly assessing this information beforehand, you could get part way through the process and not be able to finish what you have started.

Money raising options

There are many options when it comes to raising the money you need to set up your shoe business. Each comes with their own benefits and complications. The amount of money you need will determine if you can self-fund or need investors and loans.

Personal savings

It is almost impossible to start your own business without investing some of your own money. Your savings are there to act as a buffer when times are hard, or to buy something that you cannot outright afford.

Temporarily using your savings to fund your shoe business is a way to invest in your future. It may mean that you don't have any savings to fall back on for awhile, but it is a great way to get your business off the ground. Temporarily using your savings before your business generates an income for you has great benefits.

Using your own savings means that you are not charging yourself any interest on the money, so you are effectively borrowing the capital at a zero interest rate. This makes it a very efficient way to fund your shoe company. You also don't have to worry about time scales when it comes to paying it back. You can reinvest the capital if you sell the shoes quickly and need more stock. The money already belongs to you, so you can quickly decide what happens with it.

Friends and family loans

Many start-up businesses are founded on money raised from friends and family. When you have a passion for something, then it is your family and your friends that often hear the most about it. You will have shared your dreams with these people and most likely they believe in you more than an investor you have never met.

Make a professional pitch and have written agreements, but make it fun too. Keep your friends and family updated on what is going on and use their contacts in social media spaces, like Facebook, to help you get the word and excitement out there. A motivated investor will really help you to get your brand in the public eye.

Don't be afraid to ask everyone that you know, and don't take it personally if they turn you down. Having a professional attitude and treating people respectfully is key to getting them to help you. Make it easy for people to do business with you. Friends and family will want to see your new shoe company succeed.

Make sure every investor gets a new pair of shoes from your first run!

Investing partners

There are people out there that invest professionally in small businesses for which they can see a good potential return. These people may not be easy to find and they will want to see lots of facts and figures from you. They will also come with a contact list that can transform your shoe business. If they have helped others in a similar venture before you, then they will already have connections in place to help you succeed.

These people are often known as angel investors, and they operate on their own terms. They may put out their feelers and find out about companies like yours through the grapevine. This is where your social media and other marketing will help you to make contacts. Others will advertise for people to come forward and speak to them.

You need to know your business inside and out when it comes to pitching angel investors and other investing partners. This is their money and their livelihood. They are looking to make a good return on their investment. You need to think big with these investors, because selling a few shoes for a small profit is not what they are looking for. At the same time, you need to be realistic when dealing with investors, because they will have seen a thousand pitches and will know when they are not being told the full story. Make sure to polish your pitch and have all your costs and business projections in place so the angel investor will know that you are in complete control of your business.

Bank loans

You can also ask a bank for a loan to fund your shoe company. You will need to get all your information in order, as the bank will want to see your business plan as well as any costing and projections that you have worked out. Facts help here, so real quotes from your suppliers carry more weight than your own estimates. Treat this meeting in the most professional manner and the bank may consider you as a viable borrower. If you go into a meeting with the bank unprepared, they will not take you seriously and your chances of securing a bank loan will be slim.

The interest rates that banks offer are competitive, and the rate that you eventually get will depend on factors such as any collateral you can put up, your credit history, and your relationship with the bank. Visit the bank where you do your personal banking, they will have a much better picture of you as a customer, and may be able to offer you a deal that you can't get anywhere else. Your company will also appear more professional once you have a business bank account and this will aid you in securing suppliers.

Lines of credit

As an alternative to a traditional bank loan, you could secure a line of credit with a bank or other lender. This means that you gain access to a set amount of money for your business, but don't have to take it all at once. The advantage of this setup, is that you only pay interest on the amount of money that you have drawn out from the line of credit at that point in time.

If you need access to money at different times for different aspects of your shoe company, then a line of credit may be a good option for you.

Once again, you will need to have your business plans and financial forecasts in place so the lender can make an informed decision about your case. It can be complicated to keep track of your spending and the amount of interest you are incurring on your line of credit, but it is a flexible way of raising money to start your business.

Crowdfounding

The advent of the internet has given the small business access to other sources of funding. When it comes to getting new product ideas off the ground, crowdfunding is a great way to reach out to customers, and secure backing for your new shoe company.

With crowdfunding you will show potential investors what you are planning (your sales pitch), and in return they can choose to pledge small or large amounts to back your project. Once you have the money needed to launch, you can go ahead with ordering production tooling and shoes.

Crowdfunding for footwear

You can self-fund the development of your samples and buy one size of outsole tooling. Then, with a small amount of crowdfunded money, maybe less than $10,000, you can show a sample line and find backers.

If you can secure 300 to 500 backers, that should be enough to get you started. If your project funds, you will have the factory MOQ requirements met and you can use the money to purchase tooling. If you have a complicated shoe line that requires more expensive tooling, you will need more backers to launch.

Crowdfunder™ is a platform that allows people to raise capital from small individual investors and to give them a financial return. People who fund here are looking for projects where they can get their money back, plus a return on their investment. This is strictly for businesses and is a good way to see if your business plan is attractive.

Kickstarter™ will allow you to raise money in the form of a donation in return for offering a reward. The people that pledge here do not expect to see their money back, but do expect you to give them something that money can't buy. You can offer them the first pair off the production line, the ability to design the next pair of shoes, or something that they just can't get anywhere else.

Peerbackers™ is another crowdfunding website that enables people with a project to meet people that are looking to invest. It works in a similar way to the two above, and it is a great place for the budding entrepreneur to find backing for their business. Your shoe business may be able to find a group of people to help with the cost of the project, which is particularly useful if you can't get financed through traditional routes.

The advantages of crowdfunding

Another advantage of crowdfunding is the exposure for your business. Your backers will have their own network of friends, family and colleagues on places such as social media. They will be sure to let their peers know about your new shoes if they have put money into your company. This means that you immediately open up your marketing reach when your products go to market.

The reality of crowdfunding

You need to be careful with crowdfunding. A huge payout from Kickstarter™ can also mean a big tax bill before you even spend the money.

To start, Kickstarter will take their cut, about 8% of the total.

After your project funds, you will receive an income statement form (1099-M). This informs you AND the US government how much TAXABLE income you received from your campaign. Depending on your tax rate, you may need to reserve 44% of this to pay the government. This is also effected by how much you spend on your project, as expenses are deductible.

Be very careful about funding late in the year, as this money may be seen as income and taxed BEFORE you have a chance to spend it on the development and production of your shoes!

While a 5 million dollar Kickstarter result may sound awesome, it also means you need to start managing a 5 million dollar company....NOW!

If your business model is not profitable, your new shoe company may have big problems fast. Take some time and get some advice from your tax accountant about how to handle the incoming funds...BEFORE you launch your campaign.

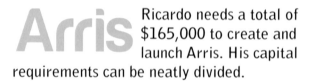 Ricardo needs a total of $165,000 to create and launch Arris. His capital requirements can be neatly divided.

Ricardo will self-finance the first $35,000 needed to develop the shoes and make the sales samples. This includes money from several of his co-workers who each offered $500. (Just in case Arris is the next Nike™, they want to be in at the beginning.)

The Arris sales force does a great job getting the Arris shoes pre-booked into Ricardo's target retailers. He has firm orders for 3000 pairs of shoes! Now he needs money to buy the shoes and open the tooling. He needs about $118,000.

Ricardo takes the orders to his local bank and asks for a loan based on the strength of the orders. His bank grants him the loan, but Ricardo has to offer his house or retirement fund as collateral. It's a big risk, but Ricardo is going to do it!

Based on the strength of the first orders, Ricardo asks the factory to amortize some of the tooling bills into the cost of the shoes. The factory owner has met Ricardo and feels the project will succeed. He agrees to delay $30,000 of the tooling payments until the second order is placed.

The factory can do this, as they have possession of the Arris tooling as collateral.

 Eve is able to beg, borrow, and steal (not literally!) the first $12,500 from her friends and family. She will need to raise about $10,000 to rent office space and "find" $5,000 for marketing. The first order of Enigma boots will cost about $97,000 to buy and ship. Eve needs a total of $124,500!
Eve will launch a crowdfunding campaign on Kickstarter™. She needs to sell about 1000 pairs to finance her first production order. Good luck, Eve!

Paying for shoes
How do you actually pay the shoe factory or footwear agent?

The main idea here is for both you and the factory to make sure you get what you want. The factory needs to make sure they will get paid for their efforts, and you need to make sure you get the shoes you paid for.

There are two common methods to make payments to factories or agents, these are the Letters of Credit (LC) and payment by Wire transfer (TT).

What is a letter of credit?
A letter of credit is a payment term mostly used for long-distance and international commercial transactions, where the two parties are not physically close to each other.

A letter of credit is a crucial part of international business transactions, because it gives security to both parties in the transaction. The seller knows that they are going to be paid, and the buyer knows that they will receive the goods. It is an official and legally-binding document that compels the buyer to exchange the agreed amount of money for the agreed goods. It allows the seller to rely on the bank that produces the letter of credit to pay up. Although no transaction can be guaranteed 100%, this us as close as you can get to ensuring that payment will be received.

As trade between companies in different parts of the country or different countries of the world has become more prevalent, so has the use of the letter of credit.

The banking laws and regulations in every country are different. The letter of credit provides peace of mind that payment will be received in exchange for the goods provided.

LETTER OF CREDIT TRANSACTION

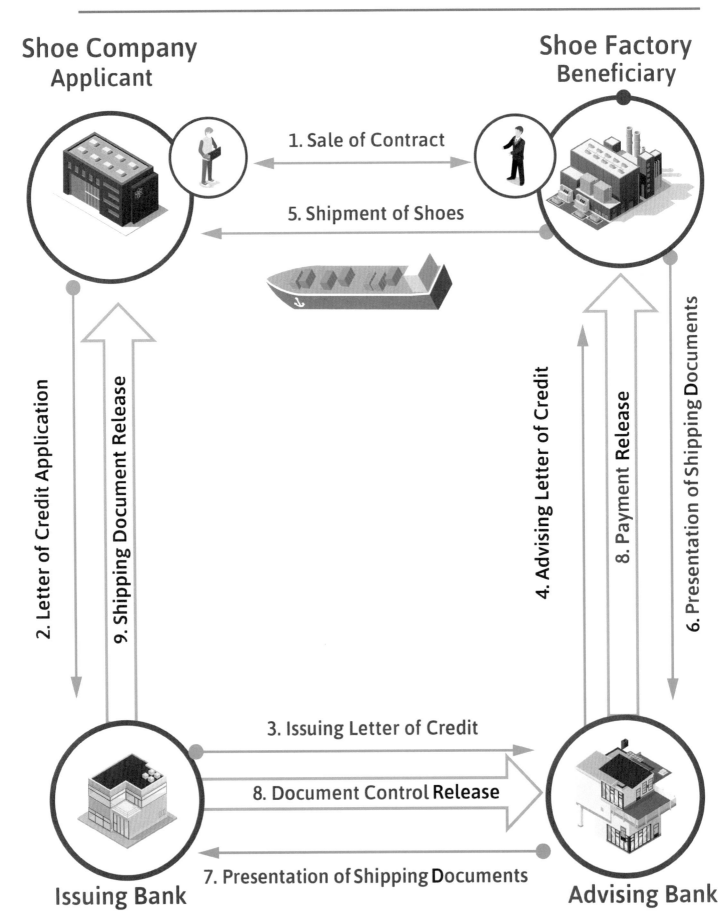

Shoe Company
Applicant

Shoe Factory
Beneficiary

1. Sale of Contract

5. Shipment of Shoes

2. Letter of Credit Application

9. Shipping Document Release

4. Advising Letter of Credit

8. Payment Release

6. Presentation of Shipping Documents

3. Issuing Letter of Credit

8. Document Control **Release**

7. Presentation of Shipping **D**ocuments

Issuing Bank

Advising Bank

How do letters of credit work?

1. The shoe company (the applicant) and the shoe factory (beneficiary or seller), agree to conduct business with each other. The shoe factory will request a letter of credit to guarantee payment for the shoes.

2. The shoe company applies to its bank for a letter of credit in favor of the seller (the shoe factory), and the bank approves the credit risk of the buyer. The shoe company must have funds in the issuing bank.

3. The issuing bank can then issue and forward the letter of credit to the corresponding bank of the seller.

4. The advising bank will authenticate the credit and forward the original credit to the shoe factory.

5. The shoe factory can then ship the goods. They will create the shipping paperwork that supports the letter of credit. This paperwork may vary greatly depending on the perceived risk involved in dealing with a particular company, and the practices of the country that they are located in.

6. The seller presents the required documents to the advising or confirming bank to be processed for payment, and the bank checks these documents.

7. The advising bank presents the documents to the issuing bank to satisfy the terms of the letter of credit. In this case shipping documents and a QC inspection certificate are required.

8. Once these documents are correct, the advising bank will claim the funds from this issuing bank on behalf of the shoe factory.

They can do this by:
- Debiting the account of the issuing bank.
- Waiting until the issuing bank remits, after receiving the paperwork.
- Reimburse to another bank as required in the letter of credit documents.

9. The issuing bank then forwards the shipping documents to the shoe company. These documents are needed to receive the goods in the buyer's home port. The documents include the bill of lading. This gives the shoe company title and legal possession of the goods.

Pros of using a letter of credit
- The LC gives the shoe factory the security that they will get paid.
  This enables you to negotiate better terms when dealing with someone for the first time.
- Your payment is backed up by a bank, so your seller has the peace of mind that they are dealing with someone legitimate.
- The LC is useful when it comes to dealing with companies in different parts of the world.
- You can set the terms of sale with the seller in advance.

Cons of using a letter of credit
- You will need to pass a credit check from your bank.
  This may not be easy for you when you first start out in business.
- It can be a long process because of all the paperwork involved.
- If some of the paperwork is missing when your product arrives, you may not get immediate customs clearance.
- You trust a third party, albeit a bank, with your money.

TT WIRE TRANSFER

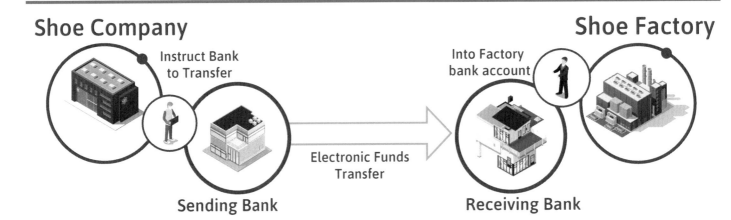

Shoe Company

Instruct Bank to Transfer

Sending Bank

Electronic Funds Transfer

Shoe Factory

Into Factory bank account

Receiving Bank

What is a wire transfer?
A wire transfer is an electronic payment service for transferring funds by wire, for example through SWIFT (SWIFT Code stands for The Society for Worldwide Interbank Financial Telecommunication.), the Federal Reserve Wire Network, or the Clearing House Interbank Payments System.

How wire transfers work
You can set-up a wire transfer through online banking or at your local branch bank. Often you will need an appointment. You may be charged a fee for transferring and some banks will limit the amount of money you can send in one transaction. You can check out the fees before you commit to sending the money. In some transactions you will need to provide a SWIFT code.

If you are transferring funds to an international account, your account will be debited the same day, and your bank will send the payment out immediately. The beneficiary's bank will generally receive the funds 1 to 2 days later. However, there are a number of factors which could delay the credit to the beneficiary. These include, but are not limited to: local bank holidays, delays by an intermediary bank or other local conditions.

Pros of using a wire transfer
- Your payment will be with the seller in a short amount of time.
- It is a highly secure form of payment.
- It ensures that your payment is final and settled with the seller.

Cons of using a wire transfer
- You will incur fees from your bank to process the wire transfer.
- There may be limits on how much money you can wire in a single transaction.
- You are responsible for shipping confirmation from the factory.

The cost of payment methods

The costs associated with sending money to another company or even another country, should be included in your decision-making when buying your shoes from a supplier. It can make a big difference to the overall cost of the transaction.

The typical fee for a buyer in a letter of credit transaction is 0.75% to 1.5%, depending on the countries involved and the size of the transaction. There are also fees for the seller, so the total cost to both parties can be higher than the 0.75% to 1.5%. A transaction of $100,000 can incur fees of between $750 and $1,500.

The typical fee for a wire transfer ranges from $15 to $50 with most major banks. This can vary depending on who you bank with, where the funds are going, the method you use to transfer, and which cuurencies you are using.

There is a lower overall fee for large transactions when you use a wire transfer versus a letter of credit.

Ricardo will use a combination of LCs and TTs to pay the factory. For smaller tooling charges and development fees, the wire transfer is more convenient.

Ricardo will use a letter of credit for the large production orders payments. The LC offers more protection for both the seller and buyer, although they can be costly and more cumbersome.

Companies with a strong working relationships will often use the wire transfer for all of their transactions.

Eve's factory prefers to use letters of credit for new customers. Once Enigma and the factory develop a personal relationship they will switch to the more efficient wire transfer.

Checklist of what you will need at the bank

When it comes to working with your bank to send money, you will need to make sure that you have certain information with you. The details that you will need vary slightly from transaction to transaction, but there are general things that you will need in all cases.

- At least one form of photo identification.

- The details of how much money you will transfer, and the equivalent in the seller's currency,

- The contract that states exactly what you will pay the factory, when you will pay it, and exactly what goods you will receive in return for your payment.

- The bank details of the person or company to whom you are paying the money.

- You may need your SWIFT code from your bank and the payees bank.

- Details of how long the wire takes to go through, so you can confirm this with your seller.

CHAPTER 7

BRAND PROMOTION AND FOOTWEAR MARKETING

Your brand promotion and marketing efforts should begin long before your shoes arrive from the factory. You should have a marketing strategy well planned before you place any orders to the shoe factory.

In this chapter we are going to review the three basic types of marketing, common footwear strategies, marketing costs and the basic components of a footwear marketing campaign.

What is marketing?

Marketing is practicing the art of seduction between you and your potential customers. It is showing off all the brilliant features of your shoes and the style of your brand, so that people desire the shoes you have made. Your marketing campaign is how you will communicate your company's brand image and values.

The first step to seducing a customer to buy your shoes is to let them know that you actually exist.

If your brand is not on your customers' minds, you won't even be considered in their footwear purchase decisions. When a customer sets out on a journey to buy a pair of shoes, you need to be visible in order to even have chance of your shoes being bought.

There is so much competition in the footwear marketplace, that you need a marketing plan to get your shoe brand out there and get customers to buy. You want to reach your audience in as many ways as possible, for as little expense as possible, so that you can grow your footwear brand and grow your profits!

Creative marketing will reach your target consumers and make them want to buy your shoes. This is the bottom line of what a great marketing campaign will do for you. There are different ways to make this happen, but at the end of the day, all your marketing efforts are geared to selling your shoes to as many people as possible.

Three types of marketing campaigns

There are three main types of marketing that we will be taking a look at here. The first is traditional marketing, which is the domain of the big marketing companies, but is also accessible to you if you know how. The second is called guerrilla marketing, and focuses on different ways to get great results. The third and newest way to interact with potential customers is social media marketing. All three of these marketing styles will be useful to your new shoe company.

Traditional marketing

Traditional marketing is based on the successful formulas that have been in place in marketing for a long time, and are practiced by big companies and their partners in the big marketing agencies.

Traditional marketing is carried out through the mainstream media, such as television and print, and can have the effect of reaching a large number of people all at once. Direct mail is a traditional marketing method that gets the name out there in one hit, and can have the effect of gaining brand recognition in a very short space of time.

The logistics of traditional marketing means that it can be an expensive way to advertise your new brand. To produce a television commercial you will need to book expensive time slots with the TV stations, hire actors and get the whole thing shot.

To deliver direct mail to tens of thousands of homes, you will incur design and printing costs in addition to the postage. You can see why traditional marketing has been the exclusive domain of brands with very deep pockets.

But this does not mean that you should shy away from the power of traditional marketing. There are some great ideas when it comes to marketing your shoe company. You just need to target your traditional marketing campaign to your specific market.

Special offer coupons can be a great way for people to sample your shoes. If you produce and distribute coupons that give the buyer a small discount on your shoes, then you immediately get your brand involved in their buying decision. The coupon doesn't have to give away a large part of your profit, but will help to get your name out there. People love to collect and use coupons, and they immediately make your shoes more appealing to the potential buyer. Make sure the coupon is branded the same way as your shoes, so that people can make an immediate connection.

Even if the coupon recipient doesn't buy the shoes, you will have raised awareness of your brand.

A customer referral program can be a great way to get people to spread the word about your shoes. These programs have been used by traditional marketers for some time, as a happy user of your shoes is the best person to convince more customers in the future to buy from you. You could include a "recommend a friend" invitation in the packaging of your shoes. Many companies make this successful by offering an incentive for the new buyer and the person who has referred as well. Your existing buyers will talk to their peer group about your shoes, and this can be an effective way of leveraging your customers.

Direct mail can be expensive if you don't know how to use it properly. Just sending out your mail to a whole area, means you are using a scattergun approach that will miss far more than it will hit.

There are companies that will provide you mailing lists that can get to your potential clients in a more targeted way. Whatever the potential demographic of your customers, maybe you will be able to narrow down these customers with a mailing list. You can then reduce the amount of direct mail you send out and reduce the cost.

"Start locally" can be a great motto for a fledgling company. You can build a brand and a reputation in your local area much easier and cheaper, than you can if you want to hit a large area all at once. Local radio is another very affordable option, and can give you access to the people in and around where you live. If you have your shoes for sale in a local store, then you could share the radio advertising costs with that store to get maximum exposure for minimal cost.

Guerrilla marketing

Guerrilla marketing involves being a little more creative than traditional marketing. It came about because people had to operate on little or no marketing budget to get their name out there.

Guerrilla marketing uses unconventional methods that many might not think of immediately. In place of the big budget, a guerrilla marketing campaign makes use of high energy and creativity to get the message out to your customer base. It usually involves making a more personal connection with one customer at a time, rather than the blanket or scattergun approach of traditional marketing.

The idea is that it is more meaningful to have a one-to-one conversation with someone you can convert to being a customer of your shoe brand for life, than to spend a lot of money on a TV ad that more than 95% of the audience will ignore. There are some great ideas out there that can make use of guerrilla marketing to help your shoe company. Here are some examples:

Give a pair of your shoes away to a fashion blogger for a review. Fashion blogging is huge, and the number of followers the top bloggers get is astounding; we are talking hundreds of thousands, if not millions, of followers for the most popular bloggers. If you want to get your brand seen, then you can give away a pair of shoes to a blogger in exchange for a review on their blog. Contact them first to make sure that they are interested. Exposure on one of these blogs can help interest in your shoes go viral. It is a great way to get noticed.

Content is king on the internet, and the way businesses are found is through search engine results. The best way to get your brand seen is to launch a blog on your website. With fresh and relevant content, you will get customers coming back to see more all the time. Remember, you are selling more than a pair of shoes. You are selling a brand and a lifestyle. If you can connect with your relevant market in a personal and meaningful way, then they will keep coming back for more.

Video marketing has really taken off over the last few years as YouTube has seemingly taken over the world! Videos that show off your latest designs or the brand that you have created will be very popular with your target market. The key to making your YouTube videos a success is the number of comments and shares that you can generate. Once your video starts to be shared from peer to peer, then you will raise awareness in your target market and gain more sales. Make your video content interesting, funny, engaging and relevant to your brand, and you will find that your customers will love it.

A "trade-in" campaign is a great way to get your brand noticed and generate new customers for your shoes. If you offer a $5 trade-in for any old shoes, then your customers will think that they are getting a bargain. It gives people the prompt to visit the store where your shoes are being sold and try on a pair. If you extend this further to say that all shoes that have been traded-in will go to charity, then you will get customers seeking you out without having to spend big.

A sticker or poster campaign is a great way to get noticed. Guerrilla marketing has the essence of the streets at its core. Just getting stickers or posters made and putting them up in prominent places is an effective and affordable way to get your name out there. This is especially effective if you live in a city. The places where people congregate, such as train stations, shopping malls and universities, are wonderful locations to get your brand seen and noticed as you launch your shoe company.

Guerrilla marketing is only limited by your time and your imagination. There are many ideas that you can pull together for very little money that will help your shoe business be successful.

Social media marketing

Social media marketing refers to the marketing activities you carry out in one or more of the wide range of social media sites that people use today. Companies large and small have seen the potential that social media offers, and a vast number of businesses have their own social media accounts.

The page that you set-up for your social media account will become the face of your company on that particular platform. It will be where other social media users will see you. The aim of social media marketing is to generate a high number of followers, so that you can get your marketing messages out to them. When people follow or like you, then your status appears in their timeline. It gives you access to send messages to them as often as you need, and also gives you access to their friends and family. Social media marketing opens up a whole new world of possibilities for the marketing of your shoe brand.

This is all a part of building the brand that you have developed for your shoe company and the products that you sell. The more people that you connect with, the greater chance you have of selling more shoes. When you can tailor those connections to the right group of people, then you can concentrate your marketing efforts on the demographic that will be the most likely to buy from you. The next step is to make the interactions you have with customers as personal as you can. You build up your fan base and your customer base one by one.

The place to start is by setting up a page for your company on the social media outlets that your customers will hang out on. This will be one of the presences that you develop on the internet that will help push your brand. Customers love to feel as though they are part of something, and a social media page is the perfect opportunity to create a meaningful connection with your customers. You will need a page where your fans can get in touch with you, keep up to date with the latest news, and ask you any questions. It is the place where you can announce the new designs that you are launching, where you can post special offers for your followers, and generate brand loyalty through exclusive competitions and content.

Your presence on social media means that you raise the awareness of your brand by reaching out to potential customers. Don't forget to mention your social media pages on all your other marketing, so that people know where to find you.

This is the ultimate brand-building tool and can work really well for your shoe company when you find and connect with the right audience. You can post links to your website, your video marketing, and your blog on the social media pages that you have created. The links you create that generate an interest in your brand are all part of the social media marketing experience, and will help generate a strong association with you and your brand. Make the most of this ad and you will create loyal customers that will come back to buy your shoes time and time again.

It does not take much time to start your social media pages but it can take time to monitor and make the most of the social media presence you generate. The people that follow you on social media will want to interact with you and require a quick response from you. This is very different from sending an email or a letter to a company, as social media users expect you to get back to them quickly. This means that you need to constantly monitor your accounts. You can set-up your smartphone to send you notifications when you get a social media interaction, so you can respond quickly and keep your customer happy.

The platforms that you choose for your social media marketing may depend on the target market that you are aiming for. In addition to the two biggest sites that I have already mentioned, there are many other options. New ones, such as Snapchat, are appearing all the time. You probably won't have time to be on all of the social media networks at once, so choose carefully the ones that will bring you the greatest return. Think about the shoes that you are selling, and look for the markets that you will sell to. Find the social media platform your target market uses, and make sure you have a presence there.

As you start your own shoe company, I'm sure that money will be tight, so you want to keep an eye on the costs. Social media accounts are free to set-up and free to use, so you can get your name out there with only the investment of your time. Use the networks you already have on social media to start.

Ask your friends and family to "like", follow, and share your pages, so that you can start getting the interest levels up immediately. The more people you reach with your message, the bigger the pool of potential customers becomes. Use social media in conjunction with some of the other ways of marketing we have looked at above, and you will find that you can supercharge your shoe brand from day one.

Footwear marketing strategies

There are many common, even classic footwear marketing strategies to consider for your new shoe company. The key point of selecting a marketing strategy is making sure it is relevant to you product market segment, and can reach your target consumers.

Sponsor athletes

Nike™ practically invented athletic sports marketing and nobody does it better, but there are still opportunities for smaller firms. There are many more athletes than companies offering sponsorships. While Nike™ pays out billions to their athletes, a start-up shoe company can have an impact in the market by supplying athletes with free product.

Product placement

Getting your products in front of your customer can be achieved by product placement in poular media. Your products may appear in TV and movies by paid placement or simply by giving products to celebrities or production companies. There are marketing firms that specialize in product placement. You may also get free product placement. If your brand has a good reputation, people will come to you asking for product.

Tigers tail strategy

This type of marketing allows a smaller company to follow the marketing campaigns of larger companies. You may supply casual shoes to snowboarding or surfing athletes. While the athletes travel the world at the expense of a major brand, your shoes will be tagging along for the ride!

Comfort is king

Because comfort is very important for shoes, many companies will make it the centerpiece of their marketing message. The comfort story may be important to casual shoe or running shoe brands, but it may not be the right focus for high performance climbing shoes or motorcycle boots.

Partnerships

Finding a marketing partner in your industry that does not compete with you is a great strategy for a small brand. Small brands working together can increase their marketing reach by sharing resources, athletes, trade show booth space, etc.

Event sponsorships

If your shoes are sport or activity specific you may have an opportunity to reach your customers through event sponsorship or event marketing. Any gathering of your target customers is useful for your brand to be present and make an impression. A shoe company does not need to select just one marketing strategy. In fact, for a smaller company, you should experiment with more than one to see what works best for your brand.

Technological expertise

You can lead a product market by offering your customers a superior or unique technology. A compelling technology story can be the driving force for a new marketing campaign. A running shoe brand may have a cushioning story, basketball shoes may have a grip story, while a back country hiking boot may have a new traction story. Make sure to spread your technology story whenever you can. Technology is a great marketing point for bloggers and magazine articles.

Performance stories

For any type of athletic shoe, telling the performance story of your product can be a very compelling message. Does you shoe provide a special cushioning benefit or is it super light-weight? Do you have any performance testing or lab results to prove your claim? Maybe your shoe is more flexible, or stiffer, or stronger, or fits better, than your competitors' shoes?

Lifestyle marketing

Lifestyle marketing is when your company presents shoes and a campaign to embody the interests, attitudes, and opinions of a group or a culture. As a lifestyle brand, you seek to inspire, guide, and motivate people; selling the idea that your shoes will contribute to your customer's way of life. Maybe low impact hiking boots with green sourcing or a special tread pattern are perfect for being in nature while not destroying it.

Cause marketing

Perhaps your company is committed to a social cause or issue. Does your company provide shoes for poor kids in Africa or raise money for breast cancer research? Maybe your brand and marketing story is a tribute to a fallen hero or lost loved one. A cause close to your heart can be the motivation for your business and the marketing message that makes your brand special.

Arris

Ricardo will use a combination of athletic sponsorships, technological expertise and event sponsorships to reach his customers. Because his customers run triathlons he can really focus his efforts.

Arris will supply shoes to race winners as prizes and Ricardo will recruit athletes currently without shoe sponsors to use his shoes. These athletes will provide a nice marketing boost to Arris and help the design team fine-tune the shoes.

Ricardo will invest capital into marketing Arris right away. As the shoes hit the market, he will run print adds in triathlon magazines and buy banner adds on a few triathlon training blogs. Ricardo will also be sending shoes to magazine editors to try out, and maybe get some free editorial coverage.

Arris will also set up booths and refreshment stations at triathlons and work with local retailers to sell shoes at race events.

The technological advancements of the Run Race Recover system will be a main focus of the Arris marketing strategy. Ricardo will work hard to tell the story of the Arris system of shoes, and will promote the fact that the system has a patent.

 The fashion footwear market is crowded with competitors. Eve will need unique ways to grab attention for the Enigma brand. She has the additional challenge of being short on capital until she can sell some shoes. Eve will have to adopt strategies she can execute with a small budget.

Eve starts with a combination of product placement, celebrity endorsements, event sponsorships, and marketing partnerships. Because Eve's market is punk rock, she can supply shoes to local bands and she can sponsor some punk concerts in Boston and New York.

Eve's marketing plans for Enigma will expand once she has more money to invest. She has priced-out ads on punk music web sites and punk music magazines for future purchase.

102

Printed catalogs and collateral

You are going to need a way to let your retail buyers and end users see your products. In years past, the only way was to print full color paper catalogs, flyers or lookbooks. While the printed catalog is still very common, the internet, universal wifi, and tablet computers now provide some great alternatives.

A slick high-quality printed catalog can be expensive to create and print. While a high-fashion luxury brand will often use an expensive catalog to project the high value of the brand, a rubber sandal company may go for an inexpensive, but colorful, throwaway flyer.

You will need to choose depending on your brand values, brand identity, and marketing budget. If you are a "green" company, you make take a stand and not print a catalog at all.

Don't skimp on product photography!

The most important thing to remember when you start to produce a catalog or marketing collateral is that you must invest in high-quality photography. The photographs of your shoes may be the only way people interact with your product before they buy it. Clean and crisp on white backgrounds are the standard for the web.

These photographs are often edited by "clipping" or trimming away the background of the image, color correcting the shoe, then adding a new drop shadow.

Photo shoots with models can be time-consuming and expensive, but are a must for marketing high fashion shoes.

 Eve will not create a paper catalog for Enigma. She will use her budget to create high fashion photos for use on her website and ads. She will create a small flyer to insert into the shoe boxes to show her customers how the Enigma style works in everyday life. She will also need clean shots for the web. Eve has a friend that can do 360° rotating images which will be a great addition to her site.

 Ricardo will create a catalog to help explain the technical benefits of the Arris system. His sales reps will use the catalog to help sell the concept to dealers. Ricardo will also create an inexpensive flyer to pass out at events and for his dealers to use on the sales floor.

Ricardo will use 3D modeling and computer graphics to make web videos. His reps will show the videos to dealers, and he will play it at events like trade shows or races. This content will be used to create a rich experience on the Arris website.

Footwear packaging

The packaging of your shoes can be a critical part of your product marketing presentation. In a retail store, a customer may see your shoe boxes stacked in the store before they see the shoes themselves. When the customer is trying on your shoes, your packaging design gives you a chance to make another brand impression.

Hang-tags and ad copy printed on your box are great places to tell your story. When a consumer is opening your packaging, you have 100% of their attention! Don't lose this chance to communicate with them.

You can tell them something, anything! You can make an impression on people not familiar with your brand, or educate them about your product or cause.

Retail packaging is not wasted with online customers. A beautiful, well-designed package will reinforce that your product is high quality, and also reinforce your customer's belief that they made the right choice.

In fact, you could even print on the packaging, "You have made a great choice."

First impressions are critical. A cheap box may save you money, but a dented or wrinkled box sends your customers the wrong message about your product! A dealer will have a hard time selling products in damaged packaging at full price. They may request replacement boxes or ask for a return.

It's important for you to study the packaging of your closest competitors, and other products that target your customers. Your shoe packaging should be appropriate to your target market. Just like when you design your shoes, you should have a design brief for your packaging.

Are your shoes being sold in a boutique or a self service big box retailer? A box for your average sport shoe will cost around $.50. A reinforced box for larger work boots, designed to be stacked 10 high for self-serve retail, may be over $2.

Fashion shoes may be boxed in beautifully embossed hand wrapped cardboard boxes with a shoe tree and drawstring bag. This high-end packaging could add $5 to the landed cost. This adds over $20 to the retail price of the shoe, but for high fashion brands this is all part of high-quality, luxury marketing.

 Ricardo's shoes will require a retail-ready packing box that helps tell his product's performance story.

Just like when he had his shoes designed, Ricardo makes a design brief for his packaging:
-Tell the Arris technical Run Race Recover story.
-Each box should be clearly marked for shoe type.
-Quality look and feel as good as Nike™ shoe box.
-Should have triathlon imagery.

Ricardo will pay a little extra to have 4-color printed graphics on the Arris boxes. This will stand out and get his shoes noticed in the store. Ricardo will have the story printed on the wrapping tissue, and each shoe will have a hang-tag labeling the shoes as run, race or recover.

The Arris boxes will have a thicker cardboard structure to help with the high-quality perception, packaging, and allow the shoes to be stacked high at retail stores. This box will cost a little more than the basic box, about $.80 per box.

 Enigma boots will require a larger box than the standard shoe. Also, the Enigma boot box is less likely to be on display in-store.

The boutiques that carry Enigma are more likely to have the boxes stacked in dark or cramped stock rooms. Eve has studied her competition and decided that sturdy brown cardboard box is appropriate. She will design a 4-color printed box end label with a large image of the boot to help store employees find the correct model.

Because Eve is planning to ship most of her boots through her website to individual customers, she will design her boot box to be strong enough for direct shipping. She could also ask the factory to double pack the boots with an "outer" shipping box for each pair instead of a bulk-packed master carton.

Point of purchase marketing materials

Point of purchase materials, often called P.O.P., will help your product get noticed at retail.

Well designed P.O.P. can draw attention to your products, educate customers, and elevate your brand by improving your shoes' in-store presentation. P.O.P. can be as simple as a poster of a sponsored athlete or reproductions of print ads.

P.O.P. requirements depend on the market you are targeting. While a poster may be suitable for a running shoe brand, the P.O.P. item for high-end fashion shoes may be a plush leather club chair with embroidered logos and a padded foot rest, for measuring customers feet.

Inexpensive printed P.O.P. items are easy to send out to dealers to help them refresh their stores frequently. New posters or header cards for display racks are common high turnover P.O.P. items.

P.O.P. displays can be expensive. Most companies will offer them for sale at big discounts or free for strong dealers.

A sandal company may offer a free display rack to dealers with an order of over 200 pairs.

You should partner with your high volume dealers in important markets to install branded build-outs. A build-out is a permanently installed fixture that may have a large logo or light box featuring your brand with space to prominently display your shoes.

Shop visits by sales reps or tech reps can assess if a dealer is using P.O.P. items as intended. It's not uncommon for a dealer to stock competitors product on your displays. Your sales rep can help fix this problem.

If you are distributing shoes on-line there may not be any P.O.P. opportunity, but an inexpensive logo printed key chain included with each purchase, may make some extra brand impressions with your customer.

There are many common P.O.P. items for shoes:
Logo printed slat wall shoe shelves
Logo printed foot measuring devices
Molded logo floor mats
Logo printed try on benches
Free standing shoe display racks
Branded in store build-out displays
Window decals
Posters
Mini catalogs

 Ricardo will need a few P.O.P. items for his dealers to help tell the Arris story and explain the 3-shoe run, race, recover system. A complicated story will require a carfully planned P.O.P. campaign.

Ricardo will have 3 different Arris shoe shelves made. He finds a clear plastic slat wall shelf and orders printed cards that fit into the shelves. When a customer is looking at the Arris shoes, they will see the three models: Run, Race, Recover.

Ricardo will also have posters and small pamphlets printed. He will send the posters to his dealers with every shipment and he will include the pamphlets inside the shoe boxes.

For his bigger accounts, Ricardo will supply a free shoe display rack with space for each model of shoe and a poster explaining the system.

Because Ricardo's shoes have some unique technical features, he will provide dealers with some of the shoe sole components. These will allow customers to see and touch the technology that is hidden inside the shoe.

 Eve's P.O.P. requirements are very different. Most of her business will be web based, and have little need for physical P.O.P. items. Eve will spend her time and efforts making sure people visit the web site.

Eve does have some fashion boutiques for the Enigma brand and she will want to make something for them. Her boutiques are more alternative and may have some unique requirements. She will work with each boutique to make something special.

For one dealer, Eve will send an original painting that was the inspiration for a shoe design. Another boutique may get a customized leather club chair for customers to sit in while they try on the boots. Creative Eve rescued the chair from a bankrupt hotel, modified it with her shoe materials, and hand painted it in her own studio.

Buying print media

Depending on the target market for your shoes, there may be magazines that serve your consumer. You should look into the rates for full-page, half-page and quarter-page advertisements. The simple truth with any magazine is that you need to pay to play. If you want editorial coverage, you need to buy ads.

Editorial is the content of the magazine. The magazine buys stories or has staff writers that create the articles. Editorial for a magazine can be a company profile, an athlete profile, product test results, product reviews, product buyer's guides, or event coverage.

Your company can get a real boost if your new shoe is featured in a positive review or a buyer's guide. So how do you get your product to appear in a magazine's editorial content? You need to buy ads. Nothing will happen unless you buy some advertising.

Will your product get a terrible review if you do not have a full page ad in the magazine? Maybe not, it may just be left out....by accident. Editorial content is expensive for a magazine to create. You can write and submit an article featuring a trip or a profile of a sponsored athlete. Magazines want your new company to succeed, they will help you plan an advertising campaign around any new product releases. If you are a steady customer buying ads every month, you can work together to insure your new ad campaign and the magazine editorial content support each other.

If you find a magazine that's important to your market, buy some ads, submit products for review, and keep the magazine staff informed about your new products with press releases.

 Ricardo finds many magazines related to triathlons and running. Ad prices are high, but the focus is good. He plans to run a few ads once his shoes arrive. He will go with the big name magazines and work to be included in the next shoe test article.

 Eve finds a few local and national punk music magazines. She also finds a local music magazine that will run a story about her new company, boots, and her band. Eve will also buy a few ads in regional magazines in areas with active punk music culture.

Online media buys

Many of the same concepts of print media apply to web based media. The major difference is the ability for you to see exactly how productive your ad buy is. With online banner ads and link backs you can see exactly how many people viewed your ads and clicked through your web pages.

You may think that online ad buys are inexpensive, think again. Banners on popular sites and display ads on search engines can add up fast.

You may consider the cost difference between your wholesale and retail selling prices as your online advertising budget.

If your shoe retails for $120 you have an online marketing budget of almost $60 per pair! With that $60 per pair, you can pay 20% to list your products on Amazon.com™, and still have money available to buy search ads on Google.com™, or hire content writers for a blog.

Banner ads

Online banner ads allow you to target specific websites focused on your target market and consumer. The more popular the site, the higher cost for ads.

Search ads

When people search on Google.com™ your ads can appear below or beside the search results. You are billed only when someone clicks on your ad. The cost per click (CPC) depends on the popularity of your targeted search term. The term "shoe" may be very expensive. The more specific term "triathalon running shoe", which targets your customers, will cost much less.

 Eve is able to arrange a product swap a with popular punk website. For just a few pairs of boots, Eve gets a month of banner ads. This is a great way to test if the web ad is effective for Enigma. Eve will record product giveways as marketing expenses on tax paper work.

 Ricardo buys some banner ads on a few triathlon training websites. He tries Google Ads™ with a small budget to see what his cost for each conversion is. The Arris ads lead to an order after about $25.00 in clicks. Not a great result but still a profitable sale.

Websites

Your website may be the single most important marketing piece you create. Your business model may call for a shopping cart, strictly informational content, or purely projecting your brand's image. No matter what your requirements are, your website has got to be first quality!

Just like you need a design brief to create your shoes, will need a design brief to make sure your website has the functions and features needed support your shoe company and your brand requirements. You need to match your website to your business model.

Brand image websites

If you are following a more traditional retail distribution model you will need to provide your customers with a complete brand image experience. This is where you show your style in a way that attracts customers to your brand and draws in new web traffic. If your shoes are fashion based, this is the kind of site you will need. Additionally, you will need great product photography showing your product in action or in inspirational settings.

Your website's most important function is to drive customers to your retail stores. You should also make sure your international customers have a way to find your shoes in their home country.

Technical and support websites

If your shoes are highly technical, used for some technical activity or require specific information for use, you will need a website geared towards support. You may need technical specifications; drawings with detailed features or photos describing the proper use of your shoes. You may want to include care instructions, spare parts, accessories, or user community forums.

E-commerce websites

If your sales strategy is web direct-to-customers, you will need a website that combines the brand image, informational support, and e-commerce online store functions. This can be a lot to pack into a website! You may need some help!

Building a website

Now that you have identified the type of website your shoe company will need, you can shop around. Finding a few websites that you like is a great first step. This will help you decide what works for your company and will help you communicate your ideas to a web designer.

Do you need a web designer?

There are many options for do-it-yourself (DIY) websites which you can use to get started. Often, you can create a professional looking result without spending too much money. The major web providers have stock templates ready for you to customize with your own logos and photos. WordPress, SquareSpace, and other providers can get you started. You can try to build a site yourself for just a few dollars, but if your site is going to need more than just information, you may need to get some professional help.

You will need to prepare a scope of project for the web designer. You should prepare a list of the pages you want, the features you will need, and organize all the content for the site. The web content includes the product photos, product copy, brand logos, and any other information you will want on your site.

How much does a website cost?

The DIY e-commerce platforms start at around $30 per month. As your site traffic grows and your product line expands, you will need a more advanced service plan. All of the major e-commerce platforms have service plans ranging from basic to professional.

These plans are based on how many products you have, pages you require, visitor traffic, and dollar volume of sales. Your shoe company may start with a plan that costs $29.99 per month but after a few years, if your sales top 1 million dollars, you may need the $199.99 per month plan.

SEO

As your websites are built you will need to work on the search engine optimization (SEO). SEO is the art and science of making sure your website appears high in search engine rankings.

If a customer searches "triathlon shoes" on Google.com™, you want to make sure your web site appears high on the first page of results. Your web designer should be asking you for the keywords or search terms you want to focus on. SEO is a long term process, usually a site is built with some terms in mind, then modified and adjusted to improve rankings for the targeted search terms.

Make sure your web designer sets up a Google analytics account and WordPress statistics review so you can start monitoring your websites' performance.

Eve needs an e-commerce platform right away! After a few demos she chooses BigCommerce.com™.

Like most popular e-commerce platforms, BigCommerce has an easy start-up process that lets Eve create her first website by herself. She selects a store template that is close to the Enigma style and makes a few changes. By selecting the basic start-up plan for $29.99, and using one of the free templates, Eve gets started without spending much money.

This basic plan has everything she needs to start selling, an e-store to show-off her boots, and credit card processing to collect payments. Eve should be able to run her website DIY style for awhile, but as Enigma grows she will need to hire some help.

 Ricardo has a double challenge. His strategy calls for two websites. ArrisRunning.com, will be a site dedicated to branding and information, not e-commerce. For this domain, Ricardo will create a WordPress™ site. He chose WordPress.com to host his site but he could have selected one of hundreds of hosting firms. Many have specific "WordPress Plans." Ricardo's plan will cost him about $15 per month. Ricardo does not have any extra time to create the site, so he collects the content and hires a professional to build it. He pays $1,000 to have a site designed and built.

Ricardo's second site, TriathlonSupply.com is a bit more complicated. This site will require a full e-commerce platform that has links to shipping services, credit card processing, and mailing list services. He chooses an advanced plan from Shopify.com™ and hires a web designer familiar with this platform to build the site and upload the product information. Ricardo pays the web designer $5,000 to build out and customize TriathlonSupply.com.

Trade shows

There are many industry trade shows you can attend to promote your shoe brand. You should plan to visit any shows related to your market. There are many contacts to be made and competitors to study. While most industry shows are closed to the general public, you can attend as a non-exhibiting vendor, as a guest, or you can ask a local shop to add you to their attending list.

Should your brand exhibit?

There are different types of trade shows, some are really only for people "in the trade," other shows are open to the general public.

If you are selling to retailers you should consider attending and exhibiting at trade shows related to your industry. Your customers will be at these shows and they will come ready to buy!

While many exhibitors and dealers are working very hard to write orders during the trade show, the real reason to attend is to meet all your buyers face-to-face and work on building personal relationships. After the show is closed for the day, it's time to meet your best dealers. If business is going well, you should be celebrating! If business is not so great, you should still be celebrating, and of course working hard to understand what the problems are.

A meal and a few drinks are a good way to get the straight story from a dealer, sales rep or distributor.

Market intelligence

Bring your product manager and designer to the show so they can see what is happening in your market. With a buyers badge you will have access to look around and see what your competitors or potential competitors are doing. You will notice that some brands have busy booths and others are empty.

Major shoe shows

MAGIC

MAGIC is the world's largest fashion marketplace, showcasing the latest in apparel, footwear, accessories, and manufacturing. Every February and August, the retail industry comes together in Las Vegas, Nevada, to show and shop the latest trends in men's, women's, juniors', and children's apparel, footwear, accessories and resources.

There are plenty of events and seminars planned throughout the 3-day trade show. (www.Magiconline.com)

World Shoe Association at MAGIC (The WSA Show or WSA@MAGIC)

The WSA Show is the largest footwear and accessories show in the world. It has been operating since 1948. It is part of MAGIC Las Vegas and located in the Las Vegas Convention Center. The WSA Show runs for 3 days every February and August. It has more than 36,000 visitors and approximately 1,500 exhibitors. Buyers and brands from more than 100 countries attend the WSA show. It is the "must attend" market for the footwear industry.
In August, everyone will be showing their spring and summer lines. Attend the February show for fall and winter fashions.

Footwear News Platform at MAGIC (FN PLATFORM)

FN PLATFORM is the global showcase for branded footwear, showcasing over 1600 men's, women's, juniors' and children's footwear brands from more than 20 countries. FN PLATFORM provides buyers with a convenient and efficient way to shop the most comprehensive selection of international footwear. www.Magiconline.com.

ISPO Munich : International Sporting Goods Trade Fair (The Internationale Fachmesse für Sportartikel und Sportmode)

More than 2600 international exhibitors and 80,000 visitors from 110 countries make this the world's largest multi-segment exhibition for sporting goods and sportswear. The following categories are displayed: outdoor, skiing, boarding, running, fitness, sportswear, beachwear, teamsports, soccer, nordic sports, biking, racket, triathlon, kids, and sourcing. ISPO Munich takes place once a year in the end of January or early February.

You may also want to look into ISPO Beijing in February and ISPO Shanghai in July, both of which are growing shows. If you have further questions regarding ISPO you can email: visitorservice@ispo.com

Surf Expo

Surf Expo is the largest and longest running surf, skate, swim and beach lifestyle tradeshow in the world. Since 1976 retailers from around the world have flocked to Surf Expo every January and September to see new trends and take care of business. Surf Expo draws buyers from more than 9,500 storefronts across the U.S., Canada, Europe and the Caribbean. The show is held at the Orange County Convention Center in Orlando, Florida, and attracts more than 27,000 attendees and 1000 plus exhibitors. It is billed as the number one order-writing show in the industry (according to Surf Expo's website). You will see products from surf, skate, sup, wake, wind, kayak/canoe, swim, footwear, resort, boutique and coastal gift categories. The show runs twice per year in September and January.
www.surfexpo.com

Outdoor Retailer (OR)

This popular outdoor gear trade show attracts thousands of buyers and features the best of the winter and summer sports market. Outdoor Retailer is held twice a year in Salt Lake City, Utah. Leading outdoor manufacturers introduce winter sports products every January and summer outdoor products every July. Go and see the largest collection of innovative gear, apparel, footwear and accessories for outdoor sports products including adventure travel, backpacking, camping, hiking, climbing, mountaineering, cycling, mountain biking, fishing, fly fishing, health and fitness, military, nutrition and natural products, paddlesports, watersports, SUP, pet products, running, trail running, surf, skate, lifestyle, triathlon, multisport endurance, and now also yoga/Pilates.
Show Dates: Winter show in January and Summer Show in July.
www.outdoorretailer.com

Agenda

Agenda is the most diverse and creative lifestyle fashion trade show. The show is made up of street wear, action sports, lifestyle and fashion. Agenda has shows in 3 US cities:
Long Beach, CA and Miami, FL in January, and Las Vegas, NV in February.
www.agendashow.com

Other shows

There are trades shows for so many other niche markets! Check out the National Shoe Retailers Association for a complete listing of upcoming shoe shows and education conferences in the U.S. and around the world.
www.nsra.org/events/event_list.asp

Ricardo has many options for footwear trade shows. Almost too many to pick from! He needs to be careful and not spend too much money.

Ricardo has found there are several triathlon and endurance sports related shows. These are small shows, but for a new company they can be a great way to get started. For his first year, Ricardo will exhibit at these small consumer shows. This will give Ricardo a chance to work with customers first hand and possibly meet other retailers that are exhibiting.

Ricardo will use the smaller shows as practice and attend the big shows as a buyer for TriathlonSupply.com to see what the major shoes are all about.

Eve looks around for trade shows that may be suitable for Enigma but she does not find any that would really attract her buyers or customers.
Eve has another problem, money. Enigma can't afford the runaway costs of exhibiting at a major show.

Eve has decided to look at punk music festivals and steam punk events. These shows are where her customers will be. She plans to show her boots and try to make contacts with other dealers that may be attending the events.

Eve has a friend with an apparel brand that is attending the Agenda Fashion Show. Eve makes a deal to help with the space rental and set-up in exchange for sharing the booth. Sharing a small booth is great way for small brands to get on the floor while saving some money.

Alternatives to industry trade shows

While industry trades shows can put your brand and shoes in front of footwear dealers and buyers, if you are planning a direct-to-consumer distribution model you will need to find other ways to get your shoes in front of end users.

Depending on your target market, there are consumer shows, not specifically for footwear, but for sports and pastimes. There are consumer shows for hunting, boating, fitness, music, steam punk, almost any pastime will have a gathering or show. You need to find the events where your customers will be.

Larger companies are also cutting back on trade show spending and looking for other ways to interface with buyers. For example, instead of setting up a big trade show booth, you could offer to fly your most important buyers to you. Buyers appreciate the special attention. Airfare, hotel, a nice meal, and a day working with your in-house team can be less expensive and more productive than a rushed presentation at a busy trade show.

 Ricardo is targeting triathletes. He will contact race organizers and arrange to display his shoes. Arris may have to provide some sponsorship money to the race organizer, but it's worth it to be directly in touch with his customers.

Ricardo can offer shoes, promotional water bottles, and free t-shirts to race winners and event staffers. Ricardo will need to experiment by attending race events. If he can bring some stock and sell shoes profitably then every triathlon becomes a sales opportunity.

An Arris logo wrapped van with a small stock of shoes can be sent to events every weekend over the summer. Ricardo starts to think, if one shoe selling van is profitable, maybe he should invest in a small fleet?

 Eve is targeting punk music. She can flow product to local bands or even pay them to wear Enigma boots and customized t-shirts on stage. Local music festivals and music related events are all places Eve will use to promote her brand.

Sample shoes

To show your shoes to retail buyers you are going to need samples. These samples are called sales samples. Depending on your sales plan, you will need either a few pairs of sales samples or a few dozen. Sales samples almost always come in just one size; 9 for men's, and 7 for women's.

If you are selling direct-to-consumer via e-commerce, then you don't need any actual sales samples. One sample, well photographed, is all you will need.

Some companies will make a sample pair for every model and colorway in their range, while other brands may select what they think is the best color for each model instead of every colorway. A complete sales sample line is often called a rainbow line, as it will have every color offered.

If your sales plan is the more traditional retail distribution model, you will need sample sets for each of your sales reps, more sets for any international distributors' sales force, and a few sets for your home office.

A small company may need 15 sets, an international brand with sales of 100 million may need 50 sets, while a mega brand with sales of 1 billion may need 300 sets.

You will also find that while your domestic sales force may not need or want samples in every color, your distributors will require every item. It's also very common to allow the distributors to order the product line piece by piece, selecting only the products that they think will succeed in their markets. Some shoe brands do not allow this, they require the distributor to take samples of every model.

Loading down your sales force with too many samples is counter productive. Sales presentations may take too long and most reps are required to pay for their samples.

A sales rep for a large sporting goods company may have a samples bill of $100,000! Once the selling season is complete, the salesmen will scramble to sell off their samples.

Sales sample production

For most shoe companies, the factory will make a special short run of the sample shoes. These are usually made by the most experienced factory staff members and extra care is taken when packing to make sure every pair is perfect.

As these shoes will be representing your brand, you must take care to have the shoes inspected before they are sent to your sales reps. A poor quality sample is worse than no sample at all! You may want to visit the factory to inspect the shoes yourself before you pay to have them shipped.

The small run samples are almost always boxed up and shipped by air to the reps. The samples will arrive months before the production shoes are ordered. The sales reps will use them to get advanced bookings BEFORE the production order is placed with the shoe factory.

If a particular model or color fails to book many orders, you may choose to cancel production before it begins. Most large shoes companies operate this way, you cannot risking making a million pairs of a shoe only to have it fail in the market.

The samples are made in only one size at this point as the shoe design has not yet been graded. The shoe company will save time and money by waiting to grade the pattern and make all the sizes until they know the shoe has "sold in" to the market.

Another common procedure is to pull the sample shoes from the top of the production run. The factory will select the first few pairs off the assembly line and air ship them to the sales force. The balance of the production is placed in shipping containers and sails by boat. By the time the main production arrives by boat, the sales force should already have orders in hand. In this case, a size run is available.

Other companies choose not to pre-sell their shoes. The samples are pulled from the production stock and the sales force can write orders for delivery "at once".

You should do your best to make sure you have customer orders BEFORE you order the production run from the shoe factory. For a small shoe company this is not always possible, and for a web only e-commerce brand it's impossible to get pre-bookings unless you have a Kickstarter campaign to collect orders.

Buying sales samples is expensive, air shipping them is expensive, but ordering a production run of shoe that customers don't want is even more expensive!

The buyers for the Arris product line are most likely athletes themselves that participate in triathlons. In order for Ricardo to win them over to the Arris concept, he is going to need samples in sizes for the buyers to test fit and even to use. Ricardo is going to need a larger than normal sample run. This will be expensive, but for this technical market he has no choice. Giving free shoes to buyers to try-out is a must.

Ricardo and his sales reps plan in advance for the Arris launch. They identify the key buyers and collect their shoe size information so they can be ready with the right shoes when they make the Arris sales pitch.

Ricardo is also planning to supply some athletes with complimentary shoes. He has befriended a few professional triathletes and they have agreed to use the shoes. Ricardo is not paying them at this point, but he is setting up Arris for future success.

Eve will need fewer sales samples than Ricardo. A few pairs of each boot should be enough. She will be selling Enigma boots on the east coast, and she hired a friend to help on the west coast. She needs a set of samples for studio shots, and a set for a photographer and model to use when she creates the Enigma "look book."

Eve will need a dozen pairs of what she feels are her strongest models so she can send them to her influencers. She has worked hard to make contact with other musicians and artists that share her style and have a public image. While she can't afford to pay people to wear her boots, she has found some like-minded friends to help promote Enigma.

Eve has also budgeted for a few dozen pairs as giveaways for her buyers.

CHAPTER 8

FOOTWEAR SALES AND DISTRIBUTION

Sales are the life blood of your new shoe company! Without profitable sales you won't have a new company for very long. Distribution is how you will get your shoes into the hands of your customers. With the right plan for sales and distribution your shoes will find their way into the market, without a plan your shoes will sit in the warehouse.

THE SALES CHAIN

The sales chain is the selling process. The sales chain starts with **you** and ends with your **end user.** There may be many people between you and your customer, each one in part responsible for making the sale. If any links in the sales chain break, you will miss a sale.

For each of these links there are ways to help insure you make the sale. There are also ways to cut links out of the chain bringing you closer to your customers and sales.

Building a strong sales chain
The sales chain starts with you believing in your shoes, and you being able to communicate, convince, and educate others of the merits of your shoes and brand. You must have the drive and energy to inspire others and attract them to your project.

Your sales team needs to believe
Your first sales goal is to rally your sales force. Your sales force, whether on salary or paid by commission, needs to believe in you and your product. Get your sales force involved in the development and marketing processes. An experienced salesmen can offer you market insights gained over many years of selling. A motivated and educated sales force will bring shoe buyers to your brand.

Turning buyers into believers
An experienced salesmen knows what the shoe store buyers are looking for. The buyer needs high quality, high margin products, that sell through quickly and don't come back as returns. Giving the buyer confidence in the product AND the brand will transform a buyer into a believer. To help the salesmen, a shoe company can offer the buyer marketing materials, generous billing terms, and may even guarantee to take back any product that doesn't sell.

On the sales floor
The shoe salesman's job is not over once the shoe buyer says, "YES." In order to make sure shoes sell well once they are on the sales floor, a shoe company can sponsor a sales clinic. The sales clinic will educate the people working the sales floor on how to sell the new products. The shoes' key features and benefits must be explained in a memorable and creditable way. More importantly, the sales clinic is a way to inspire the retailer's sales staff and get them on your side.

While a floor worker may not be happy to stay late for a clinic, free pizza, soda, or a few beers can help. Some free product like shoes, shirts, and hats can help motivate staff to sell your product above other brands. While a sales clinic may seem like a boring waste of time, a good salesman or technical sales rep will use a clinic to build a personal relationship with the floor staff, and better yet, create a bond between the floor staff and the brand. Many brands also offer prizes to top selling floor staff.

Do people want your shoes?
The sales chain has been built for the moment when a customer arrives at the store. Will they buy your shoe? This is the point where sales and marketing work together.

If the salesmen believes in your shoes, the retail buyer is convinced, and the floor staff is motivated, this is your chance to sell. Your shoes are available for purchase, but if the customer has never heard of your brand or seen your shoes before, they will most likely buy the Nike™ shoes instead.

But, this won't happen to you! Your new shoe company has invested in marketing! When the customer arrives, and the sales floor worker recommends your brand, the customer buys.

The language of footwear sales
When you set out to create a sales plan for your shoe company there are some terms and concepts you will need to understand.

Shoe buyers
Buyers and merchandisers are responsible for filling the shoe store with product. The buyers are your customers. Buyers have a budget to purchase merchandise for the store. Their goal is to buy fast selling product that makes a profit for the store. If your product is selling well, the buyer is your best friend, if there is a problem, the buyer may be asking for deep discounts long AFTER the sale.

Category buyers
A large retailer with many departments will have several product buyers, each with specific categories. You may need to meet with different buyers for men's and women's, maybe even a third buyer for kids. It's important to know the product categories your buyer is responsible for. If you plan to expand your product offering you may need an introduction to another buyer.

Getting a meeting with a shoe buyer?
First, you need to find out who the shoe buyer is. The easiest way is to call the store. For single location retailers, the store owner is usually the buyer. For large chain stores, there will be a buying office. You can call the head office or try calling the manager of a local store and asking for help. Web searches and business networking sites such as LinkedIn.com™ can be a reliable source.

There is no substitute for an experienced sales rep that knows the market. The veteran independent sales rep will know the buyers and know how to get appointments for your brand.

Buy budgets

Every buyer has a buy budget to purchase merchandise for the store. This budget is also called "open to buy" dollars. The buyer will have an amount designated for each product category per season.

Just as you plan your product line for the season, your dealer must do the same. The buyers will wait to write any orders until they have seen all the various brands competing for the "open to buy" dollars.

If you are late getting into the market for that season, the open to buy dollars will be gone. As a small brand you need to expect larger competitors will take most of the buyer's budget.

For new and small brands you have to fight to get some of the buy budget. Your product has got to be good. Getting in to see buyers early is critical for you to reserve some of that budget for your brand.

Buying strategy

Retailers will have different buying styles or strategies. Large chain stores may have a centralized buying office that controls all the incoming product. Others may allow more local control.

Buyers themselves will have very different styles. While some buyers pour over every technical detail, some may just give you a budget amount and ask you to suggest an order of hot sellers. Many salesmen and buyers will have long relationships and will trust each others judgment.

Tech reps

The technical sales representative is hired by the shoe brand to provide after sale support. After the sales rep and buyer make the sale, it is the tech rep's job to train the store's sales staff. After the shoes are delivered to the stores, the tech rep works with the floor staff to make sure they are educated about how to sell the product and happy to sell the brand. The tech rep may bring free shoes, t-shirts, stickers, soda, beer, and pizza to a shop. Whatever it takes to make the sales staff support the brand.

Selling in

When dealers or stores buy shoes from you, this is called "selling in" to the store or market. Good sell in needs to be followed by good "sell through." You may find different territories or dealers will have better or worse sell in. Poor sell in for a new model could mean cancellation before the production shoes even ship.

Sell through

Once in store, the shoes will "sell through" if customers buy them. Poor or slow sell through is a bad thing. Sell through is often measured in the percentage of sales per week. 30% per week is good, 5% per week means something is wrong.

Sales rate

Your dealers will have inventory tracking to monitor the "sales rate" of their stock of shoes. An organized dealer will have a report showing your products sales rate against other brands in the same category.

Pre-booking

The sale of product in advance of production. Pre-booking allows the shoe brand to plan inventory and production in advance. The more pre-books the better! Some shoe companies may only accept pre-booking orders, this way they can avoid being over stocked. This can mean there is no extra inventory, but on the down side, if a shoe is selling well there will not be any stock available for reorders.

At once orders

At once orders are orders placed for products without any advanced warning and with the expectation that you will have the shoes in stock. While every order is a good order, you may not have inventory to meet at once orders. After a few seasons a shoe company will have a history of pre-booking versus at once order percentages. You may learn to order 15% above bookings or you may find that cancellations of pre-booked orders will give you enough merchandise to meet any at-once orders.

Pre-booking incentives

To encourage your dealers to pre-book you can offer them discounts. A few percentage points of discount will help your dealer decide. Pre-bookings are critical to your new shoe company! Without bookings it's nearly impossible to have the right amount of the right product. Don't give away all your profit, but do what you can to get pre-book orders. The pre-booking discount should have a deadline so you can plan your factory order dates.

Volume discounts

A volume discount is a great way to reward your best customers and give your smaller accounts a "stretch goal." You can base your volume discount on the number of pairs, or on the dollar amount ordered. For example, a $5,000 account may get 2% off and a $10,000 account may get 5% off. You can design a volume discount to help grow your dealers.

New dealer discounts and bounties

A new dealer discount is a simple way to help your sales reps open up new doors. Offering your sales reps a little extra for opening new accounts is also a great way to expand your dealer network. Maybe an extra $100 or $200 per door is enough to have your reps drive to the next town or make a few extra calls before the work day is done. For new dealers, you can also offer a buy back plan if the shoes don't sell.

Representation discounts

If you find your dealers are just buying one or two items you can help drive sales of your other models by offering a "representation" discount. For example, if a dealer buys 5 models they can get a 5% discount. This is also a good way to introduce new product lines, like clothing.

On wheels

This is what you call an agreement with the dealer to accept the merchandise back at full price if it does not sell. This allows the dealer to try your product with less risk.

Markdown allowance

A dealer may demand some money to cover the cost of marking down or discounting slow selling product. This allows the buyers to maintain their margin and sell the shoe, but it will be at your expense.

Broken size runs

Because shoes are offered in many sizes, the dealers' inventory or your inventory may have some sizes sellout ahead of others. This is called a broken size run. A dealer may not want to buy a shoe model if a size is missing. Broken size runs are common at the end of a selling season, or when a model changes over. A small mistake in forecasting orders to the factory can result in a broken size run. Dealers may resist buying shoes with incomplete sizes run, so you may need to offer a discount or place a fill in order to repair or re-balance the size run.

Out of market dumping

If a product does not sell well, the overstock may be sold at a discount to another country. If you unload too much discounted product in your home market, selling new product at full price may be very difficult until the market is clear of the old shoes.

While the profit margin may be low, this unwanted merchandise can be used to open new markets overseas.

Sweeps

The warehouse sweep is when broken size runs and obsolete models are offered to a retailer in a package deal with a big discount. The warehouse sweep clears merchandise, making way for new product, and allowing the retailer to have sale merchandise with good margins. More importantly, for the shoe company, the capital can be used to buy fresh product. Sweep deals may offer shoes at cost or even below just to clean up the inventory.

Carrying costs

Shoe companies and shoe stores alike have costs associated with holding inventory. The carrying cost of inventory is the total cost of holding the shoes in stock. These costs include warehousing costs such as rent and utilities, and financial costs such as interest on borrowed money. Slow selling merchandise is a drain on your capital. Shoes may need to be discounted early to reduce carrying costs.

House accounts

Large or very important accounts may be handled by "in-house" salaried staff instead of independent or outside commissioned reps. A big account with large orders can make a commissioned sales rep the highest paid employee in the company. While this is not necessarily a bad thing, it can cause problems.

The sales rep may ignore the other accounts in the territory, only focusing on the one and not expanding the distribution. The shoe company may look at big commission checks going out and decide to save money with a salaried employee.

Count and fill

Some footwear products, like sandals for example, are fast sellers in season and can be difficult for retailers to keep in stock. The sandal salesmen can offer a count and fill service. The salesman will visit the store once a week to refresh the merchandise. He will reorganize and refill the display racks, count the back stock, and help the dealer write follow-up orders.

A smart rep will visit his stores ahead of holidays and make sure the store is stocked and ready for the busy selling days.

While this may be time consuming for the salesmen, it maximizes sales for what may be a short selling season. Some sales reps may even have a van with stock inside so delivery can be made instantly.

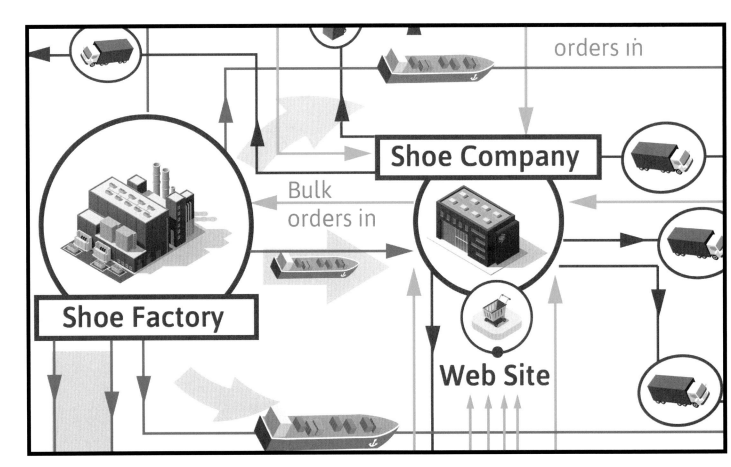

Sales and distribution models

What is the right sales and distribution model for your company? This depends on the type of shoes you are making and the markets you are targeting.

Different market segments will have very different distribution strategies to reach target customers. The type of shoe and its price point will impact where and how you distribute them.

Are you making a sport shoe that will sell at big box stores? Or, a high fashion shoe that will be seen only in boutiques? Maybe you have a special shoe for fly fishing that will sell in specialty outdoor stores? Maybe your shoe has built in features for gardening?

Does your product require post sales service, like boot fitting or custom molding? Is your shoe sport specific and found in specialty shops like golf shoes or ballet slippers? Maybe your company is making a casual shoe that can be sold anywhere?

You need to find the distribution points that attract your target consumers. These could be retail stores or maybe online.

There are two basic sales models to consider. First is the classic retail distribution channel, in which you sell your product at a discount to stores that will resell the merchandise. You are selling the shoes for about 50% of the final selling price. This is called the wholesale price.

The second is the direct-to-consumer distribution model where you remove the retail store from the middle and sell directly to the end users. You may sell your shoes in a store that you own, or online. In this case you are selling to the end user at the retail price. The retail price is double the wholesale price.

You don't have to pick just one model to distribute your shoes. You will see that large shoe companies use a combination of different distribution models.

As you learned in chapter 4, each distribution model will require its own expense and margin calculations.

RETAIL DISTRIBUTION MODEL

Retail distribution is the "classic" or traditional sales model. A shoe company salesman or independent sales representative is hired by the shoe company. The salesman shows the product line to the shoe store's merchandise buyer. The shoe store buys the product, then resells it to their customers (the shoe end users). In this sales model the store's footwear buyer is the customer. The visitors to the shoe store are in turn the dealer's customers.

This model is very simple, the dealer places an order and the shoes are shipped in bulk to the stores. The idea is the same for the shoe company, bulk orders are placed to the factory and delivered by ocean freight in large shipping containers.

For big orders going to large customers, the ocean freight containers may be packed specially for one store and routed directly to the dealers warehouse bypassing the shoe company's warehouse. For the top brands, selling direct container orders to their biggest retailers will dominate.

Pros:
Large orders can move shoes quickly and bring payments back in bulk.
Smaller numbers of employees can sell thousands of pairs.
Reduced inventory carrying costs as merchandise moves into the retail chain faster.
Pre-booking allows better business planning

Cons:
Reduced sales margins.
Dealer discounts and accommodations.
Cancellations of large orders can disrupt inventory plans.
Sales relationship hinges on a single relationship with a buyer.
Costs of owning and operating a warehouse or fulfillment center.

Retail distribution with third party distribution:
The costs of owning and operating a warehouse can be removed buy contracting a Third Party Logistics (3PL) to handle your product logistics.

Internet retailers and 3PLs providers can help with your distribution. This model gives a shoe company flexibility for how it handles order processing and shipping. Instead of operating a warehouse and shipping shoes from your office, you can contract out this function.

DIRECT-TO-CONSUMER MODEL

The direct-to-consumer model cuts out sales reps, buyers, and dealers. The shoe company is now responsible for getting the shoes into the hands of the end users. There are a few different ways to achieve this.

Operating your own stores:
The operations are similar to the standard retail model except the shoe company now captures the retail margins. However, the shoe brand must now pay all the retail store's operating expenses. The cost of retail space, retail staff wages, and carrying cost of the inventory must be counted against the profit margins.

Making shoes and selling shoes are two very different disciplines. Shoe companies can open different types of retail stores. The classic factory outlet store is a low rent location, or even a small space carved out of your warehouse used to sell off under-performing products which are unwanted by retail customers. These can be sold at big discounts while still making some profit. The modern factory outlet store is supplied with product made especially for the outlet. These shoes are different colors or made to a lower price specification so they do not to complete with your brand's other retailers. These stores are a very meaningful part of some brand's sales plan, the modern outlet store can be a large customer for the brand.

Many shoe companies will also build beautiful brand concept or showcase stores. Major cities like New York, London, Berlin, Paris, and Tokyo will have these showcase stores. Shoes sold at these stores may not have any discounts but customers will also find the complete selection of the newest products.

To reduce the risks of operating a retail location, a shoe brand may hire a firm to operate their factory outlet stores, or partner with an existing retailer to have a "brand store" inside a store.

Pros:
The shoe company captures full margin from retail margins.
The company has a direct relationship with the end users.
Price flexibility and the ability to offer discounts.
Stores can be "outlet" locations to sell off distressed merchandise.
Concept stores can project a positive brand image.
Expand sales into new markets.

Cons:
The shoe brand has all the operating expenses of the retail store.
The shoes are owned by the brand until the day they sell to the end user.
Increased financial risk of additional fixed costs.
Costs of owning and operating a warehouse or fulfillment center.

WEB BASED DIRECT-TO-CONSUMER MODEL

Internet direct sales are a sales model worth looking at. When you consider the margin dollars a retailer takes to sell your product, $50 of a $100 shoe, you just need to spend less than $50 to make the sale yourself and still come out ahead.

Web sales can allow you to capture more of the selling margin, but you will be responsible for internet marketing, collecting orders, processing payments, and shipping individual orders.

With the return rates of up to 25% for internet shoe sales, you need to have a way to repack shoes and return them to stock if they are still suitable for sale. You may also need to destroy or discount the returned shoes.

Your retail customers may also be selling your shoes on the internet, while it's possible to prohibit internet sales of your product by the terms of your sales agreement, your only recourse to an offending retailer is to close down the account.

Pros:
Your shoe company captures full margin from retail margins.
The shoe company has a direct relationship with the end user.
Price flexibility and the ability to offer discounts.
Web stores can be "outlet" locations to sell off distressed merchandise.

Cons:
Individual orders for every customer must be billed, picked, packed, and shipped.
Increased inventory carrying costs as merchandise is held until sold to end users.
Forecasting shoe orders to the factory with no pre-booking can complicate inventory planning.
Costs of processing returns, shipping, restocking and losses.
Costs of owning and operating a warehouse or fulfillment center.

WEB BASED 3PL DISTRIBUTION MODEL

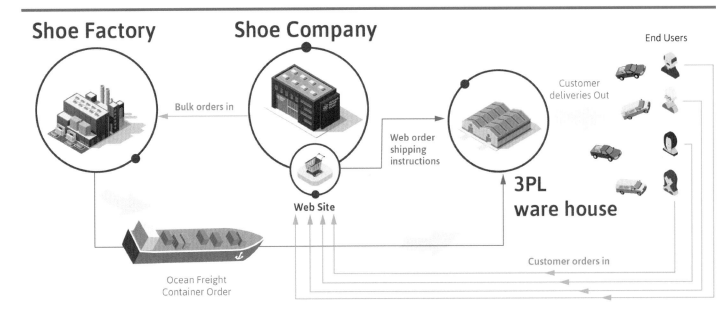

The web based 3PL direct-to-consumer model for distribution can be very efficient for a small start-up shoe company. Instead of owning a warehouse, a 3PL can help with your distribution. This model gives a shoe company flexibility for how it handles order processing and shipping. Instead of operating a warehouse and shipping shoes from your office, you can contract out your entire logistics chain.

The shoe company will contract with a 3PL firm to take delivery from the shoe factory, warehouse the shoes, and fulfill orders directly to customers.

Pros:
The shoe company captures a larger share of the margin than traditional retail.
Virtual operations can eliminate the need and the cost of warehouse space.
Virtual operations allow your workers to focus on sales and marketing and not logistics.
Individual orders can be billed, picked, packed and shipped automatically.
A company can stay small but do big business.

Cons:
A website may be the only contact with customers, low web traffic means low web sales.
Increased inventory carrying costs as merchandise is held until it's sold to end users.
Forecasting with no pre-booking can complicate inventory planning.
Return rate for internet sales can be as high as 25%.
Off-site inventory complicates inbound inspections.

WEB BASED AMAZON DISTRIBUTION MODEL

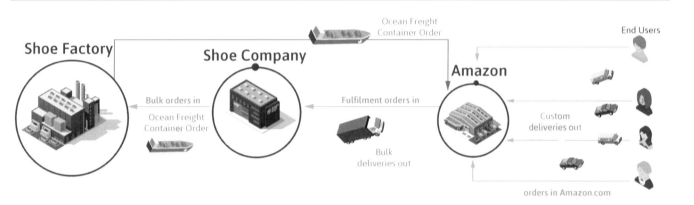

Internet retailers such as Amazon™ attract millions of customers to their web sites. For thriving brands in demand, Amazon will purchase your shoes in bulk, create an Amazon product listing, and fulfill orders to their customers. You need to be careful, once Amazon™ owns your product they may offer steep discounts beyond your MAP policy.

A small firm can do business with Amazon as they offer a 3PL service. The Amazon 3PL service is relatively expensive compared to other 3PLs but it is easy to set up and has a global reach. When you set up a listing on Amazon you can control the price and you can direct the fulfillment of the orders. You have a choice between Amazon's 3PL service, an independent 3PL, or to fulfill the orders yourself.

Amazon charges a commission on all products so this service and global reach come at a price. For footwear, the commission is 20% of the sale price. The rate for the the Amazon 3PL service is about $5 per pair.

Pros:
Amazon's™ global reach and consumer trust.
Professional online interface.
World class fulfillment and billing operations.
Easy set-up.
Avoid owning and operating a warehouse or fulfillment center.

Cons:
20% Amazon sales commission.
Relatively expensive 3PL service.
Strict inbound product marking requirements.
Little flexibility for product returns - Amazon will destroy returns or send them to you.
High return rate for internet shoe purchases.
Amazon discount policy may cause price variations.
Increased storage costs during peak seasons for slow selling product.

MIXED WEB BASED 3PL DISTRIBUTION MODEL

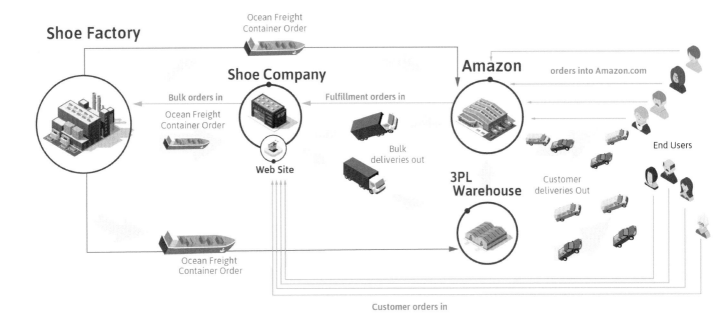

A mixed internet distribution model can give you all the benefits of selling shoes with Amazon™, while reducing potential down sides. The mixed model includes listing on your own on Amazon's marketplace, using their 3PL service, and also running your own website which will use a less expensive independent 3PL service.

Following the mixed model allows you to avoid sending bulk shipments to Amazon. You can avoid Amazon's higher storage fees by filling a small back stock as needed from your 3PL. Instead of Amazon holding a big supply of your shoes, they will only hold a 1 or 2 months supply. Your 3PL can be used to fill orders from your website and accept product returns for processing and restocking.

This model gives you access to Amazon's millions of visitors, global visibility, and world class fulfillment service while helping to preserve your product margins.

Pros:
Amazon's global reach and consumer trust.
Professional online interface.
World class fulfillment and billing operations.
Avoid owning and operating a warehouse or fulfillment center.
Real-time control of Amazon stock levels.
Amazon service for your customers without Amazon expense to your company.

Cons:
20% Amazon sales commission.
Required set up of independent 3PL service.
More flexibility for product returns.
High return rate for internet shoe purchases.
Must monitor Amazon stock levels and replenish stock regularly.

Eve is planning on a mixed sales and distribution model. Because her boots are not a main stream product, Eve is not expecting department stores or the big internet footwear retailers to sell Enigma.

She is planning to sell Enigma boots directly over the internet from her own website and she is targeting off-beat, alternative fashion retailers.

Eve will face the challenge of her retailers knowing that she also sells online. A high margin fashion boutique may not carry Enigma shoes if their customers can buy the same shoes online.

Eve will have to find the right balance of on-line and retail distribution. She hopes to have the availability of the web but also the prestige of selling in high fashion outlets.

Eve can make an excellent profit margin selling directly online if she can control her warehousing and marketing expenses.

Ricardo also plans to have a mixed model sales and distribution model. His target customers shop at triathlon and high-end running specialty shops. To serve these customers, Arris shoes will be sold wholesale to these specialty retailers. He will be hiring independent sales reps that already call on these dealers.

Because there are relatively few of these running specialty retailers, Ricardo will also sell directly at triathlons and online from Triathlonsupply.com

He needs to be careful not to upset his dealers with his idea of direct sales at events. Most retailers don't like the idea of competing with their suppliers.

Ricardo also needs to work with local retailers near any events he is planning to attend.

Global Mixed Distribution

A growing international shoe company will have a large distribution plan that delivers product into different geographical markets, different retail channels, different wholesale channels, and directly to consumer.

On pages 125 & 126 you can see what a wide open international distribution model looks like.

To supply shoes worldwide, a brand like Nike will have products coming from dozens of different factories, in many different countries, shipping to dealers and distribution points all over the world.

When your footwear brand has a global reach, you will have to develop a distribution model that can deliver product into different geographical markets and different product segments. The distribution plan for performance football cleats will be different than high fashion shoes.

Big box retailers have different requirements than smaller high fashion retailers. You will also find that the same type of shoe may have different distribution models in different countries.

124

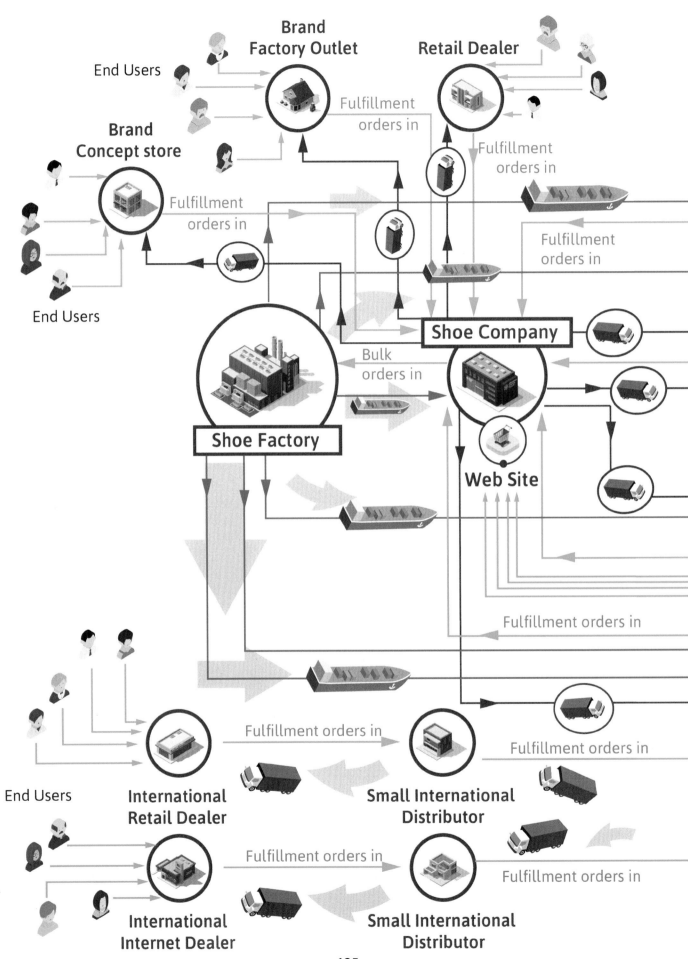

End Users

**Brand
Factory Outlet**

Retail Dealer

Fulfillment
orders in

**Brand
Concept store**

Fulfillment
orders in

Fulfillment
orders in

Fulfillment
orders in

End Users

Shoe Company

Bulk
orders in

Shoe Factory

Web Site

Fulfillment orders in

Fulfillment orders in

End Users

**International
Retail Dealer**

Fulfillment orders in

**Small International
Distributor**

Fulfillment orders in

Fulfillment orders in

**International
Internet Dealer**

**Small International
Distributor**

GLOBAL MIXED DISTRIBUTION MODEL

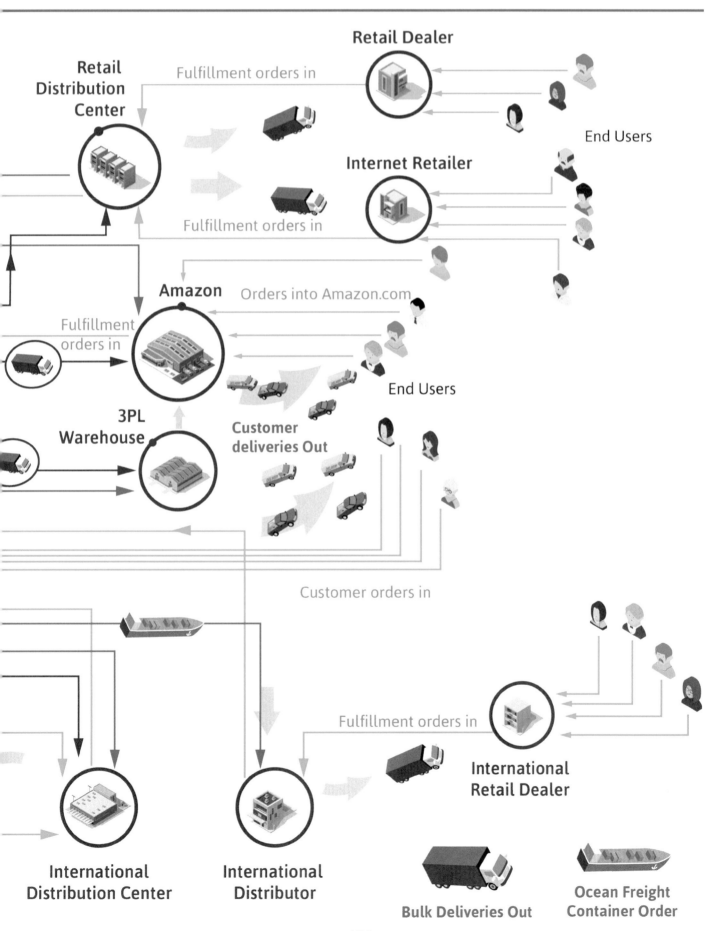

Retail Dealer

Retail Distribution Center

Fulfillment orders in

End Users

Internet Retailer

Fulfillment orders in

Amazon

Orders into Amazon.com

Fulfillment orders in

End Users

3PL Warehouse

Customer deliveries Out

Customer orders in

International Retail Dealer

Fulfillment orders in

International Distribution Center

International Distributor

Bulk Deliveries Out

Ocean Freight Container Order

CHAPTER 9

SHOE COMPANY OPERATIONS

Congratulations! Hopefully your shoes are in production and the factory is packing them up for shipment. Where are your shoes going? Are they shipping to your garage, directly to Amazon, a 3PL, a warehouse you own, or a rented storage space? Before your shoes leave the factory, you will need to map out their final destination and your new company's operational plan.

In this chapter we will review the basic operations required and the different structures you can create to meet these requirements. We will also discuss web sites, 3PL's and e-commerce integration.

What are operations?
Simply put, operations are the functions your company does to serve your customers. We have already discussed the design, development, and production operations, now we can focus on customer service and product fulfillment. You will need a way to collect the orders for your shoes and deliver them to your customers.

As your company grows, you will need a plan for your day-to-day operations. You need to handle all the accounting, supply chain, human resources, and cash flow issues. Or maybe you don't!

Depending on the sales, distribution, and operational plan you create, you may be sitting in a small office by yourself with all of these functions hired out, or in the middle of a busy office surrounded by your employees.

Customer service

Customer service is your company's forward facing contact with the outside world. When an individual consumer or dealer calls your company who is answering the phone?

The set-up of your customer service function depends on the sales and distribution model you will use.

Serving dealers

If you are selling to dealers, your customer service department will handle billing, shipping, credit, and returns for bulk orders. Your staff will answer incoming calls mainly from your sales force, shop employees, and store buyers. For a small start-up company, one or two people will be needed to take calls.

Your customer service team will have to handle the set-up and maintenance of your dealer accounts. A new dealer will need credit applications, credit references, shipping instructions, etc. If you are offering your accounts credit then you will need someone to handle collections for those slow paying dealers.

Serving consumers

If your sales are direct to consumer, your customer service team will hear from many individual callers with the same billing, shipping, and return issues that your dealers have. You will need to have a system in place to deal with hundreds of customer contacts versus a few dozen dealer contacts.

E-commerce

Before the internet, customer contact was done with a fax and a phone, each order requiring the time of your in-house staff. With modern web based e-commerce, most of your orders will be completed automatically with staff required only to handle special requests or problems. E-commerce is a must for consumer direct sales, but can also work for your dealer services.

Warehouse and logistics

Before your shoes arrive from the factory you need to organize warehouse space for the shipment. Your order may fill a 40' container and you are going to need a safe warehouse to protect the goods. You will also need a space easily accessible for shipping out.

You will need more space than just 40' x 8' x 8'. Your shoes need to be organized by model and size so they can be quickly picked for customer orders. Your parking garage or a rented shipping container may not be workable as you will need additional space to gather and pack individual orders. Your warehouse space must also be convenient for a trucking company to access for incoming and outgoing shipments.

Operational structures

Designing an operational structure for your company requires the same thought as the design for your shoes. Your operational plan must be adapted to your sales and distribution model.

If you are selling web direct, or shipping to dealers, your operational plan may be very different. Your plan will also vary depending on your personality and other circumstances.

Do you live in a big city with expensive office space and no warehousing facilities? Maybe you live in a small town where space is cheap to rent?

Are you "hands on" and want to be surrounded by the action of a growing company? Maybe you are the master planner that prefers to make the arrangements, hire out the jobs, and work behind the scenes in a quiet office?

Maybe you are on a tight budget and need to save every penny, or maybe your Kickstarter campaign brought in millions of dollars and you just need to get the office work done fast?

Your operational plan will also depend on what you are good at and what you like to do! If you are a great designer, then designing should be your focus, hire out everything else!

If you are a great organizer and dislike designing, hire out the design work and do the operations yourself.

There are many ways to organize your operations. We are going to look at several plans from the classic in-house plan to the virtual and mixed operational plans.

IN-HOUSE OPERATIONAL MODEL

Sales Department

Manufacturing

Warehousing

Management office

Customer service department

Marketing department

Shipping department

Design department

Shoe Company

Shoe store Buyer

Bulk deliveries out

Retail Shoe Store

End Users

In-house operational model

The traditional in-house operational plan is what you would imagine: a building with a busy office space divided into design, sales, marketing, and customer service areas.

Behind the office space you will find the manufacturing area and a warehouse full of shoes and shoe materials. This will be a big building! The shoe company will need a large staff to handle all of these functions.

There are some shoe companies that follow this model. They are generally smaller brands that sell high-end shoes or have invested heavily in automatic manufacturing systems.

The top shoe brands that sell millions of pairs have abandoned this operational model. These big brands would require more than 100,000 workers. Managing 100,000 employees in a dozen countries is almost impossible!

The capital requirements alone for the machinery to create new models would be overwhelming. Not to mention, what would these 100,000 workers be doing during the slow season?

Development is slowed down if a new process requires the purchase of a new machine. For the fast moving world of footwear, owning your own factory is a huge challenge. Most modern brands focus on the design, sales, and marketing challenges, while contracting out the manufacturing.

VIRTUAL OPERATIONS MODEL

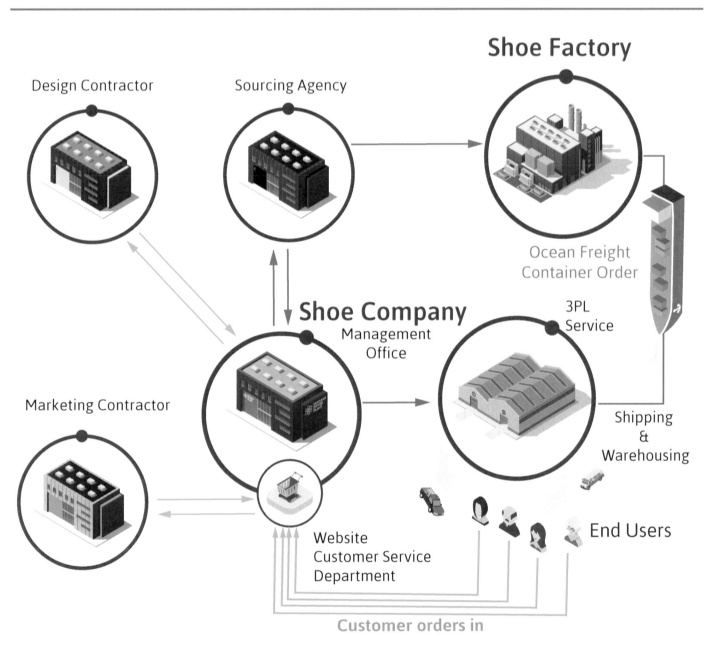

Shoe Factory

Design Contractor

Sourcing Agency

Ocean Freight
Container Order

Shoe Company
Management
Office

3PL
Service

Marketing Contractor

Shipping
&
Warehousing

Website
Customer Service
Department

End Users

Customer orders in

Virtual operations model

The virtual operation plan accomplishes the same functions as the traditional in-house and mixed operational plans but replaces employees with technology or sub-contracted specialist firms.

All the major operations are contracted out. The shoes can be designed by an outside firm. The footwear development and the shoe factory relationships can be handled by an independent sourcing agency. The agent can also provide the shipping, import, and logistical support.

The warehousing and order fulfillment operations can be contracted to a 3PL.

In this virtual model, the sales are direct to customer via website. The website's e-commerce operations can automatically collect payments and instruct the 3PL to ship the shoes directly to the customers. If arranged correctly, the process is automatic and you will not need any employees to process individual orders.

The website operations can also be subcontracted to a marketing technology company. The same firm may also provide website SEO and social media marketing operations.

MIXED OPERATIONAL MODEL

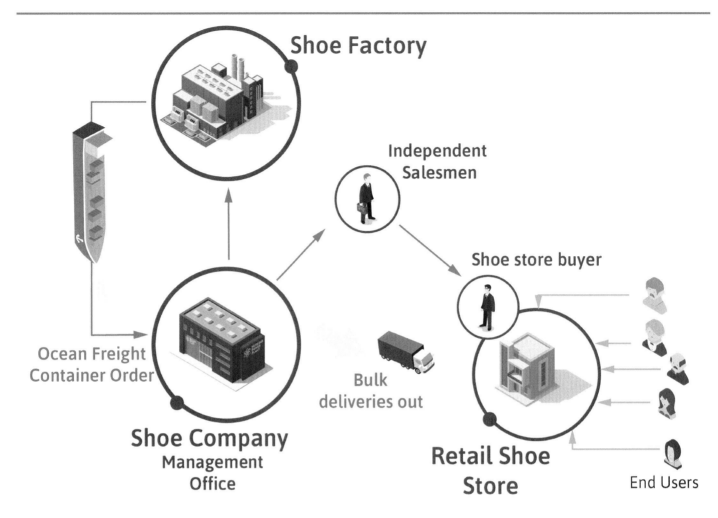

Mixed operational model

A mixed operation is very common for shoe companies large and small. In this example, the shoe company can focus on the design and marketing of shoes, while leaving the complications of shoe manufacturing to the specialist shoe factory.

In this model, the sales force of independent representatives is paid by commission and is subcontracted.

Companies like Nike use a mixed model. The size and complexity of their product lines require dozens of different supply factories in many different countries.

With such a huge product line, Nike needs an army of sales people to call on their dealers. For a large company, a sales force may be divided by regions, product categories, or dealer networks.

The strength of the mixed model is that it allows a company to focus on their strengths while contracting out other operations not core to their expertise

Nike, for example, can focus on being the number one sports marketing firm in the world while paying sub-contractors to build the shoes and sew the clothing.

Eve will follow a more traditional in-house operational plan, but with the addition of an e-commerce website to help handle customer service.

Eve is planning to make and sell 3200 pairs her first season. If Enigma's sales are successful, she will need to pack and ship all these shoes in just a few months. This could be 750 pairs a month or 175 pairs a week. The physical labor and customer service is clearly too much for one person to handle.

Eve's in-house plan will require staffing once the orders start flowing in. Eve has a group of student friends that will help her part-time.

Because Eve will be selling online and to fashion boutiques, the individual orders will be small, mostly for one or two pairs. These orders are more time consuming to pick, pack, and ship than bulk orders. Large companies with big volumes can require customers to buy shoe orders in case pack quantities.

Part of the Enigma brand story will be its Boston roots, so Eve has rented a rundown, red brick building. The space is the perfect back drop for her marketing campaign. This will be Enigma's headquarters and Eve will call it the "Safe House." The Safe House will act as the warehouse, office, design studio, and showroom for Enigma. For hard working Eve, it may also feel like home as she puts in many hours keeping her dream alive.

The Enigma Safe House requires money for rent, repairs, and utilities. Eve needs to make sure she gets the most out of her space.

While Eve plans to design the shoes and sell them herself, she is finding there are many other jobs to do too!

Ricardo will use a virtual operations plan with a more advanced e-commerce system. He will also need someone in-house to work with his growing dealer network and sales reps.

Ricardo has outsourced many of the Arris business operations. He has contracted out his shoe design and development functions and hired a 3PL service to handle all of his logistics. His websites are maintained by an e-commerce consulting firm, and he has hired a college student to manage his social media contacts.

Ricardo plans to use the same e-commerce platform to run his internet direct website and to support his dealer accounts.

As his start-up company grows, Ricardo will relocate the Arris office from his home office to a small rented space. He will need to hire one or two sales people to work the phones. With three people, Ricardo can manage the factory logistics and billing, while his small staff will operate the two websites and take calls from customers.

Ricardo's independent sales reps will work to maintain the dealer relationships but will still need support from the Arris in-house staff. Ricardo's 3PL has web enabled real time inventory so his sales reps can see exactly what shoes are in stock.

Ricardo's e-commerce platform and 3PL integration are what makes his virtual operations plan possible. Without this technology a small company like Arris could not function.

E-commerce
There are many choices available for e-commerce sites. Shopify, BigCommerce, Wordpress, Woo Commerce and Zen Cart. These systems offer high level functionality and are used by companies big and small. You can research these e-commerce providers and others online.

Is one system much better than another? If you pick from any of the top 5 providers you should be able to create a professional looking site without too much trouble. If you hire a website designer, make sure they have experience with the e-commerce platform you choose.

What to look for when selling footwear?
For selling shoes on-line your e-commerce platform must be able to show the shoe sizes available and colors. You will need a platform that keeps a live inventory of available sizes. Your platform must be able to display your shoes with color photos, different product angles, and videos. Does the platform make extra pages available for your technical information, blog posts, news etc.?

Your e-commerce platform will link to your credit card processor. There are many choices for credit card processing. Fees do vary, check out the options you have with your platform and shop around a bit. This service is behind the scenes of your website, your customers will not see it but you will. Find a service that works for you and make a quick call to your bank to make sure they don't have any issues with the credit card processor you choose.

If you are using a 3PL service to fulfill your orders, you need to make sure your e-commerce platform has an electronic link set up. The top e-commerce platforms have established these connections; this will allow your order to be sent directly to your 3PL warehouse.

There are several services that help make this connection for you. Shipwire™, Fulfillrite Order Fulfillment™, and Whiplash Fulfillment™ are some of them that can connect your web store directly to your 3PL inventory.

E-Commerce platforms
Here is a list of the top stand alone e-commerce platforms. These services are all inclusive, when you sign up they will provide everything you need.

Most also offer domain registration, hosting services, shopping cart software, credit card processing and links to 3PL shipping services.

Shopify™
Monthly Plans: $14.99 to $179.99
Website: Shopify.com

Big Commerce™
Monthly Plans: $29.99 to $199.99
Website: BigCommerce.com

Volusion™
Monthly Plans: $13.00 to $249.00
Website: Volusion.com

Squarespace™
Monthly Plans: $10.00 to $30.00
Website: Squarespace.com

3D Cart™
Monthly Plans: $19.99 to $129.99
Website: 3DCart.com

Big Cartel™
Monthly Plans: Free to $29.99
Website: BigCartel.com

Foxy Cart™
Monthly Plans: $20.00 to $300.00
Website: FoxyCart.com

Hosting services

If you are making an informational site that does not require a shopping cart there are many services that will host your website for just a few dollars per month.

Just Host™
Plans: $2.50 per month+
Website: JustHost.com

Blue Host™
Plans: $3.49 per month+
Website: BlueHost.com

Green Geeks™
Plans: $3.96 per month+
Website: GreenGeeks.com

Webhostingpad™
Plans: $1.99 per month+
Website: Webhostingpad.com

DreamHost™
Plans: $7.95 per month+
Website: DreamHost.com

GoDaddy™
Plans: $5.99 per month+
Website: GoDaddy.com

HostMonster™
Plans: $4.95 per month+
Website: MostMonster.com

HostGator™
Plans: $4.86 per month+
Website: HostGator.com

As we discussed earlier, Eve needs a basic e-commerce website to serve her online customers and her dealers. The Enigma product line is relatively small so Eve picks the "standard" $29.99 package offered by Big Commerce. Eve is building the website on her own using the free templates they offer. This plan tops out at $50,000 in sales per year. Once Eve can get Enigma sales ramped up she will need to upgrade her plan. She is now building her online store and setting up her item master with all of the Enigma products, sizes, and prices.

This plan offers a credit card gateway so set-up is not too difficult. Eve will need the Enigma bank account information for set-up.

Eve does not need a 3PL interface as her small team at the Enigma Safe House will be packing and shipping orders.

Ricardo's web hosting requirements are more complicated. He will need 2 different websites to run his operations. For Arrisrunning.com Ricardo can use a simple Wordpress.com site to provide the public face for the Arris brand. This site can also provide a link for his dealers to access his retail support and ordering site.

For his second website, Ricardo will need a very powerful and flexible e-commerce platform that allows him to serve his Arrisrunning.com wholesale and his Triathlonsupply.com retail customers. He will use Shopify.com and hire an e-commerce consulting firm to help him design and build the dual function website.

While Ricardo plans to keep his company as small as possible, he will need at least one full-time employee to update the automated business systems at Arris.

What is a 3PL?

Once your production shoes arrive in your home country you have to consider how they will be shipped to your customers. As a company owner you should consider a 3PL to handle your shipping.

So, what exactly is a 3PL? If you're new to the shipping and warehousing world, you're probably scratching your head at this term. 3PL actually stands for third party logistics. And what exactly is this? A third party logistics provider, sometimes called a 3PL or 3PL company, is a firm that provides outsourced logistics services to client companies for part, or all, of their supply chain management functions.

Why use a 3PL?

A 3PL company will handle your product logistics so that you don't have to. A good 3PL company will have an established network of warehouses, trusted shipping firms, and computerized inventory control so they can deliver your shoes quickly and efficiently.

Questions you need to ask your 3PL

When it comes to making an informed decision about which 3PL company will work for you, there are a few different questions you need to answer.

How many warehouses do they have, and where are they located? The number and location of the warehouses will ensure that you get the best coverage for your home market and can quickly deliver product to your customers.

Once an order is received, how soon until it gets shipped? You want the very best service for your customers. People expect fast deliveries and are willing to pay extra if you can offer faster service. How many orders can they handle per day and per month? If your business is growing fast, will your 3PL have the capacity to grow with you? This is important to know if you plan to ship to end users or retail dealers.

Do they have an online portal for you to check inventory levels and find the status of your orders? The ability to keep track of your inventory and orders is key to the marketing and replenishment decisions you make. An online system will make this as smooth as possible and allow you to check when it is convenient for you.

Do they have automatic low stock alerts? You never want your 3PL to run out of stock. Stock alerts can help you plan factory orders and coordinate deliveries.

Can you track serial numbers, lot numbers, and expiration dates? The ability to keep completely on top of your stock provides control and peace of mind.

Does your 3PL accept orders in multiple formats? You will want a 3PL that accepts manual or phone orders from you, automated orders from your website, and electronically generated orders from your dealers such as API, batch, and EDI formats.

Does your 3PL have a way to connect your shopping cart directly to their warehouse management system? Your fulfillment partner should have a list of supported cart systems on its website. Sometimes these connections are free while other times they have a monthly charge.

Can you speak with a human if you have a problem? You want to be able to resolve any issues quickly and completely. Does the 3PL charge for speaking with an account representative? This should be a part of the package you are paying for, but surprisingly, some charge for this service.

Are the fees clearly stated and concise? This is a big one. If at any point you are unsure, ask the fulfillment partner to give you a sample invoice including any set-up fees. You may need to do a time study and give that information to the fulfillment partner along with the storage space you'll require. You want to know all the costs associated with your 3PL to help with your planning and forecasting.

How much will using a 3PL cost?
With so many different options and so many different ways to charge it isn't always possible to do a direct comparison of the cost involved with using any particular 3PL provider. You will need to look at all the costs involved, get a sample invoice as discussed above and compare the options.

There will be initial set-up fees that can range in the hundreds of dollars depending on the complexity of your requirements. This is the cost involved to set you up in their system.

There will be fees for receiving your shoes into the 3PL warehouse. This is often charged on a per-hour basis and can typically be between $30 and $40 per hour, per person required. There will be a fee for storing products in their facility. This will be between $10 and $20 per pallet, per month, for the average provider.

For every order, there will be fees for picking, packing, and shipping. The shipping rates will be at a discount to the published rates but will include a charge between $5 and $10 for processing.

You need to look at all of these costs individually and decide which is the best 3PL provider for your shoes.

3PL Service providers

Here is a brief overview of the major 3PL providers

Fulfilled By Amazon (FBA)

If you were to believe everything that Amazon stated on their website then you wouldn't go anywhere other than Fulfilled By Amazon (FBA). It is true, they are a large company with a massive network. When you join up with Amazon, you get their full service of listing, storing, packing and shipping your shoes.

If your customers subscribe to Amazon Prime then they get the free 2-day shipping that Amazon has become famous for. The Amazon customer service team deals with any issues or returns, and they will even fulfill orders from other sales channels such as eBay™ or your own web site. Using the network and distribution that Amazon has built up over many years is an appealing draw.

As a small business owner you want to concentrate on developing your business while Amazon deals with the shipments and the customer service issues.

They have a fee calculator on their website. You can see exactly what it will cost you. FBA isn't cheap, but it's a great service.

Shipwire

This 3PL provider also has a user-friendly pricing calculator so you will know exactly what the service will cost you. They will add marketing inserts for a small extra charge, and the handling costs go down in price as your shipping volume goes up so you can save money. Like the offering from FBA, this company can help you by processing returns and providing customer service. Shipwire has 10 locations in the USA, two in Europe, and service in Australia.

eFulfillment Service

This company states that they are family-owned and you will get better customer service. There are no fees to set-up with them and they have no minimum order requirements like some of the others. They are a good place to start. Also, they do not charge for long-term storage.

Verde Fulfillment

This company's selling point is that it uses only recycled packaging and operates on green power. If you are promoting your brand as environmentally friendly, Verde service can become a useful part of your marketing plan. Their 3PL operations are also highly rated for their speed and efficiency.

One World Direct

This firm does everything you would expect from a 3PL provider. They have three distribution centers in the USA, with 24-hour call centers. They have service options for companies big and small. Set up fees are mid to high and service is top rated.

Do it yourself

If you don't sell vast amounts through Amazon there is always the option to ship your shoes by yourself. This gives you the opportunity to add a personal touch to each order. Add a free gift, or customize your packaging. It may be a little more time-consuming but can help you build and promote your brand.

This hands on approach gives you a chance to work directly with your customers. Working with your customers on a personal level is an advantage for a small brand that a huge multi-national company doesn't have.

Ship locally

If you do a quick Google search you will find loads of options when it comes to a local independent fulfillment company to deliver 3PL services for you. It is good to use local companies and you might make some connections that help you in the future. You may not find a local company that provides all the features of Amazon FBA but you will more than likely find a company that will add a personal touch for you and your customers. This might be the deciding factor.

Your logistics service is very important to customers and dealers. Lost, delayed, or improperly packed orders will leave a poor impression. You need the right logistics partner that will help you build the positive reputation you want for your brand.

 Ricardo has no interest or experience running a warehousing operation. He prefers to spend his time working with athletes and designers. He selects the virtual operations model for Arris so he can avoid logistical headaches. He will use a 3PL to handle all the Arris shipping and logistics.

Ricardo will use the independent 3PL Shipwire. Shipwire has many warehouse locations and this allows Ricardo to position the Arris stock close to the larger triathlon markets. Arris shoes can ship quickly from warehouse locations on both the east and west coast of the US. This allows Ricardo to offer express shipping at lower rates to end users and Arris dealers.

Ricardo is working hard to cultivate relationships with triathlon specialty retailers so he will limit the distribution to "core" triathlon dealers. He only wants dealers that will provide a professional shoe fitting experience for his customers.

Ricardo will avoid selling with Amazon for now. He hopes this will increase his chances for more support from his targeted retailers. Small running specialty shops have a hard time competing against products sold on Amazon. Ricardo will give them a chance to have exclusive selling rights to Arris. To show his support, Ricardo's sales terms to all dealers prohibit re-selling Arris shoes on Amazon.

Ricardo also chooses Shipwire because he needs a 3PL that can process and ship bulk orders to dealers, and single orders to customers. Shipwire's handling fees for single pair orders is low enough that Ricardo can still sell Arris shoes directly to customers profitably.

 Eve will run her own shipping operations so she will not need a 3PL for now. As Enigma grows, Eve may find that she wants to spend more time designing, selling, or working with her best dealers and less time doing customer service, order processing, and shipping.

She will look into the local Boston 3PL services and take her time to decide if she needs one in the future.

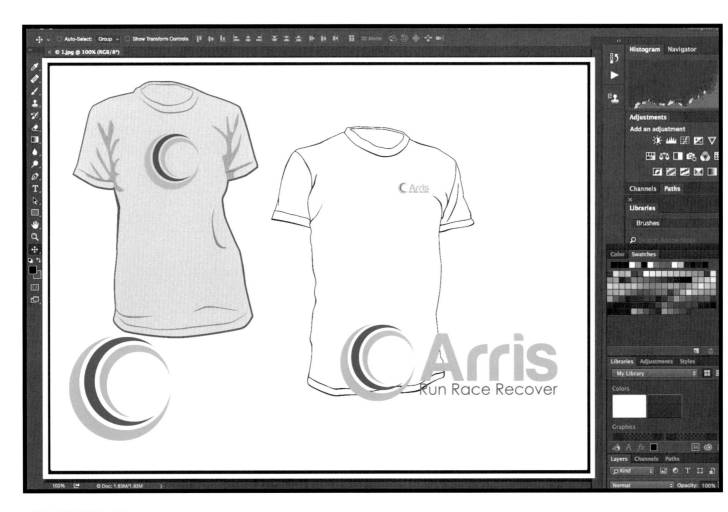

CHAPTER 10

WHAT'S NEXT FOR YOUR BRAND

Once your new shoe brand is established, you can start to think about expanding your business.
As a young start-up footwear company you will need to focus on strategies for increasing growth and improving profitability. Should you expand your line of shoes? Should you target new customers? Can you increase your market share or should you diversify into new products and markets?

Should you sell internationally? Going international is a big step! There are unique challenges with both the distribution and direct to consumer models. We will cover those in Chapter 11.

Strategies for growth
To grow your business you will need to increase the number of customers and increase the value of each sale. If you are following a retail distribution model, this means opening more doors and getting more sales per door. For web based strategies, this means more visitors to your site, higher conversion rates, and more value per conversion.

There are many ways to expand your business and your brand's reach.

Increased market penetration

Sell products into new markets

Expand your product line

Diversify your product offering

Increase your market penetration

There are a few ways to improve your brand's share of the shoe market. First, study your sales. Do you see problems? Look for geographical gaps in your distribution. For example, do you have strong sales in Boston and weak sales in New York?

You may need to hire more sales reps to cover missed territories, or reduce the size of your sales territories allowing your sales force to visit more stores. Paying your sales reps a bonus for adding new accounts is also a great way to increase your market share.

Depending on the type of shoe you are making, you may be able to sell into regional or national chain stores.

Another way to increase your market share is to add a representation discount to your sales program. This can help you win a bigger share of your dealer's buy budgets.

Be aggressive if you see a new trend in your market segment. Getting into a growing segment early will help you gain market share rapidly.

If you can identify a weakness in a competitor's product offering or sales strategy, work to exploit that weakness. If you find out a competitor has a quality problem with a $99 shoe, offer your competing shoe with a small discount.

Maybe your competitor is having financial problems? You can offer your dealers higher credit limits and longer payment terms to freeze out your struggling competitor. You can win market share by having better credit terms and excellent customer service.

Selling products into new markets

Your new shoe brand can look for growth outside your target markets. New markets can be geographical markets or user markets.

Are your shoes great for running triathlons but also good for steeple chase? A few tweaks to your marketing campaign can move your brand in a new direction.

In the 90's, a rap music star wore army boots instead of basketball shoes. A few military boot makers jumped on the trend and captured sales in a new urban market they were never planning on entering.

Keep your eyes open for trending opportunities or better yet, try to create them!

Eve needs to convince her customers to buy more of her boots. To achieve that goal she has created a new online ad campaign, "when the mood strikes you." The ads feature her range of boots along several different looks that may appeal to her customers. She is clearly showing her customers the benefits of owning more that one pair of enigma boots.

Eve knows the punk music scene she is targeting is small, she will see if Enigma can evolve beyond punk and into other markets.

She may try supporting some activist causes on her old college campus. Eve can get her boots in front of more potential customers that may not be into punk but that can still appreciate her more aggressive fashion sense.

How will Arris grow market share? Ricardo needs to sell more shoes to his existing customers. The entire Arris product strategy is based on customers buying more than one pair of shoes. To improve his conversion rate, Ricardo can offer his existing customers a discount when they buy their second and third pair of Arris shoes.

Ricardo can include mail-in rebates or coupon codes with his shoes to help drive more orders. On the website that Ricardo operates he can offer tiered discounts on follow-up orders.

He will also add more informational ad copy to his shoe box packing. Designs printed on the shoe box are essentially free, so this is a great place for Ricardo to reinforce the Arris product system.

Ricardo decides to add the Arris Run, Race, Recover, motto to the printed tissue paper that wraps his shoes.

Ricardo's shoes are great for runners too, he can start marketing beyond just the triathlon market. Ricardo can turn his same event marketing strategy to marathons and cross country running.

Expanding your product line

Once your brand is in a market with established distribution it may be easy for you to add more products to your offering. If you are lucky, your customers and dealers may already be telling you what to make! If not, your sales force will often have great ideas for you to consider.

Potential product line extensions for your footwear brand can include new price points both higher and lower than your current range, more colors of your top sellers, or increasing your size offering. You may also consider adding men's or women's genders and even kids.

You should also be looking at your competitors for product ideas. What are they doing well? What are they doing poorly? What can you do better? Ask around, question your retailers about what is going on in their stores.

Your R&D team should be out visiting accounts and observing users. New insights into the use of your product will lead you to new features and new products.

When thinking about new products one strategy is called adjective design. Can you make a shoe bigger, smaller, cheaper, lighter, softer, stiffer or maybe just more expensive?

Expanding your product line can create problems if not done correctly. New products may cause your dealer to split sales across more items rather than buying more. More choices also make your product line harder for the dealer to buy. If the product line is not clearly organized, the buyer may not know what or how to buy your product line.

Also, keep in mind that most dealers want and actually need multiple brands in their stores. You may offer a huge line but they will only ever buy a part if it. Remember that a store's credit amount will limit how much of your new product line they can purchase. The dealer will buy from your competitor to increase their overall credit limit.

A larger product line will also mean higher costs for you to develop, buy, and stock.

Sensible product line expansions will grow your business. Adding sku's improperly can back fire and reduce your market share while increasing your expenses.

 Ricardo will need to be hard hearted when it comes to slow selling models. After his first selling season the Arris product range will change. Ricardo will add sku's to successful products and re-work or cut the weaker styles.

If Ricardo's top priced models are selling well it will give him the confidence to add more expensive items to his range. Ricardo can also increase his orders to make sure he has extra stock for his web business.

Slow selling models are giving Ricardo a challenge. He will need to decide on a strategy to improve sales. Should he "cut and run"? Abandon these products or invest time and money to improve them? It can be hard for a small company to spend time both reinforcing winners and reworking losers.

 For fashion brands like Enigma, it's easy to add more styles. New print patterns, new leather colors, and emboss effects can be developed inexpensively. Because Enigma is a fashion brand, Eve will need to trend spot and update her product line often to stay current. She will need to be very careful to test new designs before she orders. A fashion brand that misses an important trend will have a very hard time selling shoes!

To keep her small company growing, Eve will also need to be very hard hearted with her designs. If a design she really likes is not selling she will have to stop production, markdown the price, and move on to a new design quickly.

With her online sales, Eve can get a read on sku's that are selling well. It's important that she uses this information to recommend the best selling styles to her retail boutique customers.

Diversify your product offering

Product diversification can be a difficult, high risk strategy to grow your brand, but not if you have a clear view of your brand's strengths.

Before you diversify you need to ask the same questions that helped form your core product strategy.

Will this new product be:
Sold by the same sales force?
Sold to the same buyers?
Sold into the same dealers?
Sold into the same distribution network?
Sold to the same end users?

You also need to consider your sourcing and operations:

Can you offer dealers higher credit limits to buy more of your products?

Do you have the in-house staff to design and develop the new products?

Do you have a partner factory that can make the new items?

Do you have the capital to fund the development and purchasing of the new items?

Your product diversification planning should start with a visit to your best retailers. Stand in their stores and look around. Do you see something you can make that relates to your current footwear offering? Do you notice anything missing? Do you see any products that you can improve upon?

Make sure to study your competitors. You should have an in-depth knowledge of your competitors' product lines. Buy their product, use it, lab test it, cut it apart. What can you learn? Study their catalogs, websites, Facebook™ pages, and Instagram™ feeds. You should know exactly what they are doing and what they are NOT doing.

Diversify or die

You may see a problem in your existing target market. Are you focused on a market niche that is fading away? Are big box stores or internet retailers putting your dealers out of business?

If you see a trend coming that will hurt your business, you may be forced to diversify or die.

Eve's accounts have been asking her to apply her personal style to accessories that would compliment her boots. Eve will start developing chain wallets, wide belts, and colorful scarves.

These new items will require Eve to find new factories for production but they will sell into the same dealers. The new items will also cost very little to develop and produce. This is a low risk diversification. Best of all for Eve, she has customers asking for these products already!

Eve sees a huge trend towards vulcanized shoes. Her target customers, GIRLS, are wearing them. Maybe it's time for Eve to put some of her creative fashion sense to work making some vulcanized shoes that can carry her brand into new footwear markets?

Ricardo has big plans for the Arris brand. He will expand the shoe offering. He can add more sizes for men and he will add women's shoes too. He will also add more colors and price points.

These are obvious ways to expand the Arris brand. The new items will be sold into the same triathlon market, to the same buyers, in the same stores, with his existing marketing campaigns, to reach his existing customers. This is a low risk diversification plan.

Ricardo is not satisfied with this simple line expansion. He can see that triathletes also need cycling shoes. Can he apply the Arris system to cycling shoes? While the development and sourcing of cycling shoes will be a new challenge, he can sell them to the same buyers, into the same stores, and to his existing customers. This cycling shoe plan will have some risk but it's not too bad.

The Arris brand also has a chance to make clothing. Ricardo knows this is a high risk diversification, but he can contract out the design, development, and sourcing of a small line to start.

Strategies for profitability

For a young company it is not uncommon to lose money the first year. Your investments in product development, production, and brand marketing may be difficult to pay off when you are a fast growing start-up.

What's important for your young company is to have a plan and goals. It is important to update your financial calculations often to make sure your new business is operating according to the plan you made. Once you have a base line for your expenses you should be able to project the number of pairs you need to sell to be profitable.

If your development expenses increase you may need to raise prices, buy more shoes, or bring in more investors to see you through. If your FOB prices come in lower than plan, you may have more capital for marketing or paying off investors.

Patching holes

If you are following the dealer distribution model the obvious step is to make sure your brand is well distributed in your home country. A careful review of your dealers and consultations with your sales force will show you any gaps. Larger sales territories can be reduced to improve service.

Your largest accounts can be made "house accounts." A house account is no longer served by a sales rep, but instead your office staff will assign an employee to serve just this one account. This is usually done when a large retailers commission check makes a sales rep the highest paid employee in the company. Of course, your sales rep will be upset and may resign. You may have to provide a small commission to keep the territory profitable.

Going after the big fish

Now that your firm is making and shipping shoes you can approach larger retailers. The biggest store chains will avoid small start-ups that don't have a proven track record for delivering shoes.

Larger retailers like Rei™, Target™, and Bass Pro™ will have labeling and logistics requirements that may be difficult for new companies to meet. Electronic Data Interchange (EDI) systems are common for processing large orders.

Wait until you have all these processes in place. Be careful, expanding into larger retailers may damage your credibility with your existing dealers.

Eve's distribution is growing but she still has many holes to fill. Her plan to have herself and her friend cover US sales is not very effective. She can see her sales are clustered around the New York and Los Angeles markets. She will need a new plan to make sure the Enigma brand is getting more sales coverage.

Eve's research also shows her that Chicago and Seattle have punk scenes perfect for Enigma to take root. Eve will hire independent sales reps to cover the Midwest and North West territories.

Enigma wants to remain a "core" brand so Eve will stay away from the big fashion retailers for now.

Arris Ricardo works very hard to make sure he has a rep force to cover the entire US. The Arris brand has 10 independent sales reps that call on Triathlon specialty and high end running stores. Because these stores are few and far between, 10 reps gives Ricardo good coverage.

He has been approached by a small chain of high end running stores. Ricardo will have to review each store location to make sure none of the new stores are close to any existing accounts. He sees that the chain store has a location very close to another Arris dealer, Ricardo decides to open the chain stores but requires the store location with the conflict not to sell the Arris shoes.

Later, Ricardo sees the new dealer is selling Arris well in the other locations, he decides to drop the exclusivity. The original store dealer may drop Arris, but now Ricardo has a more profitable dealer.

Ricardo will wait and see about the national chain stores. If he can grow the specialty market he can keep his distribution limited until he is ready to expand.

Shoe Factory

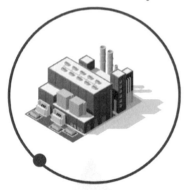

Up Stream
Diversification

Shoe Company

Down Stream
Diversification

Retail Dealer

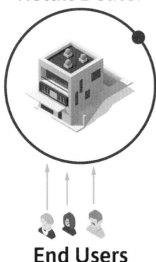

End Users

Vertical integration

Vertical integration is another form of business diversification. If your shoe company is growing strong, you may start to look at the supply chain and retail sectors of your business. Maybe you can buy or build a shoe factory and make your own shoes? This is called upstream diversification. Owning and operating a shoe factory is a very difficult undertaking, you will find the profit margins for manufacturing are in the 5% to 15% range.

While owning a shoe factory is well beyond the abilities of a small shoe brand, you can work to control some of the raw material costs going into the shoe factory. You can negotiate with raw material suppliers directly to try and improve your profit margins. This is called nominating suppliers. Some factories will cooperate with the nominated supplier while others will not.

Your shoe company also needs to be looking at the distribution and retail operations. This is called downstream diversification. Many new companies take on downstream diversification by the use of web retail and by operating their own retail or concept store.

The danger of vertical integration, both upstream and downstream, is the amplification of problems. If there is a slowdown or market disruption, your company will take the hits in three ways instead of one.

CHAPTER 11

GOING INTERNATIONAL

Going international is a great way to grow your shoe company, but with any new opportunities comes new challenges. You will need to increase staff to really drive sales. An international sales manager with some experience is a must to get your international division off the ground. Your international salesmen, teamed up with a customer service rep to handle the order flow, can get you started without too much added overhead. Travel can be expensive, but a well run international division can quickly grow to 50% of your annual turnover.

Getting ready for launch
Before your international orders start flowing in you have to prepare. First, make sure your footwear supply chain is ready. Can your factory handle more orders? You will need to protect your trademarks in your new sales territories. You will also need to understand the business models and financial implications of running an international business. Most importantly, you will need to find partner distributors.

How do I register my patent, trademark, or copyright overseas?
Patents and trademarks are territorial and must be filed in each country where protection is sought. A U.S. patent or trademark does not afford protection in another country. For more information on how to apply for individual patents or trademarks in a foreign country, contact the intellectual property office in that country directly. A list of contact information for most intellectual property offices worldwide can be found at the World Intellectual Property Office. However, the Patent Cooperation Treaty (PCT) streamlines the process of filing patents in multiple countries. By filing one patent application with the U.S. Patent and Trademark Office (USPTO), U.S. applicants can seek protection in up to 143 countries at the same time. For information about filing an international patent application under the PCT, visit the USPTO website.

What is the Madrid Protocol?

The Madrid Protocol makes it easy to file for trademark registration in multiple countries. By filing one trademark registration application with USPTO, U.S. applicants can concurrently seek protection in up to 84 countries. Information about filing an international trademark registration application under the Madrid Protocol is also available from the USPTO website.

Defending your trademarks overseas

Before you enter a new market you must register your trademarks. I suggest you either do this yourself, hire a law firm in your home country, or hire a law firm in your new market to handle the registration.

Beware: A distribution firm may offer to register your trademarks on your behalf. You should avoid this. I've been involved with several cases where the distribution firm registers the trademark naming themselves as the owner!

If your trademark falls into the wrong hands it can be difficult, expensive, or impossible to recover it. With your trademark controlled by another company, you may be forced into poor deals or locked out of a foreign country entirely. The cost of overseas trademark registrations can add up, but if your company is growing it's a worthwhile investment that can be written off as an expense.

Distribution models

To sell overseas you need people on the ground in the foreign country to replicate the marketing and customer service functions of your company. This is called direct distribution or self-distribution.

While it is theoretically possible for a small shoe brand to set-up shop in a foreign country, it is almost never done. Until your company has grown up a bit you are going to need a distribution partner.

There are many ways to get set-up with a distribution partner in a new market. The most common is to sign an agreement with an established distribution firm. You will find existing companies that specialize in distribution of foreign brands in their home countries. If your firm is growing strong, these firms will be approaching you! If you are not this lucky you will need to do some research to find them.

Finding the right distributor

A good distributor will become a valued business partner, trusted confidant, part owner, life long friend, or employee. A poor performing distributor can cause you headaches and heartaches, take your time and choose wisely.

The first place to look can be the websites of your competitors! This may seem crazy but it's not uncommon for a distributor to carry competing brands in their home market. You should also research other brands that are in your market category. If you are making hiking shoes you should look for the distribution firm that sells tents or other camping gear in your targeted county.

Don't be afraid to consult networking sites like LinkedIn™, where you can find the international sales manager of a related company and simply ask them for a reference.

What to look for in a distributor

When meeting with a distributor it is important to find out if they are an established firm. How big is their sales force? What accounts do they work with? What other brands do they carry? Do they have enough capital to actually buy your shoes? Do they have a warehouse and operations staff to move the product? Does the distributor have a marketing plan, staff, and budget planned? You should ask the perspective distributor for a list of customers and credit references.

Getting started overseas

Getting your shoes into foreign markets efficiently and at competitive retail prices can be a challenge for shoe companies big and small. Fluctuating exchange rates, grey market dealers, import duty, and shipping expenses can ruin your carefully laid plans.

As your company grows, your foreign distribution strategy will evolve. You may start with LCL orders by ocean freight to a single large retailer. A retailer with a few locations can be a good start in a small country, for developing markets this is not uncommon.

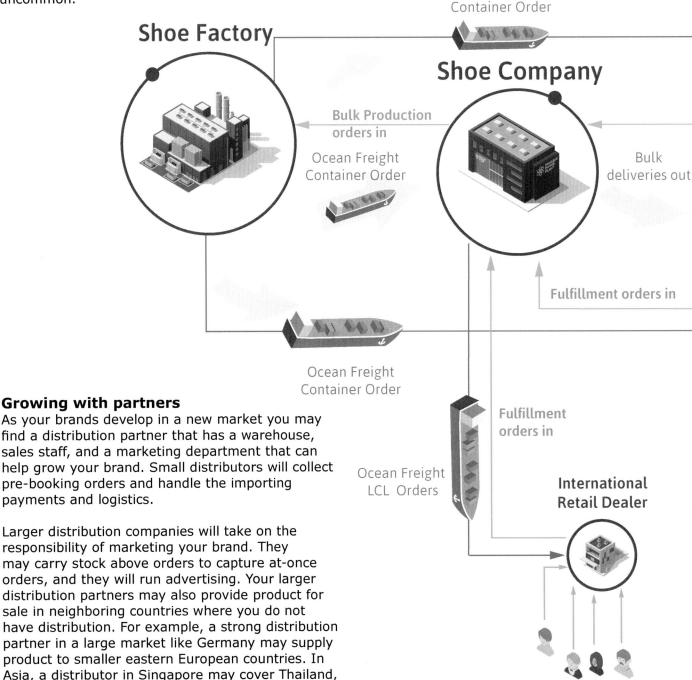

Shoe Factory

Shoe Company

Ocean Freight
Container Order

Bulk Production
orders in

Ocean Freight
Container Order

Bulk
deliveries out

Fulfillment orders in

Ocean Freight
Container Order

Fulfillment
orders in

Ocean Freight
LCL Orders

International
Retail Dealer

End Users

Growing with partners

As your brands develop in a new market you may find a distribution partner that has a warehouse, sales staff, and a marketing department that can help grow your brand. Small distributors will collect pre-booking orders and handle the importing payments and logistics.

Larger distribution companies will take on the responsibility of marketing your brand. They may carry stock above orders to capture at-once orders, and they will run advertising. Your larger distribution partners may also provide product for sale in neighboring countries where you do not have distribution. For example, a strong distribution partner in a large market like Germany may supply product to smaller eastern European countries. In Asia, a distributor in Singapore may cover Thailand, the Philippines, Indonesia, and Malaysia.

INTERNATIONAL DISTRIBUTION MODEL

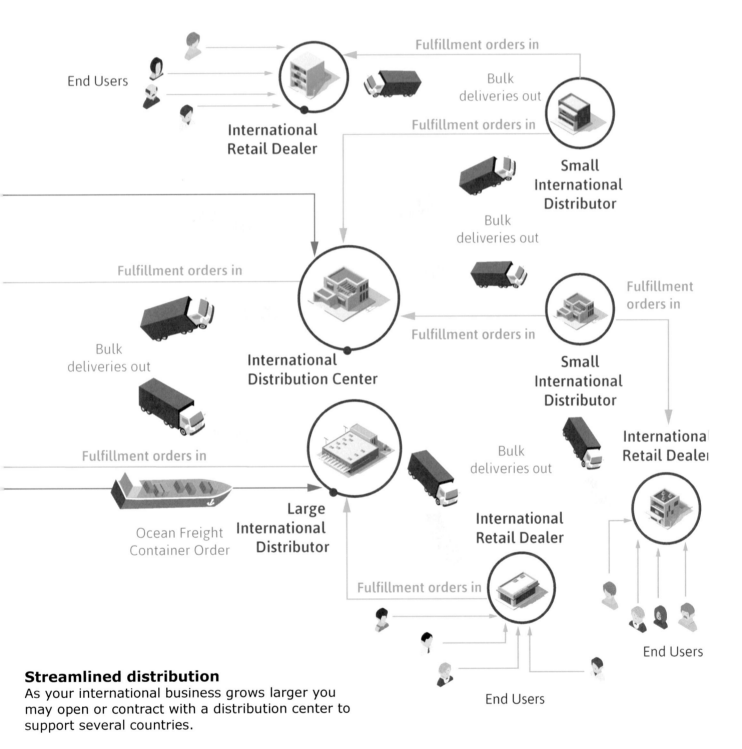

End Users

International
Retail Dealer

Fulfillment orders in

Bulk
deliveries out

Fulfillment orders in

Small
International
Distributor

Bulk
deliveries out

Fulfillment orders in

International
Distribution Center

Bulk
deliveries out

Fulfillment orders in

Fulfillment orders in

Fulfillment
orders in

Small
International
Distributor

Fulfillment orders in

Ocean Freight
Container Order

Large
International
Distributor

Bulk
deliveries out

International
Retail Dealer

International
Retail Dealer

Fulfillment orders in

End Users

End Users

Streamlined distribution

As your international business grows larger you
may open or contract with a distribution center to
support several countries.

All of your customers in the European Union can
be served with one distribution center. Rather
than trying to arrange the shipping to many
European countries, one company will collect
the orders and ship in bulk to an EU based
warehouse. This saves the duplication of efforts
and saves everyone time and money.

You want your distributors to be out selling your
product not struggling with import paperwork.

Purchase terms for distributors

For your small company you should not be offering any purchase terms or "dating." As a small firm, you will not have the cash flow to finance the production of your distributors' product. You need to demand payment of 50% upon placement of orders, and 50% upon completion. The shipments will not to be released until the final payment is made.

Your distributors' product is often shipped directly to them from your factory partners. In the trade these orders are called container orders or direct ships. The 40' or 20' container is convenient to maximize the orders and minimize shipping. Your smaller customers may be on a different schedule and they may need to take their stock from your warehouse by LCL.

From day one you need to treat your distributor like any other account. They must follow your pre-booking schedule. It's no use to have an international distributor empty out your stock that you need for your domestic customers.

You can NEVER ship products to distributors on credit unless you have known them for years and trust them. If a distributor does not pay you, you have almost no chance to recover your money.

Setting prices for distribution partners

Finding the right price for your distribution partners can be a big challenge. Your goal is to have a competitive market price in your new markets AND make a reasonable profit.

Your distribution partners should be doing the market research so you know the market price for similar products. Shipping, duty, exchange rates, and local taxes will all have an impact on the final selling price.

The economic prospects of foreign markets will also effect the price you can demand for your products.

To make your products price competitive in foreign markets, you will need to give your distributor a discount from your standard wholesale price. There is no hard and fast rule for this discount, but you can expect your profit margin on international sales to be closer to 30% if your domestic margin is 50%.

You will need different price lists for Europe, South America, Asia, and Australia.

Foreign distribution contracts

When you enter into a partnership with a distributor you will both need to sign a contract that establishes the ground rules.

The contract must include the following:

1. Clearly defined sales territory.

2. Agree not to disclose confidential information to 3rd parties. Prices, strategies, etc.

3. The distributor will not present themself as your company.

4. You agree to avoid selling product to other dealers in their territory.

5. Agree on the currency for all transactions.

6. Agree on the purchase terms. FOB or Ex works etc.

7. The distributor will pay all taxes, duties, deposits, bonds, and fees related to their territory.

8. The distributor is responsible for all claims, demands, liabilities, lawsuits, or expenses of any kind related to doing business in their territory.

9. Set the length of the contract.

10. Set performance goals.

11. Describe required sales reports.

12. Describe terms for termination.

You should not write this contract by yourself. You will need the help of an attorney or legal service with experience. A quick web search will show you many fee templates for foreign distribution contracts.

Strange Asia
In countries like Japan and Korea you will find that retail dealers are locked to distribution networks. These networks can be complex and in the case of Japan, there may be another middle man between your distributor and the retailer. These sub distributors are often linked to retail buying groups. You may ask a distributor to call on an account and they will have to refuse if they are not linked to the particular buying group.

Before signing with a distributor you should make sure they can sell to your target retail accounts. You will also find that dealers in Japan can return all the shoes, regardless of the quality. Often for no other reason than they did not sell. Quality control is critical to your survival in the Japanese markets.

Grey marketing
Grey marketing is when a product you sold into one market turns up in another market. For example, you may have a dealer in California buying discounted merchandise then reselling the shoes in Japan. The gray market importer may be avoiding import duties and selling to dealers that conflict with your distribution plan. The gray market dealer is collecting the profits but working against your brand.

For high value products, you can trace gray market goods by adding serial number bar codes to the product. This can allow you to track the original buyer of the goods.

Hard to serve countries
You may have a difficult time meeting demand in countries too small for a distributor to survive. Some small countries in South America or Europe can be served by your distributor in larger markets. You may not officially allow your Brazilian distributor to sell into Bolivia or Paraguay but you can just let it happen until you can organize a real plan.

Every country in the world has different rules to follow. You can be flexible to get your business growing but do not give small distributors payment terms. This is very risky as you may never get paid back.

Currency exchange problems
A change in currency exchange rates can have a negative impact on your distributor's buying power. Many distribution firms will lock in their exchange rate with a forward exchange contract for their projected product buy.

If their purchasing currency falls, they "win." They have contracted to exchange at the higher rate.

If their country's currency strengthens ,they "lose" and they are stuck with the lower rate. The benefit is they can plan their company operations without the danger of being wiped-out by currency devaluation.

With a distributor's margin rate around 20%, a currency exchange drop can easily destroy any chance they had for profitability.

CHAPTER 12

WHAT CAN GO WRONG?

When starting a new company there are many things that can go wrong. Knowing the common problems can help you prepare and be on the look out for small issues before they become show stoppers.

Dealing with delays

The most common problem for many start-ups is delays. In China, it seems that anything that can go wrong will go wrong. From accidental food poisoning in the factory cafeteria, to the pattern maker in the hospital, to a cargo ship on fire and adrift. So many things can go wrong and ruin your carefully organized schedule.

How to handle delays?

The only thing you can do is to start early and build some extra time into your launch schedule. Time slippage is almost inevitable, you need to plan for it! Big delays will cost money, extend development contracts, add extra wages for workers, rent, and interest. This can all add up fast if your production is delayed.

Take action

Tackle delays early in your process. Small delays in the front of your process can lead to huge delays later on. Stay up late, make more phone or video calls, or get on a plane. If you are planning a product that has a seasonal launch window it's critical that you stay on schedule. Winter boots are useless if they arrive in April and nobody will buy sandals in October.

How can you prevent delays

When you set out to make your development schedule you will need to work with your agent or factory to make sure what you want is possible. A well documented line plan and scope of project is required for the factory to fully understand. Testing new technology, finding and fitting new shoe lasts all take time. It's not aways easy to predict when something new will be ready. What seems like a simple task can derail your plans. Listen to what your factory is telling you. If you push them too hard they may agree to a timeline which they cannot realistically meet.

Avoiding unknowns

New technologies should not be put on a seasonal shoe development timeline until they are proven and ready to be commercialized. A typical development schedule may allow time to design a new midsole, but not enough time to find and qualify a new EVA formula. Make sure to review your designs with your factory technicians and developers for unknowns and plan for more time or modifications if necessary.

Avoid useless complications

While your designer may mean well, sometimes a design detail on a shoe may be more trouble than it's worth. Does a printed design need to be 8 colors? Could 5 colors achieve the same result? Is that exotic material from Italy really necessary or can it be sourced closer to the factory in China?

Make sure to check the country of origin of the specified materials. Rare, expensive, fragile, or hard to get materials should be avoided. Check to see if you can reduce the number of material suppliers. Check the lead time of each material.

Think about where your shoe factory is located and where your materials are coming from?

Raw material supply problems

Oil price fluctuations can cause price spikes in shoe materials like synthetic rubber, foam, and plastics. Do your research and make sure any price increases make sense. A 15% price hike in plastics may only effect 30% of your shoes raw materials.

Quality issues

Quality problems can kill your new company before it starts. One bad shipment can ruin all your efforts to get placed with retailers. Disappointed shoe dealers and angry customers will not be buying again.

When you choose a factory you are choosing your product quality. A shoe factory only has one quality level. The workers' care, the quality ethic, and the managers' dedication are the same regardless of the footwear customer's logo.

Footwear quality can be broken down into three issues; material quality, care in assembly, and development technique.

Material quality refers to the selection of suitable materials for your shoes and making sure the suppliers deliver stable high quality product.

A great factory can make beautiful shoes, but if the leather specified is too thin the shoes just won't last. Make sure your product specs are very detailed with every material listed and every vendor specified. You can go with the factory's recommendations, they will have vendors they trust, but make sure you have test results. Avoid "mystery materials." You need to know every component piece by piece.

A factory will have in-bound inspections to check material quality but unscrupulous factories may accept sub-standard material, at a discount, then try to pass it on at full price. Make your requirements clear!

There are many tests for materials. A good shoe factory will have a material testing lab. If you see a lab with dusty machines, maybe you should look for another factory. Material testing will check for colorfastness, bust strength, abrasion resistance, tensile strength, cracking, and crooking etc.

Care in shoe assembly is simply that! Is the shoe being made with good craftsmanship? Is the shoe sitting straight on the outsole? Do you see pressing marks, loose threads, or dirty finger prints?

Development technique is a little more complicated to explain. You are looking for a shoe designed for quality production. Does the outsole fit the upper correctly? If the sole is concave or bulging on the bottom, maybe the top net is not right? Do you see the same wrinkle on every shoe? Does an underlay x-ray through the upper in a strange way? These issues should be solved in development but they can appear in the final production.

You can get help with quality. If you have an agent they are responsible for reviewing the quality.

Make sure you have quality standards set up. What is an A grade, B grade, or C grade? Hire a 3rd party inspection service if necessary. Make sure you and the factory have a matching pair of signed confirmation samples.

Do not accept, "it's just a sample problem" or, "don't worry it will be fixed in production." Make sure you see a new sample of the shoe or a detailed photo showing the issue corrected before production begins.

You have a lot of money invested in each production run and you should arrange to visit the factory during production to make sure your shoes are right! If you see a problem, you may have to "pull the red lever" and stop production.

While a trip to the factory may be expensive, a container of poor quality shoes will end your shoe company dreams.

Shoe inspection techniques are covered in chapter 24 of the book "How Shoes Are Made."

Poor sell in

There are many reasons for poor sell in; bad weather, a missed color trend, a strong competitor. What to do depends on your product inventory situation. If you have not made the shoe yet and your bookings are small, you can try changing the price, changing the color, or just cancel the production. If you have only one item, then cancellation is hard to take, but if you have many items, the loss of one is not a problem. Large shoe brands may cut 15% of their line if the items are not booking.

If you have inventory you will need to take action quickly. First, make sure to cancel any back-up orders that are in the factory. You don't want to make your problem any larger!

Once the production is stopped you can try to find out what the problem is. Can you sell the shoes at a discount? If you are a small shoe brand you may need to change your distribution model. You may need to avoid the retail buyers and go direct to your consumer.

Poor sell through

If your shoes are in store but selling slowing you will hear complaints from your dealers. They may ask you for "mark down money" (a discount after the fact.) They may also ask you to take the merchandise back! You can be creative here. You must try to avoid losing a sale you have already made. You can offer the dealer the markdown money as a discount on new product, or offer to make a product exchange.

Your product development team will need to put in some over time to find out why the products did not sell well, and they will need to get replacement products into market as soon as possible.

Losing money

You are selling shoes but losing money! If you have made your landing margin calculations correctly you should be earning a profit from each sale. Recheck your calculations against your real purchase and importing charges. Most likely you need to raise your prices.

Look at your expenses; sales commissions, rent, salaries, and marketing expenses can add up fast. If you are lucky, you will make money your first year, but you may not. Make sure you are not going deeper in debt. Adjust your plan, get help!

Overstocked

Poor sell through and lack of repeat orders can leave you overstocked. Overstock can be dangerous to your small company especially if you have seasonal merchandise and the season is ending, or you have very tight cash flow. It's better to offer discounts early to keep the product moving as older product continues to lose value. Also, look for international dealers or offer web specials.

Sold out

A great position to be in! But, it also means there is money being left on the table. Try to switch orders to other items if you can. Ofter discounts for other slower selling items. Place rush orders to the factory or air ship products. Make sure you are not trying to rush in product that will arrive after the selling season. Gently remind dealers to increase their pre-season product buys.

Containers lost

Every so often containers go missing. They can be stolen, or a storm may wash them overboard. This is very rare. You will have insurance through your shipping firm. Check with your shipper, you can claim the cost of the merchandise and maybe even your lost profits.

In some markets containers may be "kidnapped" or seals broken and merchandise looted. In-country security for merchandise is the responsibility of the owner of the merchandise.

Lost trademarks

A popular and fast growing brand will have to work hard defending trademarks. There are unscrupulous foreign companies that will register your trademark in their home countries. You may have to sue them, pay them off, or make a deal of some sort. If the rights are valuable you can hire a distributor to fight the trademark battle on your behalf.

Damaged equipment

Shoe making equipment is generally very robust and most well made tooling can withstand 200,000 plus production cycles. However, to save money, a factory may use less expensive tooling made from resin or soft metal. The less expensive tooling does serve the useful propose of getting your shoes to market cheaper but it can cause problems later on.

Resin molds may crack, pro quality metal tooling may rust, crack, or bend. Make it a point to inspect your tooling before production and afterwards to insure it is being properly cared for.

Dealers going bankrupt

If you are selling to retailers you will have customers that go bankrupt. You may see warning signs as a dealer struggles or you may not. They will often be slow in paying before they close down. You should not offer them delayed payment terms, extended credit, or ship before checks are cleared. Set-up the account as credit card payment only. You can offer to take back unsold merchandise or send them to a collections agent.

Distributors going bankrupt

The same rules apply to international distributors. Only offer terms to your long standing customers you trust. Demand payment in advance of shipments. If a distributor goes bankrupt and owes you money do not expect to see the product or the money owed. You may have to write off the loss and move on. Make sure to protect yourself from the beginning.

The best case is to work on hiring a replacement distributor as soon as possible to reduce the lost sales in that market. It is possible to have a new distributor take over a territory and buy the stock from the bankrupt distributor.

Failing Competitors

A failing competitor can lead to big discounts in your market segment. If another brand is dumping product in the market you need to be ready with a marketing campaign, increased dealer support, and maybe some discounts to keep your product selling. You may need to reduce your factory orders until the market's extra inventory clears.

Currency exchange problems

A rapid or dramatic change in currency exchange rates can have a negative impact on your company. If your purchasing currency falls, the factory may demand a price increase. Your distributors may ask you for discounts if their home currency falls.

Currency exchange rates will effect your competitors the same as they effect you. Your goal should be to maintain your market share until the currency stabilizes. If your purchase currency increases, don't be so fast to demand increases from your factories as they will be asking for payments just as quickly if the change moves against you.

A currency exchange forward contract can be purchased to guarantee rates, but these are bets with or against the currency markets. These contracts should be viewed very carefully.

Product liability for shoes

As a company selling shoes you have legal obligations to consider so you don't end up in a situation where you could face litigation. Anyone who designs, manufactures, and sells a product must consider the possibility of product liability claims. Legal claims can be serious concern in your shoe business. If you are faced with a claim, the court costs and fines could close down your small company.

In 2012, the average amount awarded by a jury in a product liability case was more than $3.4 million. Now that we understand the potential size of the concern we will review the steps to help protect your company.

The first thing to know and take account of is that most defects in shoes fall under the part of the law governed by strict liability. When you design shoes, have them made by a third party, and offer them for sale, you are responsible for any defects.

This is the case whether you are at fault in allowing the defect to arise or not. Because you are the manufacturer and distributor, you are responsible for the shoes that you sell. In the United States, the protection offered to consumers is very high. The authorities want to ensure that US customers aren't exposed to dangerous goods, so the legislation is tough on the party responsible for bringing the product to market.

The word 'defect' can cover different types of issues and the way these can potentially affect your customers.

A design defect arises from the way shoes are planned out and developed. If there is something in the design of your shoe that is defective, then the law defines this as a design defect and you are strictly liable. For example, if the sole of the shoe is attached to the upper by means of a sharp staple that can come loose and cause injury, then you have a design defect on your hands. This means that every pair of shoes you deliver to your customers can potentially cause harm.

This is a nightmare situation and can cause major problems for any fledgling shoe company. You need to ensure that your part in the design process is clearly defined and you can rely on your manufacturer to deliver something safe. Remember, we have looked at sourcing manufacturers from overseas, they need to know how important this is when producing your shoes. Without this level of control and input you could lose everything you put into your company.

A manufacturing defect differs from a design defect. A manufacturing defect can happen if something goes wrong during the assembly process in the factory. For instance, if the wrong temperature is used to set the glue and the uppers peel away from the soles.

This means that a particular batch of shoes has been made incorrectly and may cause problems for your customers. Having strict quality control systems in place insures that you will not have these issues.

A third type of defect that can potentially cause problems is known as a marketing defect. This liability can be the result of how you advertise and describe your product to the public. Marketing defects are often linked to dangerous products such as chemicals, household machinery, or power tools but can potentially affect your shoe business too.

Do you have adequate warnings about the risks of use in your product marketing and literature? Failure to give adequate warnings is considered a defect. This can lead you down the road to a product liability claim.

As the seller of shoes you have a responsibility to your customers on many levels. You have legal obligations, but you also have moral and business obligations too. You don't want or need the negative publicity that could surround a defect in your shoes. Use caution when you design, manufacture and market your shoes. It is important to keep a strong relationship with your customers and the market as a whole. This can be done in a number of ways.

Test your shoes at every stage of the design and manufacturing process. This will help you have greater control of the way they are put together. This may cost you at the onset but will deter the costs of potential claims later on.

Indemnify yourself wherever you can with the people who make the product for you. Look to include that they take financial responsibility for the manufacturing and design should anything go wrong.

Liability insurance is available to your company so that you are covered in the event of a claim. It will cover you for the parts of the process that you are involved in. This insurance is applicable to all parties involved in the process.

If you take the right steps to insure that you design, manufacture, and sell products of a high quality, then you greatly lessen the chance that you will have any defects. This can save the reputation of your company, your customers' safety, and shield you from unnecessary lawsuits and claims.

TERMS YOU SHOULD KNOW

Amortize
To gradually pay off a large expense with installments or periodic payments. In this case, the factory may agree to distribute the cost of the tooling by adding a small charge to each pair of shoes. For example, a $10,000 tooling bill may be amortized, or paid off, by adding $.50 to the first 20,000 pairs sold.

Articles of Organization
When forming a limited liability company (LLC), you are required to file an " articles of organization" document with the state or local government. Articles of organization are similar to articles of incorporation needed to legally create and run a corporation.

At Once Orders
Orders placed by dealers for product without advance notice and with the expectation that the warehouse will have the product in stock for immediate shipping. While every order is a good order, you may not have inventory available to meet and fill "at once orders". You may decide to order 15% above pre-bookings, or you may find that cancellations of pre-booked orders will give you enough merchandise to meet any at once orders.

Bill of Lading (B/L or BoL)
The bill of lading is a document issued by a carrier (or his agent) to acknowledge receipt of a shipment of cargo. A bill of lading is negotiable and serves three main functions: the acknowledgment that the goods have been loaded, the terms of the contract of carriage, and the title for the goods.

Board of Equalization (BOE)
The BOE is a public agency in California that is responsible for tax administration and collecting various fees for specific state programs.

Booking Window
The time period from when salesmen get their samples until the first order is placed to the factory. Approximately 60 days depending on the production schedule.

Bounties
Offering your sales reps a little extra money, or a bounty, for opening new accounts is a great way to expand your dealer network. Maybe an extra $100 or $200 per door will be enough to motivate your reps to drive to the next town or make a few extra calls to open some new accounts.

Brannock™ Device

You've seen this tool in every shoe store. This is the standard for measuring feet. If you're developing footwear, you must have a Brannock device in your office. When a tester says a shoe fits loose or tight the first thing you need to do is measure their feet against this device. The Brannock device will give you accurate length and width measurements. Remember to measure both the left and the right foot!

Colorways

The color and material combination for a shoe. A single model of a shoe may be available in many colorways.

Consignee

The buyer or person who is responsible for the receipt of the shipment. Usually the receiver of the shipment.

Consolidation

Combining or uniting multiple items into a bundle or a shipment to make the best use of space.

Containers or Shipping Containers, Ocean Containers

A 40 foot long ocean container is the same as a 40 foot trailer on a semi truck. The standard container for ocean freight is 40 feet x 8 feet x 8 feet and holds about 5,000 pairs of shoes. Top selling shoes are ordered by the full container load. There is also a half size (20 footer), and an extra large 40 foot high cube (about 1 foot taller than the standard 40 foot).

Currency Forward Contract

A binding contract in the foreign exchange market that locks in the exchange rate for the purchase or sale on a future date. A currency forward is essentially a hedging tool that does not involve any upfront payment.

Design Brief

A written description for any new product that details what you are going to make, why you are going to make it, and for whom you are making it. It may include the price point, suggested materials, notes from a client meeting, etc. An effective design brief is critical in ensuring a successful project.

Designers or Shoe Designers

The shoe designer is the person who draws the shoes. Picking color trends and knowing what is cool are critical skills for any designer. Designers also work with developers to make the prototypes. Depending on whom you ask, this may be the easiest part or the hardest part of making shoes. To be a shoe designer, art school is helpful and a degree in industrial design or product design is a great place to start.

Design Proposal

Summarizes what the client is looking for and the solutions the designer will offer. The proposal describes what steps the project will entail in terms of design time, number of designs, colorways, design budget, product costing, and who to contact.

Developers or Shoe Developers

The shoe developer's job is to take a drawing and make it into a real shoe that is comfortable for someone to wear. The shoe developer is responsible for writing the technical specifications, checking the blue prints, and communicating with the shoe factory. Developers are the shoe prototype engineers and the schedule keepers. To be a shoe developer you may start as a designer, an intern, or assistant. Be ready to travel!

Ex-Works Price

The purchase term Ex-Works means the price quoted does not include any shipping. The buyer is responsible for collecting the product from the factory. All transportation costs and risks are thus assumed by the buyer.

Fictitious Name

Trade Name, or "Doing Business As" (DBA) name. The operating name of a company, as opposed to the legal name of the company. In a sole proprietorship or partnership you may choose a DBA, trade name, or fictitious business name that is different from your personal name. You may be required by your county, city, or state to register your fictitious name. Registration procedures vary. Some states require a fictitious name ad in a local newspaper. The cost for filing ranges from $10-$100. Your local bank may also require a fictitious name certificate to open a business account for you.

Free On Board (FOB):

The purchase term free on board refers to the point in which a buyer accepts ownership of purchased goods. Most of the time in South China, the shoe price will be stated as FOB Yantian. Yantian is the nearest freight harbor. The seller is responsible for the inland trucking of the goods to the freight terminal and then the buyer is responsible for all costs and transportation from that point forward. (See Ex-Works Price)

Freight Forwarding
A company that organizes shipments for individuals or corporations to get goods from the manufacturer to the customer or final point of distribution.

Grade
Grade refers to the quality of the item. A-grade is good. B-grade has small flaws and can be sold at a discount. C-Grade cannot be sold and must be destroyed or possibly repaired.

Grading or Size Grade
The word is a noun and a verb and is the process of making all the different shoe pattern sizes necessary in a size run. The sample size, or development size, is usually a men's 9 or a women's 7. Once the sample size shoe is confirmed, the extreme sizes are made, size 5 and size 12. Lastly, all the sizes in between are graded. The pattern grading is done by computer and checked by the pattern master.

Gross Sales
Gross sales are the total of all sales transactions. The gross sales amount has no deductions for sales allowances, discounts or returns.

Keystone
Any item selling at twice the price for which it was bought or produced is said to have a keystone mark-up.

Labor Overhead and Profit (LOP)
LOP is a critical part of the shoe factory's price for a shoe. The factory will add up all the material costs then add on the labor rate, overhead, and profit. The LOP for a shoe can be 30% of the total cost for a shoe. Factories may add a fixed percentage to the material cost to cover the LOP. Other factories may add a fixed flat fee.

Letter of Credit (LC)
Letter of credit is a payment term for a document between banks (usually in different countries), assuring the seller they will get paid as long as agreed upon conditions have been met. The LC is common in international trade.

Limited Liability Company (LLC)
A limited liability company (LLC) is a private limited company. It is a business structure that combines the pass-through taxation of a partnership or sole proprietorship with the limited liability of a corporation. An LLC is not a corporation; it is a legal form of a company that provides limited liability to its owners or "members." LLCs do not need to be organized for profit and are specific to the United States.

Line Planning
The schedule and allocation of orders to individual production lines. The planning takes into account which styles each line can manufacture, when it will be loaded to the line, how many pieces will be made, and when the style will be completed.

Made to Order (MTO)
Special Make Up (SMU)
Made to Order (MTO) or Special Make Up (SMU) is a special production run of shoes. The MTO/SMU shoes can be customized for a specific shoe store or international distributor. Usually a special color or material treatment is involved. The MTO product manager will work closely with the sales managers, product line managers, sales reps and designers to create the new products. MTO projects can be brought to market quickly as there is no selling or booking period required. Once the design is confirmed the order can be placed to the factory.

Manufacturer Suggest Retail Price (MSRP) or List Price
The price at which an item is sold to the public and upon which discounts are computed. Also called net price.

Mark Down Allowance
A dealer may demand some money to cover the cost of marking down a slow selling product for sale.

Market Share
The portion of a market controlled by a particular company or product. 50% share means half of the shoes sold into a market are from one company.

Merchandise Assortment Planning (MAP)
Merchandise Assortment planning is the process to determine what and how much should be carried in a merchandise category, group or department.

Minimum Advertised Price (MAP)
The minimum dollar amount that resellers agree not to advertise an item below. This amount is agreed upon between the suppliers and the retailers.

Minimum Order Quantity (MOQ)
Shoe factories and material makers often have an MOQ. This is based on dye lot size or machine operation. For example, a special mesh may require machine set-up time, so the MOQ may be 500 meters. To dye a stock material may require a MOQ of 50 meters. For suede shoes, the small

dye drum load is 1000 sq. feet of leather. It takes approximately 2 feet of sueded leather to make a basic shoe, so the factory may request a minimum order quantity of 500 pairs.

New Dealer Discount
Offering a new account a small discount is a simple way to help your company and sales reps open new doors. You can also offer new dealers a buy back plan if the shoes don't sell through.

Non-Disclosure Agreement (NDA)
An NDA is a confidential agreement and contract between parties to protect any type of confidential and proprietary information or trade secrets. Also known as a confidentiality agreement (CA), confidential disclosure agreement (CDA), proprietary information agreement (PIA), or secrecy agreement (SA). It is a contract through which the parties agree not to disclose information covered by the agreement. The NDA protects non-public business information.

Some employment contracts or severance agreements will ask an employee to sign an NDA or NDA-like agreement. This may restrict the employees' use and communication of company-owned confidential information.

On Wheels
An on wheels agreement will allow the dealer to send the merchandise back at full price if it does not sell. This allows the dealer to try your product with less risk.

Order Fulfillment
Order fulfillment involves the picking, packing, and shipping of inventory in the warehouse. Basically, a warehouse stores products until orders come in, then picks items out of available inventory (picking), appropriately packages them (packing), and sends them on their way to the designated business or customer (shipping).

Pantone TM Colors, Pantone Chips and Pantone Books
Pantone Inc. is a corporation headquartered in Carlstadt, New Jersey. The company is famous for its Pantone Matching System (PMS), a proprietary color system used in many industries. Different manufacturers in different locations can all refer to the Pantone system to make sure colors match.

Partnership
A single business in which two or more individuals share ownership, management, and profit or loss according to their partnership agreement terms.

Pattern
The design of the shoes' cut parts. The shoe pattern is fitted to the last. Just like in clothing, the designer and developers often make pattern corrections when creating a new shoe.

Pattern Cutting
Patterns are produced for the uppers, linings, insoles, heels, soles, stiffeners, backers, and toe puffs. The lasting allowance is added. The materials used in making the shoes are cut from these working patterns.

Pattern Maker or Pattern Master
The master technician that transforms the 2D drawing into a 3D pattern that fits the specified last. The designer draws the shoe and the pattern maker makes it into a real 3D shoe. A good pattern maker can improve your design while a rookie pattern maker can really make a mess of your design!

Point of Purchase (P.O.P.)
The place where sales are made. P.O.P. can be a large area like a mall or market or as small as the area for a display at the cash register where the consumer, money, and product all come together. Last minute impulse buys from point of purchase displays often happen at the cash register.

Pre-Booking
The sale of product in advance of production. Pre-booking allows the shoe brand to better plan their production numbers in advance. The more pre-books the better! Some shoe companies may only accept pre-booked orders so they can avoid making and holding extra inventory, but this can also result in lost sales.

Pre-booking Incentives
Pre-bookings are critical to your new shoe company! To encourage your dealers to pre-book you can offer them an incentive. A discount of a few percentage points off the cost will help persuade your dealer to pre-book. Without pre-bookings it's nearly impossible to produce the correct amount of each product. Don't give away all your profit, but do what you can to get pre-book orders. The pre-booking discount to your dealer will have a deadline of 90 or 120 days before store delivery.

Price point
The suggested retail price for which an item will be sold and determined to compete with prices of other products.

Product Manager or Product Line Manager

The product manager or "PM" is the person that sets the designer and developer in motion. It's the PM's job to figure out what to make. The PM will tell the designer what kind of shoe to make. The PM's responsibility is to work with the sales team and customers to find out what they need. The PM is also tasked with looking forward. What will people need next year? What color shoes will be trending? Experience in retail or sales is a big help. Designers and developers are often promoted to this position. A marketing degree will help.

Product Range or Product Line

A collection of products sold by the same manufacturer that are aimed at different segments of the market. Some may be designed to attract teenagers while others may focus on older customers.

Pullover

A prototype sample shoe upper for checking the pattern and fit. The pullover will not be made with the correct color materials, it will be made with any overstock color. During the development phase, you may make several pullovers to get the pattern correct. You will also see pullovers made for each size during the pre-production phase. The pullover will also be sent to the outsole factory to insure the shoe bottom will fit correctly.

Rainbow Line

A sample line where every colorway is presented.

Representation Discounts

If you find your dealers are just buying one or two items you can help drive sales to your other models by offering a representation discount. For example, if a dealer buys 5 models they can get 5% off.

Retail Price

The retail price is the price you pay in the shoe store for a pair of shoes.

SS-4

A form from the IRS that is used to apply for an employer identification number (EIN) which is necessary for tax filing purposes.

Sales Rate

Dealers have inventory tracking software to monitor the sales rate of their stock of shoes. This measures the sales of goods over a specific time period. An organized dealer will have a report showing the rate of sale for your products against other products in the same category.

Sales Representative and Sub Rep

Selling shoes is a great way to get involved. The sales representatives know first hand what customers are looking for. The sales force is exposed to many aspects of the shoe trade. An active sales rep can help shape the product line. A sales rep can get promoted to a product line manager position.

Sub reps work for a sales rep (or a few different sales reps) and may sell only one or two of each sales rep's lines. The sub rep may need to share a portion of their commission check with the sales rep. The sub rep may also act as the technical sales rep. The sales rep makes the sale to the footwear buyer while the sub rep trains the retail floor staff.

Sample Coordinator

A busy development office will have hundreds of shoes coming and going. The sample coordinator is the traffic cop that tracks where the shoes are. Are the samples still in China? When is the factory going to ship them? Does FedEx need more paperwork to manage the import? The sample coordinator position is a great entry-level position for learning the operations of shoe development and shoe design.

Sample size Men's 9 and Women's 7

These sizes are well proportioned and look the best for sales presentations and print ads. Size 9 and 7 are also good sizes to use for costing. The larger sizes will consume more material but the smaller sizes will consume less. 9 and 7 are the fair average.

Scope of Project

The initial task necessary when beginning a new project is to define the scope of the project. This outlines all the requirements and work that needs to be done to complete the project.

Selling In

When dealers or stores have bought shoes, you have "sold them in." A good sell in needs to be followed by selling through.

Sell Through

Shoes available to purchase in a store "sell through" when a customer buys them. Poor or slow sell through is a bad thing. Sell through is often measured in % of sales per week. 30% per week is good, 5% per week means something is wrong.

Shell Pattern
The shoe pattern fit on the surface of the last without any detail. The designer may draw on the shell pattern.

Shoe Design Brief
The shoe design brief contains all the critical information for the footwear designer to get started with the design. It will advise who the shoe is for, what sport the shoe will be used for, what the final shoe will cost, what countries it will ship to, etc.

Shoe Master Carton
The master carton or case pack for production shoes is usually a 10 or 12-pack depending on the size of the shoe and the shoes' inner box. In the master carton, the inner boxes will be arranged so the warehouse worker can easily see the shoe box end labels for size and color information.

Shoe Parts Cutting
Traditionally called 'clicking' or 'clicker cutting.' This simply implies the cutting of shoe materials. There is an art to cutting leather due to the nature of the material's grain. The cutting is done with a cutting die.

Stock Keeping Units (SKU)
A unique model/style/colorway/size. Commonly used to refer to a unique colorway. For example, if there are 2 models each with 5 colorways, there are 10 SKUs total.

Strengths Weaknesses Opportunities and Threats (SWOT)
SWOT stands for strengths, weaknesses, opportunities and threats. It is an analytical framework that can help your company assess what it can and cannot do, as well as its potential opportunities and risks.

Style Master
The style master is a customizable software program which holds all the information related to your project including images, colors, sizes, raw material inventory, production specs, tracking, cost sheets, import documents and more. A good style master is imperative to improve efficiency and organization.

Supply Chain
The network of all the individuals, companies, resources, and activities involved in the production and distribution of a product from the design, to the manufacturing, and through to the delivery to the end user.

T/T Payment
T/T stands for telegraphic transfer. T/T payments are a cheap and fast way of transferring money overseas through most banks. T/T bank transfers are one of the simplest forms of international transfers. In traditional international trade, it's risky for buyers to pay using bank transfers because their money goes into the suppliers' bank account directly – before they are able to receive their order. For companies with a long running record of trust, the T/T is fast and easy.

Try On
Try on is the initial feeling when a shoe is tested in-store. A very soft upper and footbed can give a shoe a very good try-on but will quickly flatten or compress. Also called "in store feel." The footbed and lining can make or break the try on feeling.

Volume Discounts
A volume discount is a great way to reward your best customers and give your smaller accounts a "stretch goal." You can base your volume discount on the number of pairs bought, or on the dollar amount they spend. For example, a $5,000 account may receive a 2% discount and a $10,000 account may receive a 5% discount.

Wholesale Price
The wholesale price of an item is what a shoe store pays to buy an item from the shoebrand. The wholesale price is approximately 50% of the retail price. A big store may negotiate a discount of a few %. When you see a shoe on sale for 50% off, the shoe store is just trying to break even.

Width or Shoe Width
The width of a shoe is measured in letters such as AAA, AA, A, B, C, D, E, EE, EEE, EEEE, 4A, 3A, 2A, A, B, C, D, E, 2E, 3E, 4E, 5E, 6E, or N (narrow), M (medium), R (regular), or W (wide). These letters refer to the width of the shoe as measured at the ball of the foot.

SAMPLE DOCUMENTS

In order to start your new company there are many necessary forms for local permits and tax registration. Most forms can be downloaded from the web or filled out online. Some forms will need to be picked up from your local government office. It's always a good idea to plan ahead and know what information will be required before you set out.

Form **SS-4**
(Rev. January 2010)
Department of the Treasury
Internal Revenue Service

Application for Employer Identification Number

(For use by employers, corporations, partnerships, trusts, estates, churches, government agencies, Indian tribal entities, certain individuals, and others.)

⊠ **See separate instructions for each line.** ⊠ **Keep a copy for your records.**

OMB No. 1545-0003

EIN

Type or print clearly.

1	Legal name of entity (or individual) for whom the EIN is being requested	
2	Trade name of business (if different from name on line 1)	**3** Executor, administrator, trustee, "care of" name
4a	Mailing address (room, apt., suite no. and street, or P.O. box)	**5a** Street address (if different) (Do not enter a P.O. box.)
4b	City, state, and ZIP code (if foreign, see instructions)	**5b** City, state, and ZIP code (if foreign, see instructions)
6	County and state where principal business is located	
7a	Name of responsible party	**7b** SSN, ITIN, or EIN

8a Is this application for a limited liability company (LLC) (or a foreign equivalent)? . . . . ☐ Yes ☐ No

8b If 8a is "Yes," enter the number of LLC members . . . . . ⊠

8c If 8a is "Yes," was the LLC organized in the United States? . . . . ☐ Yes ☐ No

9a **Type of entity** (check only one box). **Caution.** If 8a is "Yes," see the instructions for the correct box to check.

☐ Sole proprietor (SSN) _____
☐ Partnership
☐ Corporation (enter form number to be filed) ⊠ _____
☐ Personal service corporation
☐ Church or church-controlled organization
☐ Other nonprofit organization (specify) ⊠ _____
☐ Other (specify) ⊠

☐ Estate (SSN of decedent) _____
☐ Plan administrator (TIN) _____
☐ Trust (TIN of grantor) _____
☐ National Guard   ☐ State/local government
☐ Farmers' cooperative ☐ Federal government/military
☐ REMIC   ☐ Indian tribal governments/enterprises
Group Exemption Number (GEN) if any ⊠

9b If a corporation, name the state or foreign country (if applicable) where incorporated

State	Foreign country

10 **Reason for applying** (check only one box)

☐ Started new business (specify type) ⊠ _____
☐ Hired employees (Check the box and see line 13.)
☐ Compliance with IRS withholding regulations
☐ Other (specify) ⊠

☐ Banking purpose (specify purpose) ⊠ _____
☐ Changed type of organization (specify new type) ⊠ _____
☐ Purchased going business
☐ Created a trust (specify type) ⊠ _____
☐ Created a pension plan (specify type) ⊠ _____

11 Date business started or acquired (month, day, year). See instructions.

12 Closing month of accounting year

13 Highest number of employees expected in the next 12 months (enter -0- if none).

If no employees expected, skip line 14.

Agricultural	Household	Other

14 If you expect your employment tax liability to be $1,000 or less in a full calendar year **and** want to file Form 944 annually instead of Forms 941 quarterly, check here. (Your employment tax liability generally will be $1,000 or less if you expect to pay $4,000 or less in total wages.) If you do not check this box, you must file Form 941 for every quarter. ☐

15 First date wages or annuities were paid (month, day, year). **Note.** If applicant is a withholding agent, enter date income will first be paid to nonresident alien (month, day, year) . . . . ⊠

16 Check **one** box that best describes the principal activity of your business.

☐ Construction ☐ Rental & leasing ☐ Transportation & warehousing ☐ Health care & social assistance ☐ Wholesale-agent/broker
☐ Real estate   ☐ Manufacturing   ☐ Finance & insurance   ☐ Accommodation & food service ☐ Wholesale-other ☐ Retail
                                                                      ☐ Other (specify)

17 Indicate principal line of merchandise sold, specific construction work done, products produced, or services provided.

18 Has the applicant entity shown on line 1 ever applied for and received an EIN? ☐ Yes ☐ No
If "Yes," write previous EIN here ⊠

Third Party Designee	Complete this section if you want to authorize the named individual to receive the entity's EIN and answer questions about the completion of this form.	
	Designee's name	Designee's telephone number (include area code) ( )
	Address and ZIP code	Designee's fax number (include area code) ( )

Under penalties of perjury, I declare that I have examined this application, and to the best of my knowledge and belief, it is true, correct, and complete.

Name and title (type or print clearly) ⊠

Applicant's telephone number (include area code) ( )

Applicant's fax number (include area code) ( )

Signature ⊠   Date ⊠

For Privacy Act and Paperwork Reduction Act Notice, see separate instructions.   Cat. No. 16055N   Form **SS-4** (Rev. 1-2010)

APPLICATION FOR SELLER'S PERMIT

1. PERMIT TYPE: (check one) ☐ Regular ☐ Temporary

FOR BOE USE ONLY

2. TYPE OF OWNERSHIP (check one)   * Must provide partnership agreement

☐ Sole Owner   ☐ Married Co-ownership
☐ Corporation   ☐ Limited Liability Company (LLC)
☐ General Partnership   ☐ Unincorporated Business Trust
☐ Limited Partnership (LP)*   ☐ Limited Liability Partnership (LLP)*
                                                (Registered to practice law, accounting or architecture)
☐ Registered Domestic Partnership
☐ Other (describe) _____

TAX	IND	OFFICE	PERMIT NUMBER
S			

NAICS CODE | BUS CODE | A.C.C. | REPORTING BASIS | TAX AREA CODE

PROCESSED BY | PERMIT ISSUE DATE | RETURN TYPE ☐ (1) 401-A ☐ (2) 401-EZ

___ / ___ / ___ | VERIFICATION ☐ DL ☐ PA ☐ Other

3. NAME OF SOLE OWNER, CORPORATION, LLC, PARTNERSHIP, OR TRUST

4. STATE OF INCORPORATION OR ORGANIZATION

5. BUSINESS TRADE NAME/"DOING BUSINESS AS" [DBA] (if any)

6. DATE YOU WILL BEGIN BUSINESS ACTIVITIES (month, day, and year)

7. CORPORATE, LLC, LLP OR LP NUMBER FROM CALIFORNIA SECRETARY OF STATE

8. FEDERAL EMPLOYER IDENTIFICATION NUMBER (FEIN)

CHECK ONE ☐ Owner/Co-Owners ☐ Partners ☐ Registered Domestic Partners ☐ Corp. Officers ☐ LLC Officers/Managers/Members ☐ Trustees/Beneficiaries

Use additional sheets to include information for more than three individuals.

9. FULL NAME (first, middle, last)

10. TITLE

11. SOCIAL SECURITY NUMBER (corporate officers excluded)

12. DRIVER LICENSE NUMBER (attach copy)

13. HOME ADDRESS (street, city, state, zip code)

14. HOME TELEPHONE NUMBER
(   )

15. NAME OF A PERSONAL REFERENCE NOT LIVING WITH YOU   **16. ADDRESS** (street, city, state, zip code)

17. REFERENCE TELEPHONE NUMBER
(   )

18. FULL NAME OF ADDITIONAL PARTNER, OFFICER, OR MEMBER (first, middle, last)

19. TITLE

20. SOCIAL SECURITY NUMBER (corporate officers excluded)

21. DRIVER LICENSE NUMBER (attach copy)

22. HOME ADDRESS (street, city, state, zip code)

23. HOME TELEPHONE NUMBER
(   )

24. NAME OF A PERSONAL REFERENCE NOT LIVING WITH YOU   **25. ADDRESS** (street, city, state, zip code)

26. REFERENCE TELEPHONE NUMBER
(   )

27. FULL NAME OF ADDITIONAL PARTNER, OFFICER, OR MEMBER (first, middle, last)

28. TITLE

29. SOCIAL SECURITY NUMBER (corporate officers excluded)

30. DRIVER LICENSE NUMBER (attach copy)

31. HOME ADDRESS (street, city, state, zip code)

32. HOME TELEPHONE NUMBER
(   )

33. NAME OF A PERSONAL REFERENCE NOT LIVING WITH YOU   **34. ADDRESS** (street, city, state, zip code)

35. REFERENCE TELEPHONE NUMBER
(   )

36. TYPE OF BUSINESS (check one that best describes your business)
☐ Retail ☐ Wholesale ☐ Mfg. ☐ Repair ☐ Service ☐ Construction Contractor ☐ Leasing

37. NUMBER OF SELLING LOCATIONS (if 2 or more, see Item No. 66)

38. WHAT ITEMS WILL YOU SELL?

39. CHECK ONE
☐ Full Time ☐ Part Time

40. BUSINESS ADDRESS (street, city, state, zip code) [do not list P.O. Box or mailing service]

41. BUSINESS TELEPHONE NUMBER
(   )

42. MAILING ADDRESS (street, city, state, zip code) [if different from business address]

43. BUSINESS FAX NUMBER
(   )

44. BUSINESS EMAIL ADDRESS

45. BUSINESS WEBSITE ADDRESS
WWW.

46. DO YOU MAKE INTERNET SALES?
☐ Yes ☐ No

47. NAME OF BUSINESS LANDLORD

48. LANDLORD ADDRESS (street, city, state, zip code)

49. LANDLORD TELEPHONE NUMBER
(   )

50. PROJECTED MONTHLY GROSS SALES
$

51. PROJECTED MONTHLY TAXABLE SALES
$

52. ALCOHOLIC BEVERAGE CONTROL LICENSE NUMBER (if applicable)
___ ___ - ___ ___ ___ ___ ___ ___

53. SELLING NEW TIRES AT RETAIL?
☐ Yes ☐ No

54. SELLING COVERED ELECTRONIC DEVICES?
☐ Yes ☐ No

55. SELLING TOBACCO AT RETAIL?
☐ Yes ☐ No

(continued on reverse)

56. NAME OF PERSON MAINTAINING YOUR RECORDS	57 ADDRESS (street, city, state, zip code)	58. TELEPHONE NUMBER ( )
59. NAME OF BANK OR OTHER FINANCIAL INSTITUTION (note whether business or personal)		60. BANK BRANCH LOCATION
61. NAME OF MERCHANT CREDIT CARD PROCESSOR (if you accept credit cards)		62. MERCHANT CARD ACCOUNT NUMBER
63. NAMES OF MAJOR CALIFORNIA-BASED SUPPLIERS	64 ADDRESSES (street, city, state, zip code)	65 PRODUCTS PURCHASED

ADDITIONAL SELLING LOCATIONS   (List All Other Selling Locations)

66. PHYSICAL LOCATION OR STREET ADDRESS (attach separate list, if required)

OWNERSHIP AND ORGANIZATIONAL CHANGES   (Do Not Complete for Temporary Permits)

67. ARE YOU BUYING AN EXISTING BUSINESS?

☐ Yes   ☐ No   If yes, complete items 70 through 74.

68. ARE YOU CHANGING FROM ONE TYPE OF BUSINESS ORGANIZATION TO ANOTHER (FOR EXAMPLE, FROM A SOLE OWNER TO A CORPORATION OR FROM A PARTNERSHIP TO A LIMITED LIABILITY COMPANY, ETC.)?

☐ Yes   ☐ No   If yes, complete items 70 and 71.

69. OTHER OWNERSHIP CHANGES (please describe) :

70. FORMER OWNER'S NAME	71 SELLER'S PERMIT NUMBER
72. PURCHASE PRICE $	73. VALUE OF FIXTURES & EQUIPMENT $

74. IF AN ESCROW COMPANY IS REQUESTING A TAX CLEARANCE ON YOUR BEHALF, PLEASE LIST THEIR NAME, ADDRESS, TELEPHONE NUMBER, AND THE ESCROW NUMBER

TEMPORARY PERMIT EVENT INFORMATION

75. PERIOD OF SALES FROM: ___ / ___ / ___ THROUGH: ___ / ___ / ___	76. ESTIMATED EVENT SALES $	77. SPACE RENTAL COST (if any) $	78. ADMISSION CHARGED? ☐ Yes ☐ No
79. ORGANIZER OR PROMOTER OF EVENT (if any)	80. ADDRESS (street, city, state, zip code)	81. TELEPHONE NUMBER ( )	

82. ADDRESS OF EVENT (If more than one, use line 66, above. Attach separate list, if required.)

CERTIFICATION

All Corporate Officers, LLC Managing Members, Partners, or Owners must sign below.
I am duly authorized to sign the application and certify that the statements made are correct to the best of my knowledge and belief.
I also represent and acknowledge that the applicant will be engaged in or conduct business as a seller of tangible personal property.

NAME (typed or printed)	SIGNATURE	DATE
NAME (typed or printed)	SIGNATURE	DATE
NAME (typed or printed)	SIGNATURE	DATE

FOR BOE USE ONLY

SECURITY REVIEW	FORMS	PUBLICATIONS
☐ BOE-598 ($ _____) or ☐ BOE-1009	☐ BOE-8 ☐ BOE-400-Y	☐ PUB 73 ☐ PUB DE 44
REQUIRED BY APPROVED BY	☐ BOE-162 ☐ BOE-519	
	☐ BOE-467 ☐ BOE-1241-D	
	REGULATIONS	RETURNS
	☐ REG. 1668 ☐ REG. 1698	
	☐ REG. 1700 ☐ _____	

1600 PACIFIC HIGHWAY, SUITE 260, SAN DIEGO, CA 92101
P.O. BOX 121750, SAN DIEGO, CA 92112-1750
(619) 237-0502
Return Mailing Address:

Name:_____

Address:_____

_____
City   State   Zip Code

Ernest J. Dronenburg, Jr.
County of San Diego
Recorder/County Clerk
www.sdarcc.com

IN PERSON

THIS SPACE FOR USE OF RECORDER/COUNTY CLERK

FICTITIOUS BUSINESS NAME STATEMENT

TYPE OF FILING AND FILING FEE (Check one)
☒ Original- $42.00 (FOR ORIGINAL FILING WITH ONE BUSINESS NAME ON STATEMENT)
☒ Renewal- $42.00 (NO CHANGES IN THE FACTS FROM ORIGINAL FILING)
  EACH ADDITIONAL COPY IS $2.00 AND EACH ADDITIONAL CERTIFIED COPY IS $3.00
  $5.00- EACH ADDITIONAL OWNER IN EXCESS OF ONE OWNER
  $5.00- EACH ADDITIONAL BUSINESS NAME FILED ON SAME STATEMENT, DOING BUSINESS AT SAME LOCATION.

FOR OFFICIAL USE ONLY
TYPE OF IDENTIFICATION PROVIDED: [ ] REG [ ] AGENT
[ ] DRIVER'S LICENSE   [ ] MILITARY ID   [ ] ACK
[ ] PASSPORT   [ ] OTHER_____

(1) FICTITIOUS BUSINESS NAME(S):   PLEASE NOTE: YOU WILL BE REQUIRED TO PRESENT A VALID PHOTO ID TO FILE THIS STATEMENT IN PERSON.

a._____

b._____
                    PRINT FICTITIOUS BUSINESS NAME(S)

(2) LOCATED AT: _____ / _____ / _____ / _____ / _____
          PHYSICAL BUSINESS ADDRESS (No P.O. BOXES OR POSTAL FACILITIES)   CITY   STATE   COUNTY   ZIP Code

   MAILING ADDRESS:_____

(3) REGISTRANT INFORMATION: (Individual, Corp., LLC, Gen. Partner, etc.)

a._____
   If individual-spell out first and last name

   _____
   Residence Address, if Corp. or LLC enter physical address (No P.O. BOXES OR POSTAL FACILITIES)   City   State   Zip Code

   _____
   If Corporation or LLC – Print State of Incorporation/Organization

b._____
   If individual-spell out first and last name

   _____
   Residence Address, if Corp. or LLC enter physical address (No P.O. BOXES OR POSTAL FACILITIES)   City   State   Zip Code

   _____
   If Corporation or LLC – Print State of Incorporation/Organization

(4)   THIS BUSINESS IS CONDUCTED BY: (Check one)

☐ A. An Individual   ☐ E. Joint Venture   ☐ I. A Limited Liability Company
☐ B. A Married Couple   ☐ F. A Corporation   ☐ J. Limited Liability Partnership
☐ C. A General Partnership   ☐ G. A Trust   ☐ K. An Unincorporated Association-Other than a
☐ D. A Limited Partnership   ☐ H. Co-Partners   ☐ L. State or Local Registered Domestic Partners

(5) THE FIRST DAY OF BUSINESS WAS: _____/_____/_____ OR IF NOT STARTED YET, CHECK HERE ☐ NOT APPLICABLE

I declare that all information in this statement is true and correct. (A registrant who declares as true any material matter pursuant to Section 17913 of the Business and Professions code that the registrant knows to be false is guilty of a misdemeanor punishable by a fine not to exceed one thousand dollars ($1,000).)

(6) Signature _____
          (Only one is required)

   Typed or Printed Name _____

   Title of Officer, if Limited Liability Company/Corporation_____
          The form must be legible – no erasures, whiteouts, strikeovers acceptable if accompanied with initials.
          THIS STATEMENT WAS FILED WITH THE RECORDER/COUNTY CLERK OF SAN DIEGO COUNTY AS INDICATED BY THE FILE STAMP ABOVE.

NOTICE: IN ACCORDANCE WITH SUBDIVISION (a) OF SECTION 17920, A FICTITIOUS NAME STATEMENT GENERALLY EXPIRES AT THE END OF FIVE YEARS (5) FROM THE DATE ON WHICH IT WAS FILED IN THE OFFICE OF THE COUNTY CLERK, EXCEPT, AS PROVIDED IN SUBDIVISION (b) OF SECTION 17920, WHERE IT EXPIRES 40 DAYS AFTER ANY CHANGE IN THE FACTS SET FORTH IN THE STATEMENT PURSUANT TO SECTION 17913 OTHER THAN A CHANGE IN THE RESIDENCE ADDRESS OF A REGISTERED OWNER. A NEW FICTITIOUS BUSINESS NAME STATEMENT MUST BE FILED BEFORE THE EXPIRATION.
THE FILING OF THIS STATEMENT DOES NOT OF ITSELF AUTHORIZE THE USE IN THIS STATE OF A FICTITIOUS BUSINESS NAME IN VIOLATION OF THE RIGHTS OF ANOTHER UNDER FEDERAL, STATE, OR COMMON LAW (SEE SECTION 14411 ET SEQ., BUSINESS AND PROFESSIONS CODE).
IF SUBMITTING THE STATEMENT IN PERSON, THE REGISTRANT OR AGENT WILL BE ASKED TO PRESENT A VALID PHOTO ID FOR ALL THE FICTITIOUS BUSINESS NAME FILINGS.
IF SUBMITTING THE STATEMENT BY MAIL, THE REGISTRANT OR AGENT MUST ATTACH A COPY OF A VALID PHOTO ID OR A NOTARIZED CERTIFICATE OF ACKNOWLEDGEMENT.
CC231M (Rev. 05/11/15)

Confidentiality / Non-Disclosure Agreement

It is understood and agreed to that the below identified discloser of confidential information may provide certain information that is and must be kept confidential. To ensure the protection of such information, and to preserve any confidentiality necessary under patent and/or trade secret laws, it is agreed that

1. The Confidential Information to be disclosed can be described as and includes: Invention description(s), technical and business information relating to proprietary ideas and inventions, ideas, patentable ideas, trade secrets, drawings and/or illustrations, patent searches, existing and/or contemplated products and services, research and development, production, costs, profit and margin information, finances and financial projections, customers, clients, marketing, and current or future business plans and models, regardless of whether such information is designated as "Confidential Information" at the time of its disclosure.

2. The Recipient agrees not to disclose the confidential information obtained from the discloser to anyone unless required to do so by law.

3. This Agreement states the entire agreement between the parties concerning the disclosure of Confidential Information. Any addition or modification to this Agreement must be made in writing and signed by the parties.

4. If any of the provisions of this Agreement are found to be unenforceable, the remainder shall be enforced as fully as possible and the unenforceable provision(s) shall be deemed modified to the limited extent required to permit enforcement of the Agreement as a whole.

WHEREFORE, the parties acknowledge that they have read and understand this Agreement and voluntarily accept the duties and obligations set forth herein.

Recipient of Confidential Information:

Name (Print or Type):

Signature

Date:

Discloser of Confidential Information:

Name (Print or Type):

Signature:

Wire Transfer Form

Member # _____   From Account _____

Member Name _____

Member Address _____

Member Phone # (_____) _____ - _____   (_____) _____ - _____

Member email _____

| Funds Verified by: | |
| Fee amount: | Approved by: |

Amount to Be Sent $_____
All funds are sent in US Dollars

WIRE TRANSFER INSTRUCTIONS - ☐ Domestic   ☐ International

Receiving Bank Name _____

Address _____

Phone # (_____) _____ - _____   Contact Person_____

ABA# _____

Further Credit To (Financial Institution name) _____

Address _____

Phone # (_____) _____ - _____   Contact Person_____

ABA# _____   Swift Code _____

BENEFICIARY INFORMATION - ☐ SELF   ☐ LEGAL OWNER   ☐ THIRD PARTY

Credit to – Beneficiary's Name _____

Address _____

Phone (_____) _____ - _____   (_____) _____ - _____

Account Number _____   Account Type _____

Special Instructions _____

_____

Member's Signature _____   Date _____   Time_____

Made in the USA
Middletown, DE
21 June 2018